# NOWHERE TO GROW

# SOCIAL INSTITUTIONS AND SOCIAL CHANGE
*An Aldine de Gruyter Series of Texts and Monographs*

EDITED BY James D. Wright

# NOWHERE TO GROW

## Homeless and Runaway Adolescents and Their Families

LES B. WHITBECK and DAN R. HOYT

ALDINE DE GRUYTER

New York

# About the Authors

**Les B. Whitbeck** is a Professor of Sociology at Iowa State University and faculty affiliate in the Institute for Social and Behavioral Research. Dr. Whitbeck has published numerous articles on at-risk youth. Whitbeck and Hoyt are co-investigators on a new longitudinal study of homeless adolescents.

**Dan R. Hoyt** is an Associate Professor of Sociology at Iowa State University and faculty affiliate in the Institute for Social and Behavioral Research. He has published on the sociology of mental health and research methods.

ALDINE DE GRUYTER
A division of Walter de Gruyter, Inc.
200 Saw Mill River Road
Hawthorne, New York 10532

This publication is printed on acid free paper ⊗

**Library of Congress Cataloging-in-Publication Data**
Whitbeck, Les B.
    Nowhere to grow : homeless and runaway adolescents and their families / Les B. Whitbeck and Dan R. Hoyt.
        p.   cm.
    Includes bibliographical references and index.
    ISBN 0-202-30583-X (alk. paper). — ISBN 0-202-30584-8 (pbk. : alk. paper)
        1. Homeless youth—United States.   2. Runaway teenagers—United States.   3. Runaway teenagers—United States—Family relationships.
    4. Problem families—United States.   I. Hoyt, Dan R., 1949-   .
    II. Title.
    HV4505.W43   1999
    362.74—dc21                                                99-19051
                                                                    CIP

Manufactured in the United States of America

10  9  8  7  6  5  4  3  2  1

# Contents

## PART III.  TAKING CHANCES:
## ADOLESCENTS ON THEIR OWN

## PART IV.   NOWHERE TO GROW
## THE DEVELOPMENTAL CONSEQUENCES OF RUNNING AWAY

# Acknowledgments

This work could not have been completed without our agency partners in St. Louis, Kansas City, Wichita, Des Moines, and Lincoln. Not only did we rely on their knowledge of the streets and the youths we interviewed, they were involved in every aspect of the project. They contributed to questionnaire development, they were the interviewers and supervisors of interviewers, they edited questionnaires, and they gave us feedback on research procedures. This was a true partnership and we hope this book reflects their hard work and devotion to the young people they serve, the faces behind the numbers we report. Thanks, especially to the M.I.N.K. (Missouri, Iowa, Nebraska, Kansas) Youth Services Consortium for believing in us enough to get the project started.

We also thank Linda Hoyt, Debbie Bahr, Chris Kinley, and all the folks at the Data Acquisition Unit at the Institute for Social and Behavioral Research at Iowa State University for sharing their expertise in data collection, interviewer training, questionnaire development, and computer-assisted telephone interviewing. Thanks also to the Institute's support staff. We know it was a difficult project to manage and we appreciate the extra time you took to solve problems inherent to doing research directly on city streets.

We were particularly lucky to have had the pleasure of working with a wonderful group of graduate research assistants. Graduate assistants Kevin Yoder, Kim Tyler, and Sheri Jenkins and our postdoctoral student Wan Ning Bao analyzed data, did qualitative interviews, and created code books, technical reports, and agency reports all with good humor and great competence. They made all those data analysis meetings seem like fun.

A project like this could not have been accomplished without significant research support. For this we are indebted to the National Institute of Mental Health (MH50140). Special thanks to our project officer Della Hann for her advice and support as we learned the funding process.

Finally, we thank the kids who agreed to share the stories of their lives with us.

# I

# SOCIETY'S FORGOTTEN CHILDREN

# Runaway and Homeless Adolescents in America

*She's a really neat kid, but seems to be thirteen going on thirty. At one point her mom told her that if you can make it one week on your own, then you don't need me. Her mom locked her out at this point.*

—Interviewer comment

If you live in or have visited even a medium-sized city recently, you have seen runaway and homeless young people. They congregate in certain downtown areas, "the loop" in Des Moines, "the wall" in St. Louis, or "the ave" in Seattle. During inclement weather, they hang out in malls. Larger cities may have several areas defined by geographic and ideological barriers; for example, in Seattle, there is First Avenue, Broadway, and the University District. Unlike many homeless adults, runaway and homeless adolescents may be difficult to identify. Mostly, they look like the other kids: Sometimes outrageous in costume, sometimes in Windbreakers and sneakers, maybe in gang colors. The difference is that they won't be going home tonight.

Defining homelessness is difficult. As one nationally respected researcher has put it, "[H]omelessness is not and cannot be a precisely defined condition" (Wright, 1991, p. 19). Defining homelessness among young people is even more difficult than for adults. Many unhoused young people have homes they can return to—if not the home they left, then that of a relative or family of a friend. Many drift in and out of settings that may or may not include adult caretakers, changing environments frequently with little adult monitoring. A significant proportion cannot return home and literally have

3

no family that will take them in. Even these children may have institutional options for housing from which they have run or become disenchanted by rules, multiple moves, or a "revolving door" of caseworkers and foster parents. Homelessness for young people is a continuum that ranges from living at home with parents and running away for a night to independently making one's way on the streets. In between, there are stays with friends, stays with relatives, foster care, group homes, juvenile detention, and a range of shelter options, both supervised and unsupervised. The duration of being unhoused may be as short as a single night.

One difficulty in defining "homelessness" that is unique for young people is the distinction between being unsupervised and unhoused. For a minor, being away from home overnight and unsupervised constitutes homelessness, even though he or she may be housed with minor friends or unrelated adults (e.g., trading sex for shelter or living with an adult "boyfriend"). Definitions, therefore, must take into account the dual criteria of being unhoused and unsupervised. Traditional definitions distinguish between being a "runaway," "throwaway," and "street youth." "Runaway" refers to someone who is away from home at least overnight without parental consent or knowledge (National Network of Runaway and Youth Services, 1991, p. 3). "Throwaway" refers to a child's having been told that he or she may not return home or having been kicked out or locked out of the parents' house. "Street youth" may be used to refer to runaways and nonrunaways. It usually refers to young people who hang out on the streets, and who may or may not have homes to return to at night (Shane, 1996). These are largely unsupervised young people who may be essentially on their own regardless of having the choice to return home at night. For the purposes of this research we will use the National Network of Runaway and Youth Services definition of "runaway." "Chronic runaways" will refer to children who have run away three or more times (Pennbridge, Yates, David, & Mackenzie, 1990). We will refer to "homeless" youth as someone eighteen years or younger who cannot return home or has chosen to never return home and who has no permanent residence (see GAO, 1989).

## NATIONAL ESTIMATES OF THE NUMBER OF HOMELESS AND RUNAWAY ADOLESCENTS

No one knows how many runaway and homeless young people there are in America. According to a recent review article, "There have been no comprehensive studies of the number of homeless youth in the United States" (Rotheram-Borus, Parra, Cantwell, Gwadz, & Murphey, 1996, p. 370). Reliable estimates of the number of chronic runaway and homeless youth are scarce (Committee on Health Care for Homeless People, 1988) and can vary widely. Of the estimates commonly cited in the research literature, many are dated: some are over twenty years old. In a report to Congress, the Department of Health and Human Services (House Committee on Education and Labor, Subcommittee on Human Resources, 1984) estimated that as many as 1.3 million youth ran away in 1984 and that 500,000 of these were homeless. A 1989 GAO report of shelter populations between October 1985 and June 1988 indicated that 44,274 youth had received at least overnight care at federally funded shelters. The Office of Juvenile Justice and Delinquency (Finkelhor, Hotaliñg, & Sedlak, 1990) estimated 450,700 runaways in 1988 and concluded that the number of runaways had not increased since their last national survey in 1975. More recently, the National Network of Runaway and Youth Services estimated that one million children ran away in 1992, of whom 300,000 were homeless (Shane, 1996).

Without reliable data it is difficult to accurately portray the extent of the problem. This is exacerbated by the fact that most of the systematic research has focused on large population centers usually deriving data from one service system or shelter (Rotheram-Borus et al., 1996). The prevalence and consequences of the problem in small and midsized cities are virtually unknown. What information exists regarding smaller cities tends to be anecdotal or service-related. To our knowledge, there have been no systematic regional studies in the United States that included cities of widely varying populations.

## RESEARCH ON HOMELESS AND RUNAWAY ADOLESCENTS

As a nation of immigrants, the United States has a long history of young people making it on their own both in their initial immigration to North America and later during the westward migration (Libertoff, 1980; Wells & Sandhu, 1986). In the past we have tended to romanticize precocious independence, calling up visions of Huckleberry Finn, the young cowboy, or later the young hobo of the Great Depression. As late as the 1960s we viewed running away as largely a matter of choice. Young people were rebelling against society and their parents and "dropping out." Research from the 1950s, 1960s, and 1970s reflects this early ideology. Then, as now, the work often was descriptive, unrepresentative, and based on availability samples in single locations (Brennan, 1980).

Much of this early descriptive work focused on establishing classification systems or typologies of runaway adolescents. These typologies reflect the cultural ambivalence toward early independence. For example, Berger and Schmidt (1958) dichotomize runaways into "spontaneous and reactive runaways." The spontaneous group were adventurers; the reactive groups were running from problems. Homer (1973) also suggested that there were essentially two types of runaways: those running to something and those running from something. The "running to" group were viewed as adventurers or pleasure seekers. Other typologies innocently downplayed the seriousness of most runaways. Haupt and Offord (1972) distinguished between "gesture runaways," who were making a cry for help and "real runaways," who intended to escape a particular situation. Similarly, Shellow and colleagues (Shellow, Schamp, Liebow, & Unger, 1967) categorized runaways into those who were "pathological" and those who were "normal." The "pathological" young person was on the run for personal or family troubles and was a chronic runner. The "normal" runway left home only one or two times, did not evidence high levels of family troubles, and showed little delinquent behavior. The Scientific Analysis Corporation (1974; cited in Brennan, 1980) identified three types of runaways: the "sick," the "bad," and the "free." The "sick" referred to those with identifiable psychopathology, the "bad" were those who engaged in delinquent behaviors, and the "free" were those who were engaged in pleasure-seeking, adventure, or exploration.

The need to categorize runaways persisted into the more empirically oriented work of the late 1970s and early 1980s. Indeed, practitioners continue to come up with typologies in the 1990s (Zide & Cherry, 1992). Brennan (1980) developed an extensive categorization of runaways based on two general classes: (1) not highly delinquent, nonalienated runaways; and (2) delinquent, alienated runaways. The former category describes the young people as either: (1) "young, overcontrolled escapists," (2) "middle-class loners," or (3) "unbonded, peer-oriented runaways." It is noteworthy that, with the advent of systematic empirical studies of runaways such as that by Brennan, Huizinga, and Elliott (1978), the "adventurer" category disappeared.

Recent work has shown convincingly that runaways are running from something or drifting out of disorganized families rather than running to something. Early separation is not about "seeking one's fortune" in contemporary society. It is about troubles within a family. More homeless and runaway adolescents typically rate their families as having problems than do nonrunaways. Schweitzer and colleagues (Schweitzer, Hier, & Terry, 1994) found that homeless adolescents scored higher than housed children on measures of deprivation based on the Parental Bonding Inventory (Parker, Tupling, & Brown, 1979) and the Family Environment Scale (Moos & Moos, 1981). Stefanidis and others (Stefanidis, Pennbridge, MacKenzie & Pottharst, 1992) reported homeless adolescents who did not do well in transitional living and other intervention programs scored significantly lower on measures of attachment than those who were responsive to agency stabilization efforts. Control group studies also have indicated that homeless adolescents report higher levels of parent marital problems and lower levels of parental care and acceptance than adolescents who live at home (Daddis, Braddock, Cuers, Elliott, & Kelly, 1993).

A substantial proportion of runaways are leaving family situations that pose serious risk. Although rates of adolescent reports of abusive family backgrounds vary widely across studies, they all indicate severe risk for physical and sexual abuse. Janus, Burgess, and McCormack (1987) found that 71.5% of the male runaways they interviewed reported physical abuse, and 38.2% reported sexual abuse. Silbert and Pines (1981) study of juvenile and adult street prostitutes indicated that 60% had been sexually abused. In the Kurtz, Kurtz, and Jarvis (1991) report based on shelter intake records of 2,019 runaways from eight southeastern states, 28% of the runaways identified themselves as having been sexually or physically abused. About 30% of Kufeldt and Nimmo's (1987) sample of 474 runaways reported physical abuse. Bridge, Inc., in Boston (Saltonstall, 1984) has reported a 65% physical abuse rate. Only 5% of its sample "clearly stated there was no abuse in their homes" (ibid., p. 78). A Los Angeles County shelter/drop-in center study (Pennbridge et al., 1990) reported a 47% abuse/neglect rate. Using the Conflict Tactics Scale (Straus & Gelles, 1990), Whitbeck and Simons (1993) found adolescents reported physical abuse rates ranging from 80% for slapping to 48% for being "beaten up" for a sample of 150 street youth in Des Moines, Iowa. Thirty-seven percent of the young women reported forced sexual activity by an adult caretaker. According to the National Network of Runaway and Youth Services, 70% of adolescents in shelters have been physically and/or sexually abused (Kennedy, 1991). As we will discuss in Chapter 5, parent/caretaker reports corroborate runaway reports of high levels of family violence and add the dimension of adolescent to caretaker violence (see also Whitbeck, Hoyt, & Ackley, 1997b).

Because research reports tend to be bound to single shelters or cities, we cannot make generalizations about the characteristics of runaway and homeless youth with great confidence. Recent research on runaway and homeless adolescents is inconclusive regarding gender ratios. However, there is considerable evidence that, like their adult counterparts, the young men are more likely to be living directly on the streets and young women somewhat more likely to be in shelters (Schaffer & Catton, 1984; GAO, 1989). Without regard to shelter arrangements, adolescent males and females tend to run away at about the same rates (Nye, 1980; GAO, 1989). Runaways tend to reflect all ethnic and racial groups in their proportion to the general population (GAO, 1989), but there is some evidence that they are more likely to come from lower income (Nye, 1980) and stepparent families (Finkelhor et al., 1990). There is general agreement that with the exception of some "magnet" cities such as San Francisco (Kennedy, 1991; Rotheram-Borus, Luna, Marotta, & Kelly, 1994) or Los Angeles (Pennbridge et al. 1990) most runaways stay in or close to their own communities (Crystal, 1986; Ferran & Sabatini, 1985; Nye, 1980; Schaffer & Catton, 1984; Whitbeck & Simons, 1990).

One characteristic that all runaway youth share is the extreme risk of serious harm while they are on their own. Researchers have been surprisingly silent regarding street victimization. A well-cited review of the literature spends several pages on victimization at home and risky street behaviors but does not mention street victimization even in a section on health problems of runaways (Robertson, 1992). A more recent review devotes only a few lines to street victimization (Rotheram-Borus et al. 1996). Even some of the best diagnostic assessments of street youth do not take street victimization and the trauma of being homeless into consideration. Rather, diagnoses are based on stressors from within the family of origin (Feital, Margetson, Chamas, & Lipman, 1992). The recent focus on what young people are running from is so pronounced that some researchers have made the case that the choice to run is a rational one given dysfunctional and abusive families (Bucy & Obolensky, 1990). Clearly, runaways are substituting one source of risk for another. As one homeless adolescent we interviewed put it:

> A lot of times they [runaway adolescents] feel they'd rather be abused by the world than the ones they love. I would much rather be abused by the people I don't know than the ones I do know. (Eighteen-year-old male)

In the studies that choose to document it, there is plentiful evidence of the hazards of street life.

Kipke and colleagues (Kipke, Simon, Montgomery, Unger, & Iverson, 1997) reported that 51% of their sample of Hollywood street youth had been beaten up since being on the streets, 45% had been chased, and 26% had been shot at. Nineteen percent had been stabbed while living on the streets, 15% sexually assaulted, and 7% wounded by gunfire. Aside from the obvious traumatic effects of serious victimization, there is constant anxiety and fear associated with precocious independence. More than 50% of Kipke's respondents feared being shot or stabbed and almost 50% feared being sexually assaulted or beaten up. Rotheram-Borus and associates (Rotheram-Borus, Rosario, & Koopman, 1991) reported that in a New York sample of runaways, 20% had been physically assaulted, 20% sexually assaulted, and 20% robbed in the three months prior to seeking shelter. Hagen and McCarthy (1997) deal with victimization anecdotally but do not tie it specifically to their discussion of delinquent behaviors. Shane (1996, p. 46) presents studies on victimization of adults and generalizes from these to homeless youth, but cites no studies that systematically document victimization. Like many researchers on homeless young people, Janus and colleagues (Janus, McCormack, Burgess, & Hartman, 1987) provide poignant case studies that include street victimization, but do not systematically chronicle its prevalence or include its effects in their analyses of psychological outcomes.

Our early work in Des Moines indicated high levels of victimization among both adolescent and adult homeless people (Whitbeck & Simons, 1993). Regardless of age, men were more likely to be beaten, threatened, or assaulted with weapons. Half the adolescent males reported having been beaten up on the streets, 57% had been threatened with a weapon, and 42% actually assaulted with a weapon. One-third of the adolescent females had been beaten up, one-third had been threatened with a weapon, and almost one-fourth had been assaulted with a weapon. Adolescent homeless women reported more than twice the rate of sexual assault (37.5%) than adult homeless women (14.7%).

The developmental significance of such serious victimization is enormous. By the time young people are pushed out, drift out, or actively make the decision to leave home, they are likely already to have been physically or sexually abused. Once on their own, the likelihood of further harm, witnessing someone being harmed, or experiencing fear and anxiety about one's safety is almost certain. Simply the vulnerability of being homeless creates serious psychological stress regardless of actual victimization or the witnessing of victimization (Goodman, Saxe, & Harvey, 1991). We cannot accurately assess the emotional health and well-being of runaway and homeless young people without taking these stress effects into account.

In fact, we know very little about the mental health status of runaway and homeless young people (Mundy, Robertson, Robertson, & Greenblatt, 1990). The small number of available reports show that homeless and runaway adolescents typically score higher on measures of behavioral and emotional disorders than do nonrunaway youth. Schweitzer and Hier (1993) found that over 53.7% of their sample of Australian homeless adolescents scored within the clinical range on the externalizing and/or internalizing Youth Self-Report (Achenbach 1991) subscales compared to 5.2% of the control group adolescents. Among U.S. runaways most studies have found heightened rates of depressive symptoms, suicidal behavior, and substance abuse (Smart & Walsh, 1993; Yates, Mackenzie, Pennbridge, & Cohen, 1988). Research using diagnostic protocols typically has been based on small samples and indicates a range of diagnoses. Feital and colleagues (1992) using the Diagnostic Interview for Children and Adolescents-Revised with a sample of 150 shelter adolescents reported that 59.3% met criteria for conduct disorder, 49.3% for major affective disorder, 37.3% for dysthymic disorder, 31.8% for posttraumatic stress disorder (PTSD), and 41.3% for alcohol and drug abuse. Based on diagnostic interviews with 97 street youth in Los Angeles, Mundy and associates reported that 20% exceeded the cutoff for a clinical level of mood disturbance. Thirty percent of these adolescents endorsed four or more psychotic symptoms. Evaluations of 296 runaway and homeless adolescents in Seattle based on the Diagnostic Interview for Children—Revised (DISC-R) indicated that two-thirds of the adolescents met criteria for at least one diagnosis (Cauce, Paradise, Embry, Lohr, & Wagner, 1997). The most prevalent diagnosis was conduct disorder (48.2%).

Accurate diagnosis is problematic with homeless adolescents because it is often difficult to distinguish early developmental disorders from onset of symptoms when homeless (North, Smith, & Spitznagel, 1993). Also, it is almost impossible to separate normal responses to the stresses of street life from psychological symptoms. Symptoms such as paranoid ideation, anxiety, and depression are likely to be overrepresented and indicative of a healthy response to the vulnerability of living in public places (Goodman, Saxe, & Harvey, 1991). Current research tends to confuse the emotional and behavioral effects of running away and unsupervised living with those of early family history. We believe that over time, the day-to-day stress of persistent vulnerability, coercive interactions, witnessing violence, and actual victimization experienced by runaways amplifies existing mental health problems originating in highly disorganized and dysfunctional families.

Regardless of duration, spending time directly on the streets, or experiencing victimization, precocious independence marks a significant developmental transition. More than any other adultlike behavior, the act of running away asserts separation and independence from monitoring and supervision of caretakers. The earlier and more often the child chooses to leave adult supervision, the greater the cumulative effects of the behaviors. Normal processes of individuation and separation are accelerated and accentuated by precocious independence. As we will show in the following chapters, adolescents who run at early ages are more likely to run again and again. The developmental trajectory of chronic runaways is one of diminishing parental control, increased independence, and institutional involvement. Our data indicate that running away often sets in motion pernicious chains of events that become more and more difficult to escape as the duration of independence increases.

## A LIFE COURSE DEVELOPMENTAL APPROACH TO PRECOCIOUS INDEPENDENCE

All adolescents must eventually separate from the control of adult caretakers and become independent young adults. The course of this transition is typically gradual, marked by forays into independence and returns to the security of home. Errors of judgment, rebellious behaviors, and early experiments with adult behaviors such as tobacco use, alcohol use, and sexuality mark the course of the transition. Such early experimentation ordinarily consists of "practice" behaviors at being adult or, in the case of more severe antisocial behaviors, attempts to rebel against and assert independence from adult control. Moffitt (1997) has distinguished between life course trajectories of adolescents who experiment with adult behaviors (adolescent-limited) and those who develop a persistent pattern of antisocial behaviors that will continue into young adulthood (life-course persistent). According to Moffitt, "adolescent-limited delinquency is ubiquitous. . . . [N]umerous rigorous self-report studies of representative samples have now documented that it is statistically aberrant to refrain from crime during adolescence" (ibid., p. 15). Given the extent of adolescent delinquent behaviors, the factors that predict a continuous trajectory of antisocial behaviors rather than age-limited delinquency become extremely important.

From a life course perspective, the developmental process is one of interrelated, self-perpetuating chains of events. Children most at risk from neurological or psychological impairment (e.g., attention deficit disorder, oppositional disorder, hyperactivity) frequently are those whose temperament and social location expose them to ineffective parenting. Irritable, developmentally delayed, and highly active children are difficult to parent even for those who are most suited for the task. As Moffitt points out, however, often these subtle neurological characteristics are inherited (see Huesmann, Eron, Lefkowitz, & Walder, 1984) or the result of low birth weight or other prenatal insults associated with very young and very poor mothers. The children who are most likely to have early behavioral problems are many times those whose parents are least able to cope with them. Such early deficits are sustained and amplified over time through negative interactions such as harsh or inconsistent discipline by parents and tantrums and oppositional behaviors by children.

Caspi and colleagues have delineated the life course processes underlying the continuity and accentuation of behaviors across time (Caspi & Bem, 1990; Caspi, Bem, & Elder, 1989). Interaction styles are reinforced over time in two ways: (1) individuals select into environments and relationships that positively reinforce the behaviors, and (2) in novel situations expectations of similar interaction styles are projected on others so that the style is perpetuated (Caspi & Elder, 1988). "Interactional continuity" occurs when interaction styles are reciprocated or otherwise reinforced and through self-confirming expectations (e.g., hostility elicits hostile reactions from others). At a more general level, "cumulative continuity" is the result of the process where "an individual's behavior patterns—adaptive or maladaptive—are sustained across the life course by the progressive accumulation of their own consequences" (Caspi et al., 1989, p. 277).

Moffitt (1997) builds on these concepts to distinguish between experimental adultlike and delinquent behaviors that are part of the developmental process of becoming adult and a more pernicious developmental process that results in lifelong patterns of antisocial behaviors. She identifies two sources of cumulative continuity for antisocial young people. First, these young people fail to learn conventional behaviors that serve as alternatives to antisocial behaviors. The developmental process is straightforward. Children who are neurologically or psychologically impaired (e.g., attention deficit disorders, hyperactivity, oppositional disorders) are likely to be those whose parents may have the fewest personal and social resources needed to cope with them successfully (younger, lower socioeconomic status parents who may share the child's impairment). In such families, children learn very early that aggressive behaviors (temper tantrums, whining, nagging) are usually successful (Patterson, 1982). These early problems with temper and aggressive behaviors result in school failures. The children may be less attentive, create more classroom problems, and have learning problems. Their aggressive behaviors on the playground may result in rejection by conventional peers, and they will drift into deviant peer groups where they learn to engage in delinquent behaviors (Dodge, 1983; Patterson, 1982). These children miss out early on opportunities to develop prosocial skills that can provide alternatives to antisocial behaviors. They experience academic failures that close educational options. They do not acquire the social skills necessary to develop relationships with conventional peers and mentoring adults.

Second, the adolescents progressively become entrapped by the consequences of their own behaviors. The accumulation of negative chains of events diminishes opportunities for change. Educational opportunities are lost because of poor performance. Alcohol and drug problems, poor or no work histories, and an evolving criminal record all serve to preclude opportunities for positive developmental outcomes. Criminal records and poor academic and work histories rule out high-paying occupations. Pregnancies and early parenting may eliminate opportunities for young women. As the accumulation of negative experiences grows, options narrow, doors close.

Runaways are setting the stage for such cumulative negative developmental consequences in several ways. First, running away is the most extreme of the adultlike behaviors an adolescent can assert. Smoking, alcohol use, and early sexuality all may assert adult status. Running away enacts that status. The adolescent is choosing independence from caretakers. Second, as we will demonstrate in this volume, running away puts in motion negative chains of events that meet all of the criteria for Moffitt's conceptualization of a life course–persistent antisocial trajectory. Running away interrupts parental control and supervision. It disrupts educational progress. It exposes the adolescent to deviant peers on the streets and in shelters and predatory adults on the streets. There are few legitimate means of self-support for homeless young people, so that running away encourages deviant survival strategies while they are on their own. Finally, in the absence of adult supervision and control, it encourages other adultlike behaviors such as drug and alcohol use and early sexuality.

Third, the runaway is selecting into a caretaker-free environment that precludes opportunities for adult support and advice. The influences in their environment become peers in similar circumstances. Finally, and possibly most important, running away at an early age strongly predicts subsequent runaways. Once the adolescent asserts independence, he or she is highly likely to begin a chain of subsequent independent behaviors. As we will demonstrate, the developmental trajectory for chronic runaways is away from parental supervision and control and toward independence or institutional control. Once on their own, it is difficult, if not impossible, to return to childhood routines of rules and supervision.

## OVERVIEW OF THE BOOK

This book is about the developmental trajectories of runaway and homeless adolescents. After an overview of our sample (Chapter 2), Part II begins with their life histories (Chapter 3) and the ways disorganized family histories of multiple transitions loosen primary ties to parents and caretakers. We trace the trajectories of their life transitions. Transitions controlled by parents and caretakers decrease across time; those controlled by the adolescent and institutions increase. In Chapter 4 we extend the investigation of developmental history to include the parent/caretaker generation. Here we examine the effects of parent characteristics on adolescents' lives. For example, analyses investigate the extent that parents/caretakers' alcohol and drug, history of mental health problems, and legal problems affected life at home. Chapter 5 is an in-depth look at the parent/caretaker-child relationship from both points of view. This chapter examines parenting behaviors and compares the parents/caretakers of runaways to parents of nonrunaway adolescents. We also compare reports of runaway adolescents to their nonrunaway counterparts on measures of parental warmth and supportiveness, rejection, and monitoring. Finally, we review parents/caretakers' and adolescents' descriptions of violence within the family, from parent to child, and child to parent.

Part III focuses on adolescents' experiences when they are on their own. Following our theoretical perspective, we begin with their social networks and peer influences (Chapter 6). We turn next to an examination of their survival strategies when on their own, how they gain subsistence and shelter, their contacts with helping agencies and health care providers (Chapter 7). The analyses investigate factors that predict high-risk survival strategies when the adolescents are on their own. In Chapter 8, we discuss adolescent sexual histories and their sexual behaviors when they are on their own. This chapter includes pregnancy histories, concern about and risk for HIV infection, and the contexts of sexual relationships. Our analysis focuses on the precursors of high-risk sexual activities. In the final chapter in Part II we deal with victimization and trauma when on the streets (Chapter 9). Here we chronicle types of serious victimization both quantitatively and qualitatively using the respondents own words to describe traumatic incidents. In our analyses we delineate factors associated with serious victimization.

Part IV focuses on adolescent developmental outcomes. In Chapter 10 we discuss internalization problems among adolescents and their parents. Here our analysis addresses precursors of depressive symptoms and posttraumatic stress disorder among adolescents. Chapter 11 focuses on externalization problems including delinquent behaviors and alcohol and drug use.

In the final two chapters of the book we return to our theoretical framework to propose and evaluate a risk-amplification model of development for runaway and homeless adolescents (Chapter 12). This model proposes that the negative developmental effects originating in the families the adolescents leave are accentuated by their experiences when they are on their own. It tests empirically Caspi and colleagues' conception of cumulative continuity by assessing the direct and indirect effects of early family history and later street experiences on adolescent victimization and emotional well-being. The model indicates that effects of early psychological harm from coercive abusive families are amplified through their influence on behaviors while the adolescents are on their own by increasing the likelihood of victimization. The final chapter (Chapter 13) looks into the futures of runaway and homeless adolescents. We examine characteristics of adolescents who may do well despite their histories of running away. The adolescents discuss their futures in their own words and provide advice regarding interventions.

The intent of the book is to work the reader through the various risk factors associated with precocious independence beginning in the family and then extending to the adolescents' environments and behaviors when they are on their own. At each stage we examine how the factors under consideration contribute to risky behaviors and discuss their consequences for adolescents' development. The book is about cumulative consequences for young people who have few good options. Often the choice is to stay in a disorganized or abusive home or risk life on one's own. Perhaps just as often, no clear choice is ever made. Early independence simply occurs as a result of family disintegration and the child drifts into independence. Once the adolescents are on their own, their options narrow even more. Precious "growing up" time is being lost and it is not recoverable.

**2**

# The Midwest Homeless and Runaway
# Adolescent Project

## INTRODUCTION

Our initial efforts to field a study in smaller urban areas of the Midwest were met with considerable skepticism. We were told that this was a problem unique to major population centers, particularly coastal "magnet" cities such as New York, Los Angeles, and San Francisco. The number of homeless youth in smaller cities, particularly those in the Midwest, was thought to be minimal and their conditions dissimilar to those in larger cities. I recall the representative of one potential funding source responding incredulously, "Street kids? In Des Moines?" It took three years of pilot work funded by small university research grants and staffed largely by graduate students and undergraduate volunteers to provide the empirical evidence necessary to attract national funding. Yes, there were street kids in Des Moines, a whole street culture in fact, and they were being victimized at rates similar to those in New York and Los Angeles (Whitbeck & Simons, 1990; Simons & Whitbeck, 1991; Whitbeck & Simons, 1993).

As in our pilot work, the Midwest Homeless and Runaway Adolescent Study was based on partnerships with street outreach agencies. Through the M.I.N.K. (Missouri, Iowa, Nebraska, and Kansas) Youth Services Consortium we met with representatives of youth services agencies serving runaway young people. The agencies proved eager to work with us. Underfunded and often ignored in a political climate more interested in punishing runaway young people than providing supportive services, agency workers wanted the stories of the youth they saw every day told. And they wanted their own data to make their case with legislative and community policymakers. Agencies in the M.I.N.K. consortium were selected for participation in the study based on their having an existing street outreach program in addition to shelter and/or transitional living facilities. All but one of the study agencies had a street outreach van. This agency had an inner-city drop-in center that catered to street youth. In all, we worked through six agencies to obtain our sample: two in St. Louis, one each in Kansas City, Wichita, Lincoln, and Des Moines.

Our partnerships were based on agencies providing access and expertise in outreach to runaways and homeless young people. The outreach workers were very familiar with local street cultures and were already known and trusted by many of the runaways. They were all trained youth workers with considerable experience interviewing and interacting with this group of young people. Agencies were paid for the parts of positions assigned to data collection or were paid an interview fee and interviewer expenses on a per interview basis. In return for allocation of time to the project, we developed measures and provided data to the agencies in the form of a general summary of project findings and individual agency reports that could be used for program evaluation and fund-raising. These reports have since found their way into state legislative committees and service-oriented grant proposals for several of the participating agencies.

We provided training in systematic data collection for selected staff who served as project interviewers. A trainer and project coordinator from the Data Acquisition Unit of the Institute for Social and Behavioral Research at Iowa State University visited each site for two days of orientation and training. During this time, interviewers went over the protocol question-by-question, were provided an extensive training manual, role-played interviews, and repeatedly practiced difficult sections of the questionnaire such as the life events matrix and the pregnancy history section. Informed-consent issues and procedures as well as reimbursement procedures were practiced. An on-site supervisor was appointed for a local check of completed questionnaires. Comprehensive editing was assigned to Data Acquisition Unit staff, who reviewed questionnaires as soon as they arrived at the research institute. Each individual interviewer was monitored and lapses or mistakes were followed up by the project manager.

## DESIGN OF THE STUDY

The research design had several unique characteristics compared to other studies of homeless and runaway adolescents. First, it focused on "nonmagnet" cities in largely agriculturally based states in the Midwest. If street kids could be found in some of the cities we targeted, we believed they could be expected in any metropolitan area in the nation. Second, the design involved multiple sites with widely varying populations. Not only did the study include a variety of urban areas, we also had interviewers in Nebraska and Iowa visit smaller shelters in small cities (e.g., Cedar Rapids, Mason City, and Davenport, Iowa; Scottsbluff, Nebraska). These varying data collection sites provided information on contextual effects based on community size. Third, the design included intensive histories of the adolescents' life transitions from birth to the present, including changes in family configuration, and parent-initiated, institution-initiated (e.g., child welfare or juvenile court interventions), and child-initiated changes in residence or living situation (e.g., leaving home to live with another parent, running away). These life histories provided information on adolescents' family life prior to first runaway as well as the number and timing of subsequent runaways. Fourth, where possible, the research design included multiple reporters offering, for perhaps the first time, an intensive investigation of parent/caretaker reports regarding parent/caretaker characteristics, home life, and developmental histories of runaway adolescents concurrent with the adolescent self-reports. Reports of parents/caretakers and adolescents will be compared throughout the book.

Multiple reporters across multiple data collection sites provide increased confidence in the findings. For example, our finding that parents/caretakers and runaway adolescents tell essentially the same story regarding parenting (Chapter 5; see also Whitbeck, Hoyt, & Ackley, 1997) increases confidence in adolescent self-reports regarding home life prior to running away. Similarly, parent/caretaker and adolescent agreement on reports of externalizing behaviors provide increased confidence of self-reports of adolescent behavioral problems provided in single-reporter research designs.

## SAMPLE

Six hundred two adolescents and 201 of their parents/caretakers were interviewed during a period of approximately 18 months from early 1995 through August, 1996. Adolescent interviews were conducted in outreach vans, restaurants, shelters, transitional living facilities, and drop-in centers as part of regular agency outreach. Interviews lasted about one and one-half hours. Respondents were paid $15 for participating. Our response rates ranged from a low 71% for one of the St. Louis agencies to 100% for the Kansas City and Lincoln shelters, with an overall response rate of 93%. Reimbursement rates and a majority of shelter respondents account for the high adolescent response rates.

Informed consent for the adolescents included an overview of the types of questions they would be asked and information regarding mandatory reporting of maltreatment or indications of intent to harm themselves. They were told they had the right to terminate the interview at any time and that they could refuse to answer any question. Further, they were assured that refusal to participate in the study would have no effect on shelter status, referral for services, or any other provision of services to them. Parental permission to interview was obtained when the adolescents were in shelters and parents could be located. Obtaining or attempting to obtain parental permission to provide services was part of shelter policy in all of the shelters with which we worked.

During the informed-consent procedures the adolescents were told that at the end of the interview they would be asked if we could contact a parent or guardian. They were assured that the information they gave would remain confidential and that a separate interviewer would contact the parent or guardian by phone in two to three weeks. Parents/caretakers would only be told that at the time of contact their child was all right. If they had questions about the runaway, they would be referred to the agency that had conducted the interview. This procedure met both the needs of the research project and those of participating agencies. The goal of each of the participating agencies was to work with families where possible. Adolescents were assured that their decisions regarding parent contact would have no effect on reimbursement for the interview.

Of the 602 adolescents interviewed, 281 (46.7%) gave consent for parent/caretaker contact. Of these, 201 (71.5%) parents/caretakers agreed to participate in the study. Only 18 (6.4%) refused to be interviewed; 62 (22.1%) could not be located. Problems locating parents were mostly attributable to incomplete or incorrect phone numbers or addresses provided by adolescents.

## ADOLESCENT SAMPLE CHARACTERISTICS

We obtained usable interviews for 241 young men and 361 young women. The adolescents ranged in age from 12 to 22 years. The average age was about 7 months higher for young men (16.6 years) than for young women (16 years). Modal categories were 17 years (21%) for the young men and 16 years for the young women (25%). Ages were almost normally distributed (Figure 2.1) with very few falling into the oldest or youngest age brackets.

Although the majority (61%) were European-American, almost one-fourth of our respondents were African-American with the remainder Hispanic, Native American, or "other." Prior to running away, over one-half had lived in large metropolitan areas (more than 100,000 people) or a suburb of a large urban area (Table 2.1). Only 7% of the sample came from very small communities or had lived on farms. Most of the adolescents had been housed the week prior to their interview (Table 2.2). Almost one-half (49%) had spent the previous week in a shelter, 23% had been living with friends, and 14%

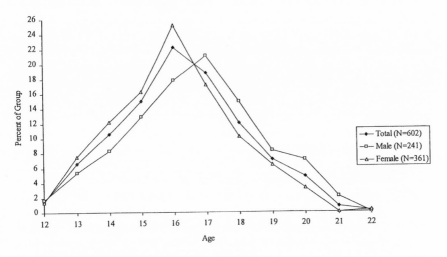

*Figure 2.1.* Adolescent age distribution by gender.

*Table 2.1.* City of Origin

| City Size (Population) | Number (N = 600) | Percentage |
|---|---|---|
| Metropolitan area (100,000+) | 287 | 47.8 |
| Suburb of metropolitan area | 41 | 6.8 |
| Medium-sized city (50,000 to 100,000) | 119 | 19.8 |
| Town (10,000 to 50,000) | 58 | 9.7 |
| Small town (2,500 to 10,000) | 52 | 8.7 |
| Very small town (2,500 and less) | 38 | 6.3 |
| Country/farm | 5 | 0.8 |

*Table 2.2.* Where Adolescents Spent Most of Their Time in the Week Prior to Their Interview

| Location | Number (N = 599) | Percentage |
|---|---|---|
| Shelter | 292 | 48.7 |
| Friends | 135 | 22.5 |
| Parents or other relative | 85 | 14.2 |
| Institution (hospital, group home, juvenile detention) | 40 | 6.7 |
| Street (abandoned house, car, van) | 17 | 2.8 |
| Other | 30 | 5.0 |

Table 2.3. Parental/Caretaker Occupation

| | Percentage of Group | | | | | |
| | Adolescent Report of Caretaker's Occupation | | | Caretaker Report of Own Occupation | | |
| Occupation | All (N = 541) | Male (N = 216) | Female (N = 325) | All (N = 134) | Male (N = 50) | Female (N = 84) |
|---|---|---|---|---|---|---|
| Managerial and Professional Specialty | | | | | | |
| Executive, administrative, and managerial | 5.9 | 6.5 | 5.5 | 10.4 | 6.0 | 13.1 |
| Professional specialty | 12.4 | 13.4 | 11.7 | 9.7 | 18.0 | 8.3 |
| Technical, sales, and administrative support | | | | | | |
| Technicians and related support | 2.0 | 0.5 | 3.1 | 4.5 | 2.0 | 6.0 |
| Sales | 8.7 | 7.4 | 9.5 | 7.5 | 8.0 | 7.1 |
| Administrative support/clerical | 13.5 | 12.0 | 14.5 | 21.6 | 28.0 | 17.9 |
| Service | | | | | | |
| Private household services | 4.6 | 3.2 | 5.5 | — | — | — |
| Protective services | 1.1 | 0.9 | 1.2 | 1.5 | 0.0 | 2.4 |
| Other services | 21.3 | 20.4 | 21.8 | 23.9 | 26.0 | 22.6 |
| Farming, forest, and fishing | | | | | | |
| Farm operators or managers | 0.2 | 0.0 | 0.3 | — | — | — |
| Other farm-related | 0.7 | 1.9 | 0.0 | — | — | — |
| Other agricultural related | 0.6 | 0.9 | 0.3 | — | — | — |
| Precision production, craft, and repair | | | | | | |
| Mechanics and repairers | 0.9 | 0.5 | 1.2 | .7 | 2.0 | 0.0 |
| Construction | 2.6 | 4.6 | 1.2 | 1.5 | 2.0 | 1.2 |
| Precision production | 3.3 | 2.8 | 3.7 | 1.5 | 2.0 | 1.2 |

| | | | | | | |
|---|---|---|---|---|---|---|
| Operators, fabricators, and laborers | | | | | | |
| Machine operators, assemblers, and inspectors | 7.0 | 6.0 | 7.7 | 9.0 | 6.0 | 10.7 |
| Transportation and material moving | 2.0 | 3.2 | 1.2 | 6.0 | 2.0 | 8.3 |
| Handlers, equipment cleaners, helpers, & laborers | 5.7 | 7.4 | 4.6 | 2.2 | 4.0 | 1.2 |
| Miscellaneous | | | | | | |
| Odd jobs | 0.6 | 0.9 | 0.3 | — | — | — |
| Homemaker | 0.2 | 0.0 | 0.3 | — | — | — |
| Military | 0.9 | 0.9 | 0.9 | — | — | — |
| Drug dealer | 0.6 | 0.5 | 0.6 | — | — | — |
| Sex workers | 0.7 | 0.5 | 0.9 | — | — | — |
| Not codeable | 2.6 | 2.8 | 2.5 | — | — | — |
| Missing | 1.8 | 2.8 | 1.2 | — | — | — |

had been with their parents. Only about 3% had spent the previous week directly on the streets.

To obtain estimations of social origins we asked the adolescents about their primary caretakers. Because of the number of caretaker transitions most of these young people had experienced, respondents were asked to designate the most important adult guardian in their lives, "the adult who cared about you the most, lived with you and helped raise you as you were growing up." Two-thirds (64%) named their mothers as their primary caretaker, 12% their fathers, and about 8% their grandmothers. The remaining 16% of the caretakers were widely scattered among steprelatives, adoptive parents, and nonrelatives. Ten of the children listed foster parents as primary caretakers; 5 gave a professional person (e.g., caseworker) as the one that cared about them the most.

Table 2.3 provides adolescent and caretaker reports of occupations of primary caretakers. Occupational categories (U.S. Employment Service 1991) were well-distributed. Of the 90% of parents/caretakers who were employed, 18% were reported to be professionals or managers, almost 25% were technicians, administrative support, or sales persons, 27% were service workers, and 15% were laborers. Seven of the young people listed their primary caretakers as sex workers or drug dealers. Two-thirds of the adolescents reported that their primary caretakers were employed full-time (66%). Twelve percent were unemployed. Almost one-half of the adolescents said that their primary caretaker had been on "welfare" at some time when the adolescent was still at home; of these, three-fourths (73%) reported having received food stamps while living with their primary caretakers. According to the adolescents, about 22% of the primary caretakers had not completed high school, 18% had completed college or a technical/trade school, and 3% had an advanced degree.

## PARENT/CARETAKER SAMPLE CHARACTERISTICS

On receipt of the consent form with the primary caretaker address from the agency interviewer, parents/caretakers were contacted for a 20–30 minute computer-assisted telephone interview. At the end of the interview, they were offered $25 to complete a mailed questionnaire. Of the 201 parent/caretakers interviewed by phone, 167 (83%) returned usable mailed questionnaires. Parents/caretakers who talked with us were predominantly female (83%). Their average age was 41 years with a range of 28 to 70 years. Eighteen percent of the parents/caretakers reported less than 12 years of education, 7% had 16 years, and 4% reported more than 16 years of education. Fifty-six percent of the parents/caretakers reported they were employed full-time and 11% part-time. Thirteen percent were homemakers, with the remaining unemployed or retired. Of those employed, 20% gave their occupation as professionals or managers; 34% as technicians, sales persons, or administrative support, 25% as service sector employees, and 21% as laborers (Table 2.3). Parents/caretakers reports of household income (Table 2.4) indicated that almost one-fourth (23%) of the adolescents came from homes with annual incomes of less than $15,000. Eleven percent were from households with incomes in excess of $55,000. Most of the parents/caretakers were currently married (58%) or living with someone (3%). Five percent were currently separated and 25% were divorced. About one-half (51%) had been married more than one time. Of these, 61% had been married twice and 24% had been married 3 times, and 16% had been married 4 or more times. Seventy percent of the married parents/caretakers reported that their spouses worked full-time.

## ANALYSES OF REFUSAL RATES

As noted, there were two refusal points in our sampling frame for the matched parent/caretaker-adolescent sample: adolescent refusal of consent to contact primary caretakers and the actual caretaker refusals. We performed a series of statistical analyses at both refusal points to determine systematic differences between consenting and nonconsenting adolescents and participating and nonparticipating adults.

Adolescent males and females were about equally likely to give consent to contact primary caretakers (46.9 and 46.5%, respectively). European-American youth were slightly more likely to give consent to contact than

*Table 2.4.* Caretaker Report of Total Household Income

|  | Percentage of Group | | |
|---|---|---|---|
| Total Income | All Adolescents (N = 201) | Male Adolescents (N = 71) | Female Adolescents (N = 130) |
| Below $5,000 | 3.0 | 2.8 | 3.1 |
| $5,000 to 10,000 | 8.5 | 11.3 | 6.9 |
| $10,000 to $15,000 | 11.9 | 8.5 | 13.8 |
| $15,000 to $20,000 | 11.4 | 11.3 | 11.5 |
| $20,000 to $25,000 | 8.0 | 4.2 | 10.0 |
| $25,000 to $35,000 | 19.4 | 18.3 | 20.0 |
| $35,000 to $45,000 | 11.4 | 15.5 | 9.2 |
| $45,000 to $55,000 | 9.5 | 9.9 | 9.2 |
| Above $55,000 | 10.9 | 11.3 | 10.8 |
| Don't know | 2.0 | 2.8 | 1.5 |
| Refused/missing | 4.0 | 4.1 | 4.0 |

their minority counterparts. Fifty-three percent of white, non-Hispanics gave consent, compared to 45% of Hispanic young people, 37% of African-Americans, and 40% of Native Americans. Younger adolescents were significantly more likely to give consent (mean age for consenters = 16.07, nonconsenters = 16.44). Adolescents who described themselves as gay, lesbian, or bisexual had a lower consent rate (32.1%) than self-described heterosexuals (47.6%). Youth from large urban areas, suburbs, and other towns were about equally likely to give consent to contact parents/caretakers. However, youth from very small towns were much more likely to consent (76.3%). These were largely shelter children who had had much less experience on their own and fewer runaway episodes.

In general, the more conventional the adolescent, the more likely he or she would give consent to contact the primary caretaker. Adolescents who were involved in drug and alcohol use were significantly less likely to give consent than nonusers. Those who had attended some school in the previous year were more likely to grant permission to contact (48.7%) than those who had not. Those who reported engaging in deviant subsistence strategies (e.g., panhandling, theft, survival sex) were less likely to give consent. Consenters were significantly less likely to have been seriously victimized while on their own. However, there were no differences in consent based on the amount of time spent actually living on the street or the total amount of unsupervised time (e.g., living with friends, housed but unsupervised by an adult).

Besides being behaviorally more conventional, consenting adolescents were closer to their parents/caretakers than were the nonconsenting adolescents. Young people who gave permission to contact rated parents/caretakers significantly higher on measures of parental warmth and supportiveness and parental monitoring than those who refused permission to contact. Otherwise, adolescent descriptions of parents/caretakers had little effect on their likelihood of consenting to contact. Consenting youth did not differ from nonconsenting youth on measures of parent/caretaker education, employment, or participation in welfare programs.

As noted, the majority of the parents/caretakers whom we were unable to interview could not be located with the information provided us by the adolescents. Only 6.4% of the adults actually refused our request for an interview once contacted. The remaining 22% of the nonrespondents could not be reached because of incomplete addresses or incorrect phone numbers. The noncontact adults differed from those whom we interviewed in much the same ways as the adolescent refusals. Parents/caretakers of young men were more likely to be noncontacts than those of young women. They were also more likely to be of an ethnic minority, parents/caretakers of a gay or lesbian adolescent, and from large metropolitan areas. Adolescents of parents/caretakers whom we were unable to contact were more likely to have been arrested. Contact rates did not differ by adolescent reports of physical and sexual abuse or by social characteristics of the parent/caretaker (e.g., education, employment, or having been on welfare).

Once contacted, the parents/caretakers of young men (77%) were more likely to agree to an interview than those of young women (63%). The social characteristics of parent/caretaker respondents were similar to those of the entire adolescent sample. The parent/caretaker response rate was unaffected by levels of education, employment, and having ever participated in a welfare program. Parent/caretakers of majority youth (77.5%) and Hispanic youth (77.7%) were most likely to participate in the study, African-American (58.5%) and Native American (50.0%) parents/caretakers least likely. Parents/caretakers from suburbs (84.2%) and very small towns (79.3%) were more likely to agree to an interview than those from urban areas, regardless of city size.

Caretakers who refused participation were viewed by their adolescents as more rejecting and less warm and supportive than those who agreed to become part of our study. Similarly, refusal rates were higher for parents/caretakers whose adolescent viewed them as neglecting. Surprisingly, no significant differences were found for caretakers whose adolescents reported physical and/or sexual abuse. Also parent/caretaker response rates did not differ on the basis of adolescent drug and alcohol use. The longer the adolescent had been on his or her own, the less likely the parent/caretaker agreed to be interviewed.

In summary, two somewhat similar scenarios for participation emerged. Among adolescents, consent to contact a parent or caretaker was more likely among younger, less deviant runaways, who remained somewhat attached to their parents/caretakers. For the adult generation, angrier, more rejecting parents of older, more emancipated youth were less likely to agree to be interviewed. The bias of our matched parent/caretaker-adolescent subsample therefore is quite conservative. The "most troubled" parents and children refused our attempts to interview across generations. Instead, our subsample of 201 parents/caretakers and adolescents tend to represent the more successful, least dysfunctional families of runaways. This is important to note in that these parents and children are reporting significant family problems including behavioral problems, mutual violence, and problems with parenting.

## SOME LIMITATIONS AND CAUTIONS

We understood from our pilot work and discussions with street workers that we would be limited in amount of productive interview time with these adolescents. We believed we were "stretching" the parameters of valid responses by setting the time at ninety minutes even though we built a snack break into the process. For this reason we do not have all of the information we would have liked and do not have multiple reports on several of the measures.

There are at least two sources of systematic bias readers should keep in mind. The first involves the quality of the adolescent self-report data. To assess this we obtained interviewer evaluations of each interview as part of the research design. Interviewer assessments indicate that the young people tended to be interested and involved in the interview process. Only about 13% were rated by interviewers as not very or not at all interested. Few of the interviewers judged the young person as somewhat or very uncomfortable during the interview (11%). Subjects were not interviewed if they appeared dangerous or were not sober or coherent at the time of the interview. *Most of the interviewers believed that any systematic reporting bias was in the direction of under- rather than overreporting negative experiences and behaviors* (see Appendix Table 2A.3). Over one-fourth of these seasoned street workers believed that the young people were at least somewhat underreporting physical abuse (28%) and sexual abuse (24%). Almost one-third of the adolescents were thought to be underreporting drug/alcohol use (32%).

As a second cautionary note, readers should keep in mind characteristics of the matched parent/caretaker-adolescent subsample when evaluating our results. The systematic bias that exists is undoubtedly conservative. That is, the nonrespondents are probably from more disrupted and more dysfunctional family systems. Third, although the study was designed to reach adolescents directly on the streets, the time and energy constraints on our "real world" agency staff meant that interviews often took place at opportune times and locations. The majority of our interviews are shelter interviews. However, many of the sheltered youth had spent significant time on the street, and we have a wide distribution of unsupervised living arrangements and length of time unsupervised.

Finally, our data are cross-sectional. To truly evaluate the effects of precocious independence on adolescent development we need longitudinal data (see Hoyt, Whitbeck, & Cauce, under review). However, our life events matrix provides retrospective developmental histories from which we can draw some guarded conclusions. Also, our analyses based on life course theories are suggestive of amplification processes at work as these young people experience the effects of early independence.

In summary, we believe our data provide a systematic investigation of runaways in typical American cities. The sample allows comparisons of runaways in cities that vary widely in population. In addition, the reports of parents/caretakers provide invaluable information regarding the family lives and developmental histories of these young people. As their stories unfold, keeping in mind that these are often the best functioning families will be difficult. These are troubled, often disorganized families. However, it is also important to note that the parents/caretakers in our study often are reporting on the behaviors of "any adult caretaker" who had been in the children's lives and not necessarily their own behaviors. Many of these adult caretakers are struggling to make amends for early harm done their children through no fault of their own and may be attempting to rebuild or hold together a disintegrating situation.

# II

# THE FAMILY LIVES OF RUNAWAY AND HOMELESS ADOLESCENTS

# 3

# The Early Lives of Runaways

*She has almost no memories of childhood. I was really saddened by this kid's story. She doesn't have any contact with any family. She hasn't had any long term place to grow up at. When you have to pick a foster mom as your significant guardian and you can't even remember her name—that's sad. She identified us [the agency] as her support person in two areas—she barely knows us.*
—Interviewer comment

## THE LIFE-EVENTS MATRIX

We wanted in-depth developmental histories of the adolescents but we did not have interview time to do a traditional family history with each adolescent. To accomplish this in the short time we had available, we created a life-events matrix that allowed the interviewer to construct a table of consecutive life transitions beginning at birth and ending with the adolescent's current living situation. The young person was first asked "What adults were living with you and looking after you when you were first born?" Next they were asked the location (city and state), then why that situation changed (approximate month and year), and when they left it (approximate month and year). After establishing family configuration and location at time of birth, each subsequent life transition involving a change in family configuration or location was probed consecutively: "What adults were living with you and looking after you next?" and "What situation did you (live in/move to) next?" The life-events matrix provided sequential information regarding life changes that included approximate dates so that by age we could chronicle changes in family structure (divorces, remarriages, live-ins), geographic moves with family members, number of parent-initiated changes in the liv-

31

ing arrangement of the child (e.g., moves to live with grandmother, divorces that resulted in moves), institutional or legally initiated changes in the living arrangement of the child (e.g., child welfare interventions, juvenile detention), and child-initiated changes in living arrangements (e.g., deciding to move in with his or her father or a friend's family, running away). Not only did the matrix allow us to count important life transitions, it also provided information on the number of runs, approximations of the amount of total amount of time spent unsupervised (total time on own, housed or unhoused), and the amount of time actually living on the streets (total time unhoused).

## LIFE TRANSITIONS

The life-events matrix chronicled multiple levels of disorganization in the adolescents' young lives. The stories that emerged were lives full of changes. Our respondents have moved from residence to residence, caretaker to caretaker, beginning at early ages. Once on their own the process seems to accelerate. One young woman described 31 separate self-initiated moves by age 18 years. These included runs from home, from residential facilities and foster homes, as well as moves in and out of friends' homes. The average number of adolescent-initiated moves was 5.5.

About two-thirds of our respondents (62% males and 64% females) had experienced institutionally initiated moves to and from residential facilities, shelters, foster care, and juvenile detention. The maximum for institutional moves was 26 for a young man aged 16 years. Similarly, two-thirds (68%) of the males and almost three-fourths (73%) of the females had experienced a change in family structure. The highest number of such changes was 13 for a young woman aged 16 years at the time of our interview.

Changes in the children's lives were also initiated by their parents either by placement or by changes in family configuration. Two-thirds of the adolescents told us that their parents had initiated changes in the child's living arrangement. These involved moves between parents, moves to relatives, and institutional placements. One adolescent boy reported 12 parent-initiated changes in residence by the time he was 14 years old. Over half of the changes in family structure were due to the divorce or separation of a parent (Table 3.1). Further changes in family configuration through remarriages or having a parent or parent's boyfriend or girlfriend move in or out of the family were experienced by almost two-thirds (63%) of the adolescent females and 40% of the males. About 7% of the females and 5% of the males had lost a parent through death. Seven percent of the females and 4% of the males had had a parent spend time in prison.

Life for the majority of the adolescents had been a "revolving door" of various living situations often beginning early in life. Reasons for parent-initi-

*Table 3.1.* Categories of Changes in Family Structure by Gender: Percentage Reporting and Means

|  | Male | | Female | |
|---|---|---|---|---|
|  | % Ever | Mean | % Ever | Mean |
| Divorce/separation | 53.1 | .69 | 54.0 | .70 |
| Remarriage | 16.3 | .18 | 25.5 | .28 |
| Boy-/girlfriend moved in | 10.9 | .14 | 20.2 | .27 |
| Parent returned | 7.9 | .09 | 9.7 | .12 |
| Boy-/girlfriend moved out | 5.4 | .06 | 7.8 | .10 |
| Death of parent | 5.0 | .05 | 6.6 | .07 |
| Parent sent to prison | 3.8 | .05 | 6.6 | .08 |
| Abuse/violence by parent | 2.9 | .03 | 5.5 | .06 |
| Evicted | 2.1 | .05 | 3.3 | .04 |
| Parent in hospital or treatment | 1.7 | .02 | 2.8 | .03 |
| Both parents left | .8 | .01 | 1.7 | .02 |
| Other | 5.4 | .08 | 9.1 | .12 |
| Total | 67.8 | 1.56 | 73.1 | 2.00 |

*Table 3.2.* Categories of Parent-Initiated Changes by Gender: Percentage Reporting and Means

|  | Male | | Female | |
|---|---|---|---|---|
|  | % Ever | Mean | % Ever | Mean |
| Rules and behaviors | 18.7 | .22 | 17.2 | .24 |
| Let child return | 17.0 | .24 | 24.9 | .35 |
| Kicked out | 16.6 | .21 | 16.3 | .22 |
| Change in custody | 14.1 | .27 | 10.5 | .16 |
| Parent placed in foster care | 13.7 | .17 | 15.2 | .17 |
| Parent unable/not wanting to care | 10.0 | .10 | 10.0 | .12 |
| Sent to relatives | 5.4 | .07 | 8.0 | .11 |
| Other | 16.6 | .19 | 20.2 | .26 |
| Total | 66.1 | 1.49 | 67.0 | 1.63 |

ated changes were widely distributed (Table 3.2). Even though the adolescent is the reporter on the life-events matrix, parent-initiated moves were primarily attributed to the adolescent behaviors. Failure to comply with rules and behavioral problems were the reasons most mentioned. The next most mentioned parent-initiated change was a parent/caretaker kicking the young person out of the house. The profile that emerges is one of a parent abdicating the caretaker role by placing the child in foster care, arranging for him or her to leave home due to problem behaviors (destination unknown), sending the child to a relative, or simply telling the child to leave. Simple custody changes between parents accounted for only a small proportion of the parent-initiated changes (14% males, 11% females). Rather, the reasons listed by the adolescents for why their parents/caretakers moved them are suggestive of frustration (e.g., not following rules, behavioral problems, kicked out) and resignation (unable or unwilling to care for child, placed in foster care).

A quite different picture emerges when we focus on child-initiated transitions (Table 3.3). Here the adolescents were most likely simply to say they left home (no reason given) or to attribute their leaving home to intolerable or dangerous circumstances. Forty-two percent of the females and 33% of the males reported leaving home due to abuse or neglect. Similar percentages left due to fighting and arguing (39% females, 37% males). About one-fourth attributed their leaving to rules to which they would not comply and to their own behavioral problems. Almost one-third simply said they wanted to live elsewhere. The profile of child-initiated moves suggests remarkable detachment. These children appear to be leaving home after a considerable period of emotional separation, simply drifting out at some point and not returning for a period of time. Over one-half report that at some point they returned home of their own accord. As the adolescents become more separated from the family, more precociously independent, they leave when the situation gets too difficult (family fighting, violence) or when they believe their freedom is being infringed upon by rules or behavioral constraints.

It is important to keep in mind that multiple forces are working simultaneously to push and pull these young people into and out of their families. Adolescents who experience parent-initiated moves are also initiating their own changes in residence. At the same time many are also becoming "system kids." Over one-fourth report spending time in foster care or a group home (26% males, 27% females) (Table 3.4). Forty-two percent of the

*Table 3.3.* Categories of Child Initiated Transitions by Gender: Percentage Reporting and Means

|  | Male | | Female | |
| --- | --- | --- | --- | --- |
|  | *% Ever* | *Mean* | *% Ever* | *Mean* |
| Left/no reason given | 74.3 | 2.32 | 67.9 | 2.16 |
| Returned home | 52.3 | .98 | 51.2 | .98 |
| Abuse/neglect | 33.2 | .48 | 41.6 | .64 |
| Arguing/fighting | 36.5 | .60 | 39.1 | .59 |
| Wanted to live elsewhere | 32.4 | .55 | 30.7 | .62 |
| Rules and behavior | 26.6 | .40 | 26.6 | .33 |
| Sought shelter from street | 13.3 | .20 | 10.0 | .13 |
| Total | 96.7 | 5.44 | 93.9 | 5.46 |

*Table 3.4.* Categories of Institutional Initiated Transitions by Gender: Percent Reporting and Means

|  | Male | | Female | |
| --- | --- | --- | --- | --- |
|  | % Ever | Mean | % Ever | Mean |
| Released from institution | 36.5 | .70 | 33.5 | .60 |
| Arrested/juvenile detention | 34.4 | .63 | 42.1 | .80 |
| Foster care/residential | 25.7 | .45 | 27.4 | .38 |
| System transfer | 19.1 | .39 | 16.3 | .31 |
| Psych/substance abuse | 9.1 | .16 | 8.9 | .12 |
| Other | 17.8 | .24 | 13.5 | .15 |
| Total | 61.5 | 2.56 | 64.0 | 2.35 |

females and 34% of the males had been arrested at some point and spent time in juvenile detention. Almost 10% had spent time in a residential treatment program. A significant proportion (19% males, 16% females) had been transferred within the system.

## CASE STUDIES

The revolving door for some of these young people never seems to stop. They move from family to friends, to foster care or group homes, to on their own, perhaps never having a single reference point that is "home." As transitions grow in number, a pattern evolves. The adolescent moves from family-oriented transitions to greater involvement in institutional transitions and self-initiated transitions. To illustrate the disarray of these young lives we chronicle the life-events of two representative adolescents.

### Robert

Robert is a 16-year-old who first ran away at age 11 years and has been on his own off and on since then. He recalls first running after having an argument with his mother and deciding to spend the night at a friend's house. The following day he was located and his mother had him placed in a local children's hospital. Upon release from the hospital, Robert promptly ran away again, staying in an abandoned car for several nights. He was located and again hospitalized. After his release from the hospital he was soon arrested for breaking and entering and served three months in juvenile detention. When he was returned to his mother's home she was heavily abusing drugs and he was soon on his own again. With nowhere to go he "stooped" in vacant buildings. Tired of living on his own he approached a residential center, which released him again to his mother's custody. He was soon arrested again, this time for assault. He was briefly detained in juvenile detention and again was admitted to a children's hospital, where he spent about two months. When he was released to his mother's custody, Robert found her living with a lesbian lover. Arguments with his mother's lover and being in trouble with gang activity caused him to move briefly to his girl-friend's home. After an argument with his mother he overdosed at a party and was again hospitalized. This time he was released to his grandmother. After a few weeks there he moved in with a male friend with whom he developed a sexual relationship. After this relationship broke up, Robert returned to live with his mother. During this time he was in and out of the hospital and trans-ferred within the system to residential care and group homes for the next sev-eral months. He was arrested again and charged with burglary, arson, and attempted murder. He served a third sentence in juvenile detention. Since his release, he has lived primarily on the streets, supporting himself by selling drugs. He remains active in a local gang. While on the streets Robert has traded sex for food, drugs, and shelter. At the time of the interview he was staying at a homeless shelter.

### Amy

Amy was also 16 years old at the time of our interview. Her parents divorced when she was five and she lived with her mother until her father took her and her sister away from her mother illegally. When her mother regained custody she was living with a boyfriend. During the next several years, her mother had four live-in boyfriends. When Amy was 12, her mother, while high on drugs, told her and her brother to leave. Having no idea what to do or where to go, they spent that night at a friend's house. Soon after they returned home, her mother, still using drugs, became physically abusive. After a family argument that became violent, Amy again spent some time with friends. Child Protective Services became involved when the mother abandoned the family. Amy was then placed in a group home, where she attempted suicide. After a brief hospitalization she was returned to the group home and again made a suicide attempt. After another hospitalization she was released to a foster home that didn't work out. From there she was placed again in a group home, from which she ran away. She was caught by police and returned to a shelter. During her time in the shelter, her baby brother died but she was not allowed to return home for the funeral.

Over the next nine months Amy ran away from a group home a total of 26 times. After yet another hospital stay, a foster home was tried again, but she was asked to leave due to behavioral problems. So it was back to the group home. After another series of runs she wound up in juvenile detention. When released she tried living with her mother again and then living with an uncle. When things did not work out at the uncle's house, she returned to live with her mother. Authorities removed her from her mother's house because of the parent's ongoing drug habit and returned her to the group home. Amy admits to serious drug use herself and has used IV drugs. She has recurring nightmares and obsessive thoughts regarding a stranger-rape during the past year. She was living at a group home at the time of our interview.

## TRANSITION PATTERNS

The recurring developmental theme is one of family disorganization and multiple life transitions at very early ages for these young people. As the number of child transitions increases, family ties appear to weaken or are never truly established. Linkages erode and the opportunity for, or necessity of, early independence expands. Children leave, drift out, or are cast out in various ways. They may be turned over to agencies, sent to live with the other parent, grandparents, or other relatives, or simply told that they may not return home.

We graphed transition patterns across time to illustrate this process of decreasing parent involvement and increasing adolescent independence and institutional involvement as the numbers of transitions expand (Figure 3.1). Changes in family configuration and parent-initiated changes were primarily early transitions. Family structural changes (divorces, remarriages,

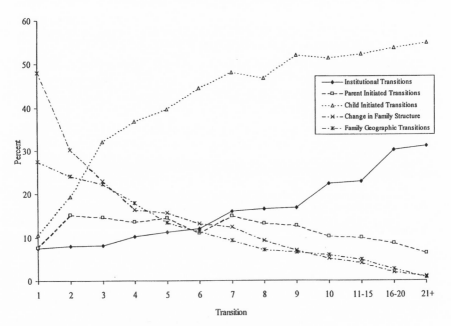

*Figure 3.1.* Transition patterns of runaway adolescents.

live-ins) were frequently noted as early transitions and were seldom mentioned as later life changes. Parent-initiated transitions also tended to be mentioned earlier and then dropped in number and leveled off. Geographical moves with the family followed a similar pattern. Child-initiated transitions, however, increased markedly above all other types of transitions. Later transitions were predominantly child-initiated or, to a lesser extent, institutional-initiated placements.

The transition patterns indicate increasing child independence and decreasing parent involvement. Parent/caretaker-child linkages appear to weaken as the number of transitions grows. Parent/caretaker influence in the child transition process is largely replaced by institutional control by the seventh transition. Child-initiated transitions surpass all subsequent changes by the fourth transition. Once begun, the runaway process appears to have cumulative effects. The adolescents moved persistently toward separation from family as the number of transitions increased either through increasing independence or institutional placements.

## AGE AT FIRST RUNAWAY AND RISK FOR SUBSEQUENT RUNS

The age at first runaway has important implications for subsequent development. The more precocious the independent behavior, the greater is the likelihood that subsequent adultlike independent behaviors will follow (Moffitt, 1997). Numerous studies have focused on the dysfunctional characteristics of the families that adolescents leave, but very few have documented the effects of family disorganization and instability. Mundy and colleagues reported correlates and effects of residential instability on adolescents in an inpatient psychiatric facility (Mundy, Robertson, Greenblatt, & Robertson, 1989). They found that family instability was associated with other types of family-of-origin dysfunction and severity of disorder. Based on attachment theory, Stefanidis and associates reported long-term adjustment effects for adolescents with histories of family disorganization and multiple out-of-home placements (Stefanidis, Pennbridge, MacKenzie, & Pottharst, 1992). However, typically the effects of family disorganization are lost due to its strong association with other aspects of nonoptimal parenting.

We believe that this basic disorganization is fundamental to the process of precocious independence. It weakens boundaries so that drifting out or choosing to leave becomes easier for the adolescent. Ties may erode as caretakers come and go. Geographic mobility reduces support systems linked to home and neighborhood. The pace of change itself may contribute to the need for independent behaviors. If one of the consequences of parental divorce is to accelerate adolescent separation (McLanahan & Sandefur, 1994), multiple changes in family configuration may be expected to accentuate that effect.

This coupled with other types of family change pushes the child toward early independence.

Using the retrospective data from the life-events matrix, we constructed a path model that used the number of family transitions prior to the first run to predict age at first run and the number of subsequent child-initiated transitions. We hypothesized that the number of adolescent-reported changes in family structure prior to the first run and the number of prior family changes in residence would be negatively associated with the age at which the child first ran away. That is, the greater the number of family structural and geographic changes, the earlier is the age at first run. The model also predicts the number of subsequent child-initiated changes in residence based on age at first run. The earlier the child seeks independence, the more likely he/she will continue to act independently.

The number of changes in family structure was measured by taking the total number of changes in family configuration prior to the child's first run and dividing it by the child's age at the time of first run to obtain an average per year change in family configuration. The mean for changes in family structure was .120 with a standard deviation of .137. The number of family changes in residence was similarly constructed and had a mean of .088 and a standard deviation of .140. Age of child's first run was assessed by the age given when the child first left home to be on his/her own or was kicked out to be on his/her own. The number of child-initiated transitions after first runaway represents a count of all child-initiated changes in living situations recorded on the life-events matrix after the child first experienced being on his/her own. The mean for this measure was 3.9 with a standard deviation of 3.2. The model controlled for gender of adolescent.

The young people in our study on average first ran at age 13.5 years for both adolescent males and females. Very few ran prior to age 10 years. The majority (80%) had run by 16 years. All were on their own by age 19 years. There were few differences between adolescent boys and girls in the timing of first run. The age curve for timing of first runaway climbs very steeply from about age 11 through 17 years, indicating that the cycle often begins prior to becoming a teenager.

The results of our path model (Figure 3.2) indicate that both the number of changes in family structure ($\beta = .21$; $p = .0001$) and number of family changes in residence ($\beta = -.07$; $p = .07$) were negatively related to age at first run regardless of the gender of child. The greater the average number of family changes per year prior to running, the earlier is the age at first run. Multiple family changes appear to erode children's ties and encourage earlier separation. This is consistent with other research indicating that basic changes in family configuration such as divorce of a parent accelerate the adolescent separation process and hence participation in adultlike behaviors (McLanahan & Sandefur, 1994).

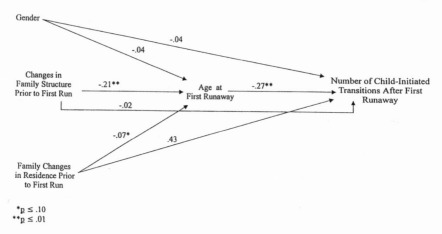

*Figure 3.2.* Regression model for family transition and age at first runaway.

Our findings suggest that multiple family transitions not only lead to earlier drift out, but the timing of first independence predicts subsequent child-initiated transitions ($\beta = -.27$; $p = .0001$). The younger the child at first run, the more likely he/she will run again. As we will note throughout this volume, once the transition to adultlike behaviors occurs, a process is set in motion that is difficult, if not impossible, to turn around. Precocious independence is a life-altering transition in the context of a disorganized, multiple-transition family. The adolescent's adaptation, though developmentally harmful in most instances, indicates an effort to take control of chaotic or—as we shall see in subsequent analyses—often dangerous situations. Once asserted, it is not easy to relinquish such control.

## AGE AT FIRST RUNAWAY AND RISK OF SPENDING TIME ON THE STREETS

About one-third of the adolescents had spent time directly on the streets. Males (41.1%) were more likely to have spent time without shelter than females (28.8%). Males were also more likely to end up on the street at an earlier age. The risk for spending time without shelter begins early (about age 10 years) and climbs dramatically from ages 12 to 17 years for both males and females. At this point, the risk levels off for females but continues to increase through age 20 years for the adolescent males.

When adolescents separate early, their exposure to risk as a consequence of their own behaviors and the environment increases. Adolescents have fewer resources, no access to institutionalized sources of independent income (e.g., welfare or food stamps), little work experience, few skills, and little access to legitimate means of self-support. We extended our model to examine the relationships between early independence and the risk of spending time directly on the streets (e.g., spending the night without shelter, in cars, in abandoned buildings). Using logistic regression we ran two models (Table 3.5). The first took into account the effects of gender, changes in family configuration, and changes in residence on whether the adolescent ever spent time on the streets. Of these variables, only gender predicted street time. Adolescent males were more likely to spend time on the streets than were females ($\beta = .52$). When age at first run was added in the second model, it significantly increased the likelihood of street time in addition to gender ($\beta = -.09$). Multiplicative odds ratios (see columns for exp *B* in Table 3.5) indicated that males were about 1.5 times more likely than females to spend time on the streets and that each year that a child delays running away decreases the likelihood of ever spending time on the streets by about 10%.

## LEAVING DISORGANIZED FAMILIES

These results lay the foundation for what will be a recurring theme in this volume: Early independence for children is the result of a long process of events originating within the families from which they leave. The developmental histories of these adolescents point to multiple sources of change in caretakers and in residence. At some point these children become independent participants in the change process, an attempt perhaps to exert more control over their lives. The more transitions children experience in family structure and residence, the earlier they will initiate change on their own.

*Table 3.5.* Logistic Regression for Family Disorganization, Age at First Run on Ever Spending Time Directly on the Streets

|  | Model 1 | | Model 2 | |
|---|---|---|---|---|
|  | B | exp B | B | exp B |
| Gender | .52* | 1.68 | .51* | 1.66 |
| Family structure | .55 | .58 | .90 | .41 |
| Family geographic | .30 | .74 | .43 | .65 |
| Age on own | — | — | .09* | .92 |
| Intercept | −.80 | | .41 | |
|  | $G^2 = 10.73$ (3 df), $p = .013$ | | $G^2 = 16.5$ (4 df), $p = .002$ | |

* $p \le .05.$

The earlier this process is begun, the more likely the young person will independently initiate subsequent changes in residence and, in turn, the more likely he or she will spend time at serious risk, directly on the streets.

Delineating family transitions is only the beginning of the story. Families don't become chaotic by accident. There are histories of individual and relationship problems that contribute to the lack of stability in location and structure. In turn, these histories lead to problematic interactions and behaviors that erode ties and promote changes on every level. Often the pattern of multiple transitions is passed across generations. We turn next to the family histories of the runaways we interviewed reported by the adolescents themselves and by their parents/caretakers.

**4**

# Troubled Generations

*When I went to school, I would in the back of my mind, I would think that they (classmates) went home to storybook families, and I was going home to this nightmare.*

—Male, aged 18 years

For the majority of families in our study, troubles did not begin with the runaway child. Rather, the adolescents left homes characterized by loose family ties and multiple transitions. These family characteristics often originated in the troubled lives of the adult caretakers. Frequently, problems spanned generations. In this chapter we chronicle the lives of parents/caretakers and other family members and examine the ways they have influenced the runaway adolescents. We also investigate three-generation models of alcohol and drug problems and serious criminal behaviors.

## ADOLESCENT REPORTS OF FAMILY PROBLEMS

The adolescents reported family histories characterized by alcohol and drug problems, mental health problems, and troubles with the law. Over one-half (56%) of the adolescents reported that at least one of their parents had an alcohol problem (Table 4.1). Nineteen percent told us that both parents were problem drinkers. Over one-third (35%) of the adolescents believed that at least one of their parents had a problem with hard drugs; 10% of these said both parents used hard drugs. About 15% reported that at least one parent had a "marijuana problem." When we added together reports concerning all of the multiple parents and stepparents with whom the adolescents had lived, two-thirds (65%) had been exposed to a parent or stepparent who had an alcohol problem and 44% had lived with a parent who had a problem with hard drugs. Clearly, substance abuse had played a significant role in many of the adolescents' lives.

We asked the young people who reported family alcohol and drug use about its consequences for them. About one-half to two-thirds reported that it contributed to arguments with the substance abusing family member (Table 4.2), most often with mothers (61%) or stepfathers (66%) who drank or used drugs excessively. Almost 50% reported that drug and alcohol use contributed to arguments with siblings. More than one-half (56%) told us that substance abuse contributed to violence directed toward them by their stepfathers; almost one-half (45%) said it had resulted in violence toward them by their mothers. About one-half of the adolescents said that alcohol or drug use by mothers (52%), stepmothers (41%), or stepfathers (50%) contributed to their decision to leave home.

More generally, substance abuse resulted in the adolescents witnessing arguments with others and violence toward others. This was particularly true for violence by males in the family (e.g., stepfathers and brothers). Exposure to violence was the norm for the majority of adolescents who had any fam-

Table 4.1.  Adolescent Reports of Parents' Alcohol/Drug Problems

|  | Alcohol | | Marijuana | | Hard Drugs | |
|---|---|---|---|---|---|---|
| Relationship to Target | N | % | N | % | N | % |
| Mother & father | | | | | | |
| One parent | 223 | 37.0 | 62 | 10.3 | 151 | 25.1 |
| Both parents | 114 | 18.9 | 26 | 4.3 | 57 | 9.5 |
| Total | 337 | 55.9 | 88 | 14.6 | 208 | 34.6 |
| Stepmother & -father | | | | | | |
| One parent | 88 | 14.6 | 27 | 4.5 | 44 | 7.3 |
| Both parents | 6 | 1.0 | 1 | 0.2 | 7 | 1.2 |
| Total | 94 | 15.6 | 28 | 4.7 | 51 | 8.5 |
| All parents | | | | | | |
| One parent | 183 | 30.4 | 72 | 12.0 | 142 | 23.6 |
| Two parents | 123 | 20.4 | 32 | 5.3 | 84 | 14.0 |
| Three parents | 59 | 9.8 | 15 | 2.5 | 26 | 4.3 |
| Four parents | 17 | 2.8 | 7 | 1.2 | 9 | 1.5 |
| Five parents | 8 | 1.3 | 2 | 0.3 | 6 | 1.0 |
| Total | 390 | 64.7 | 128 | 21.3 | 267 | 44.4 |

Note:  "All parents" includes mothers, fathers, stepmothers, and stepfathers.

Table 4.2. Adolescent Reports of the Affects of Relatives' Alcohol/Drugs on Their Lives

| Has relatives' alcohol/drug use led to: | Arguments with you | | Violence toward you | | Leaving home | | Arguments with others | | Violence with others | | Other problems | |
|---|---|---|---|---|---|---|---|---|---|---|---|---|
| Relationship to target | N | % | N | % | N | % | N | % | N | % | N | % |
| Mother | 158 | 61.2 | 116 | 45.0 | 134 | 51.9 | 168 | 65.1 | 137 | 53.1 | 102 | 39.5 |
| Father | 134 | 44.2 | 91 | 30.0 | 82 | 27.1 | 176 | 58.1 | 154 | 50.8 | 115 | 38.0 |
| Stepmother | 8 | 47.1 | 3 | 17.6 | 7 | 41.2 | 8 | 47.1 | 9 | 52.9 | 6 | 35.3 |
| Stepfather | 70 | 66.0 | 59 | 55.7 | 53 | 50.0 | 78 | 73.6 | 63 | 59.4 | 44 | 41.5 |
| Brothers | 33 | 47.1 | 22 | 31.4 | 6 | 8.6 | 47 | 67.1 | 42 | 60.0 | 18 | 25.7 |
| Sisters | 26 | 47.3 | 15 | 27.3 | 12 | 21.8 | 39 | 70.9 | 30 | 54.5 | 17 | 30.9 |

ily member who had an alcohol or drug problem (Table 4.2, column 5). Regardless of the relationship, if family members abused alcohol or drugs, more than one-half of them had been involved in a violent incident in the presence of the adolescent respondents.

Often family substance abuse was pervasive. As one 16-year-old male told us:

> My aunt on my mom's side, she had a real heavy thing with cocaine. My brother always had it in the house. I heard stories about my aunt, I heard stories about my uncle, my father, and I figured, you know, they're adults, they don't die from it, so I'm not going to either. And my brother's cool, and he does it, so I did.

Sometimes their families just dissolved around them because of extensive substance abuse:

> I was never really raised. My father was too drunk or too high to know what the hell was going on, and like I said, my mother was too depressed to even be able to take care of herself. So, the only raising I got was from my brothers and sisters on the street. (male, aged 15 years)

Intergenerational family problems weren't limited to alcohol and drug abuse. Many of the young people reported that a parent, caretaker, or other relative had been involved with the criminal justice system. Over one-third (37%) told us that at least one parent had been involved in a "serious law violation" (Table 4.3). "Serious law violations" were defined as those involving property or persons. "Nonserious law violations" referred to more minor violations such as drunken driving, child support nonpayment, and trespassing. Summing all of the parents and stepparents with whom the adolescents had lived showed that 42% of them had been arrested for a serious law violation. These ranged from murder/manslaughter to petty theft, drug dealing, or pimping. Almost one-third (29%) had been arrested for a nonserious law violation.

Fewer of the adolescents reported a parent or caretaker with mental health problems. About one-fourth (24%) described a parent or caretaker as depressed; only about 2% reported a parent with symptoms of thought disorder.

## PARENT/CARETAKERS' REPORTS ON FAMILY PROBLEMS

When we asked the parents/caretakers about extended family alcohol or drug abuse, a truly intergenerational profile emerged. In the matched sample of 201 parents/caretakers and adolescents, one-fourth of the parents/caretakers told us that either their mother or their father (the adolescents' grandparents) had an alcohol problem; 9% said that they had a parent who

*Table 4.3.* Adolescent Reports of Parents' Legal Problems

| | Nonserious crimes | | Serious crimes | |
|---|---|---|---|---|
| Relationship to Target | N | % | N | % |
| Mother & father | | | | |
| One parent | 125 | 20.8 | 171 | 28.4 |
| Both parents | 20 | 3.3 | 52 | 8.6 |
| Total | 145 | 24.1 | 223 | 37.0 |
| Stepmother & -father | | | | |
| One parent | 35 | 5.8 | 55 | 9.1 |
| Both parents | 2 | 0.3 | 6 | 1.0 |
| Total | 37 | 6.1 | 61 | 10.1 |
| All parents | | | | |
| One parent | 145 | 24.1 | 166 | 27.6 |
| Two parents | 21 | 3.5 | 75 | 12.5 |
| Three parents | 6 | 1.0 | 9 | 1.5 |
| Four parents | 0 | — | 0 | — |
| Five parents | 0 | — | 1 | 0.2 |
| Total | 172 | 28.6 | 251 | 41.8 |

*Note:* "All parents" includes mothers, fathers, stepmothers, and stepfathers.

had problems with hard drugs; 11% had a sibling (the adolescents' uncles or aunts) with an alcohol problem; 9% had a sibling who had used hard drugs.

We also replicated the question asked adolescents regarding the effects of family alcohol and/or drug use on the runaway adolescent with the parent/caretaker as the reporter. Nearly one-half (46%) of the parents/caretakers told us that alcohol or drug use within the extended family (e.g., the caretakers' parents, siblings) had led to arguments with the adolescent runaway. One-half (54%) of the parents/caretakers said that extended family substance abuse resulted in the adolescents witnessing violent confrontations; one-fourth reported that it resulted in violence directed toward the adolescent. Twenty-one percent of the parents/caretakers said that it contributed to the child's leaving home. Regardless of the reporter, or the generation reported on, the respondents told us that family alcohol and drug abuse contributed to family conflict, violence, and the adolescent leaving home.

## PARENTAL SUBSTANCE ABUSE PROBLEMS AND THE PARENT-CHILD RELATIONSHIP

Substance abuse not only contributed to family conflict: it also directly affected the quality of the parent/child relationship. For the adolescents' mothers and fathers, we examined separate regression models that investigated the effects of parents' substance abuse on adolescents' perceived warmth and supportiveness from parents, parent monitoring, parental rejection, parental physical abuse, and sexual abuse. All of the regression models were based on adolescent reports and controlled for gender and age of the adolescents.

*Parental warmth and supportiveness* was measured with a 10-item scale in which the adolescents responded to questions regarding the degree to which the parent and child worked together to solve problems, whether the parent asked the child's opinions on matters affecting him or her, and the extent to which the parent let the child know that he or she was cared about. Response categories ranged from 1 = always to 5 = never. Items were recoded so that a high score indicated higher levels of parental warmth and supportiveness. Cronbach's alpha for the measure was .91.

*Parental rejection* was assessed with a 5-item measure developed to assess the quality of the parent-child relationship (Brennan, 1974). The scale focuses on the degree to which the parent is perceived to care about the adolescent, trust him or her, and the extent to which the parent blames the adolescent for things. Response categories ranged from 1 = strongly agree to 5 = strongly disagree. Items were recoded so that a high score indicated greater parental rejection. Cronbach's alpha for the measure was .79

*Parental monitoring* was measured with 4 items in which the adolescents were asked to indicate how often their parent knew where they were, who they were with, whether they had a set time to be home on weekends, and if the parent knew whether the adolescent had come home by the set time. Response categories were 1 = always to 5 = never. Items were recoded so that a high score indicted greater parental monitoring. Cronbach's alpha for the scale was .75

Five items from Straus and Gelles's (1990) Conflict Tactics Scale were used to assess parents' *physical abuse* of children: threw something at you in anger, pushed, shoved, or grabbed you in anger, slapped you in the face or head with an open hand, hit you with some object, and beat you up with fists. Items pertaining to threat and assault with a weapon were dropped to normalize the distribution. Response categories ranged from 1 = never to 4 = many times. Cronbach's alpha for the measure was .85.

*Sexual abuse* was measured with 2 items that asked the adolescents whether a parent or adult caretaker had made a verbal request for sexual activity or engaged in forced sexual activity with them. Response categories ranged from 0 = never to 3 = many times. The two items were summed for a range of 0–6 with a high score indicating higher levels of sexual abuse. Cronbach's alpha for the measure was .90.

*Parent substance abuse* had a dichotomous measure that indicated adolescents' positive response to questions regarding whether the parent had a problem with alcohol or drugs.

As the regression models indicate (Table 4.4), adolescent reports of parental substance abuse problems were associated with all of the measures of the parent-child relationship but one (father's monitoring). Substance abuse problems were negatively associated with perceived parental warmth and supportiveness ($\beta = -.13$ mothers, $= -.11$ fathers), and positively associated with parental rejection ($\beta = .09$ mothers, $= .08$ fathers) for both parents. It was negatively associated with mothers' monitoring of the adolescents' behaviors ($\beta = -.09$). Parents' substance abuse problems were positively related to physical abuse ($\beta = .21$ mothers, $= .16$ fathers) and sexual abuse ($\beta = .14$ mothers, $= .09$ fathers). Bivariate correlations for the variables used in the regression model are provided in Appendix, Table 4A.1.

Parental drug or alcohol problems debilitate family processes, resulting in heightened conflict, the adolescent witnessing violent behaviors, and violence directed toward the adolescent. The spillover effect on parenting was consistent with the overall family patterns. Parents perceived to have substance abuse problems were likely to be less effective with their children. They were apt to be perceived as abusive and rejecting. They were less apt to be perceived as warm and supporting or interested in their children's whereabouts or well-being.

## ACROSS GENERATIONS

As noted, the parents/caretakers told us that substance abuse and other family troubles often were intergenerational. Because we had information from parents/caretakers on their parents (the grandparent generation), we were able to construct multiple-reporter models of substance abuse and serious criminal behaviors that spanned three generations. These analyses were based on the matched sample of 201 parents/caretakers and adolescents. The first model we examined incorporated parent/caretaker reports of their parents' substance abuse problems, adolescent reports of parent/caretakers' substance abuse problems, adolescent reports of parental physical and/or sexual abuse, and adolescent reports of their own substance abuse. The measures for the grandparent generation were simply whether the parents/caretakers identified either parent as having an alcohol or drug problem. The measures of physical and sexual abuse discussed previously were combined into a single *family abuse measure*. Cronbach's alpha for the combined measure was .86. *Adolescent reports of parent substance use* was the summation of mother and father alcohol and drug use. The *adolescent substance abuse* measure consisted of 11 items in which the adolescents were asked how often they had used a particular substance during the past 12 months. Items were coded 0 = not used and 1 = used during the past 12 months and summed. Cronbach's alpha was .86. The models controlled for age and gender of the adolescents.

*Table 4.4.*   Effects (β) of Substance Use Problems on Parenting (Adolescent Reports)

| | Model 1: Warmth | | Model 2: Rejection | | Model 3: Monitor | | Model 4: Physical Abuse | | Model 5: Sexual Abuse | |
|---|---|---|---|---|---|---|---|---|---|---|
| | Mothers | Fathers | Mothers | Fathers | Mothers | Fathers | Mothers | Fathers | Mothers | Fathers |
| Parent substance use problems | −.13** | −.11** | .09* | .08* | .09* | −.01 | .21** | .16** | .14** | .09** |
| Age | −.08 | −.08 | .08* | .08* | −.05 | −.05 | .17** | .17** | .09* | .09* |
| Gender (0 = males) | −.10* | −.11** | .13** | .13** | .10* | .09* | .14** | .15** | .21** | .22** |

\* $p < .05$.     \*\* $p < .01$.

In the intergenerational substance abuse model (Figure 4.1) we hypothesized a fully recursive path model where parent/caretaker reports of their parents' substance abuse problems would be positively associated with adolescent reports of substance abuse problems of the parents/caretakers. We also predicted direct effects of the grandparent generation substance abuse problems on the adolescent generation's substance abuse problems and direct effects on adolescent reports of parental physical and sexual abuse. In turn, a positive association was hypothesized between parents/caretakers' alcohol and drug problems and parental physical and sexual abuse. Finally, we predicted a positive relationship between parents/caretakers' alcohol and drug problems and adolescent alcohol and drug problems, and a positive relationship between parental physical and sexual abuse of the adolescent and adolescent alcohol and drug problems.

The results provide evidence for intergenerational patterns of substance abuse in the families of homeless and runaway adolescents. Parent/caretaker reports of their parents' (adolescents' grandparents) substance abuse problems was associated with adolescent reports of parent/caretaker substance abuse problems (β = .16). Parent/caretaker substance abuse problems increased the likelihood of physical and/or sexual abuse of the adolescent runaway (β = .39). In turn, a history of parental abuse (β = .20) was positively associated with adolescent reports of substance abuse problems. Adolescent girls were more likely to report family abuse (β = .22). Adolescent boys were more likely to report drug and alcohol use (β = −.20). Age was positively related to reports of family abuse (β = .19). The model explained 21% of the variance of adolescent reports of family abuse and 8% of the variance of adolescent substance abuse.

The model investigating the intergenerational transmission of serious criminal behaviors was less straightforward (Figure 4.2). As was the case with substance abuse, our measure for serious criminal behaviors was the parent/caretaker report that one of their parents had had "trouble with the law." As noted earlier, types of legal problems were coded as "serious" (involving

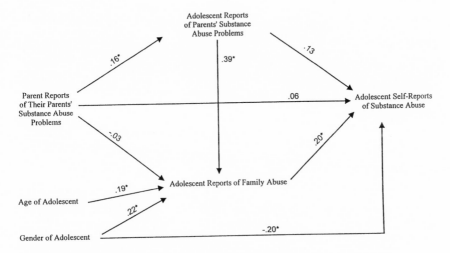

*Figure 4.1.* Intergenerational model of substance abuse. Standardized regression coefficients. *p* = .05.

crimes against persons or property) and "nonserious" (involving victimless crimes, or misdemeanors such as OWI, nonpayment of bills or child support). *Adolescent report of parents' serious crimes* was the summation of adolescent reports on mothers and fathers. *Adolescent reports of their own criminal activity* was assessed with summation of three items: Whether the adolescent had ever taken money from someone, broken in and taken things, or dealt drugs. This formed a continuous variable that ranged from 0 = no to all three to 3 = yes to all three. The model controlled for gender and age of adolescents.

Parent/caretaker reports of their parents' (the grandparent generation) serious criminal behaviors were not associated with either adolescent reports of the parent/caretaker's serious crime or perceived parental abuse (Figure 4.2). However, there was a direct intergenerational effect between criminal behavior in the grandparent generation and the grandchild generation (β = .22). Also, parent/caretakers who had been involved in serious criminal behaviors were more likely to have engaged in physical or sexual abuse of the adolescent (β = .19). In turn, family abuse was associated with adolescent serious criminal activity (β = .20). Older adolescents were more likely to report a history of family abuse (β = .20). Adolescent girls were more likely to report family abuse than adolescent boys (β = .27). Adolescent males were more likely to have been involved in criminal activity than females (β = −.39). The model explained 10% of the variance of family abuse and 21% of the variance of serious criminal behavior by the runaway adolescents. Bivari-

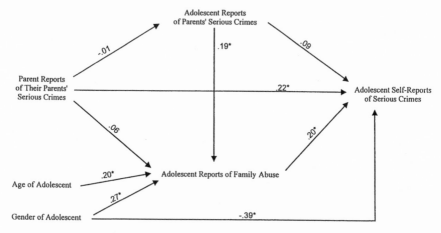

*Figure 4.2.* Intergenerational model of serious criminal activity. Standardized regression coefficients. *p* = .05.

ate correlations for both intergenerational path models are provided in Appendix, Table 4A.2.

## THE FAMILIES OF RUNAWAY AND HOMELESS ADOLESCENTS

Although the tendency of policymakers has been to focus on runaways as problem adolescents, it is apparent from our data that there is much more to the stories of these young people's lives. The majority of the adolescents in our study (65%) had lived with a parent or stepparent who they believed had a problem with alcohol. Almost one-half (44%) had lived with a parent or stepparent whom they perceived to have a problem with hard drugs. About one-half (42%) had lived with a parent or stepparent who had had serious problems with the law. Both parents/caretakers and adolescents told us that these family environments, at best, were difficult for the adolescent, at worst, dangerous. Furthermore, parent/caretaker substance abuse was associated with diminished basic parenting skills such as monitoring, warmth, and supportiveness, and greater perceived parental rejection. It also was associated with a greater likelihood of physical and/or sexual abuse.

In addition, we found evidence that these problems were intergenerational. Adolescents whose grandparents were substance abusers were more likely to have parents who had substance abuse problems and who were physically and/or sexually abusive. Given these family attributes, the adolescents were also more likely to abuse substances themselves. Similarly, criminal behaviors spanned three generations both directly from grandparent to grandchild and indirectly through increasing the likelihood of abusive behaviors on the part of parents/caretakers.

Given the seriousness and the nature of the family problems reported by both the adolescents and their caretakers, the degree of family disorganization and family transitions we documented in Chapter 3 is not surprising. The emerging family portrait is one of multiply troubled family members, high levels of family conflict, and fragile, often temporary family situations. The majority of adolescents are leaving families that have little to hold them. At one level, the number of transitions and levels of disorganization weaken family ties. At another level, troubles within the families may make them an uncomfortable place to be. At a third level, interactions between parents/caretakers and children may be socializing aggressive/coercive behaviors that penalize the young people in establishing supportive buffering relationships inside and outside the family. We turn next to an examination of this socialization process as we investigate the parent-child relationship.

# 5

## Getting Along at Home
### *The Parent/Caretaker-Child Relationship*

*My mama, she used to get beat by her boyfriend and anytime I seen that hap-*
*pen, you know, I would run out there and help my mama. . . . And my little*
*brother do the same. And he would like punch us or something. . . . So yeah,*
*we . . . I have been physically abused . . . but not really.*

—Male, aged 17 years

Thus far, we have found that multiple family transitions and significant levels of alcohol and drug problems characterized the families of the adolescents we interviewed. We also have found evidence that parent/caretaker
alcohol and drug problems resulted in significant discomfort for the adolescents, diminished parenting skills of caretakers, and increased likelihood of
exposure to violence and abuse. These family conditions spanned generations for some of the families. In this chapter we expand our discussion of the
adolescents' development with an in-depth look at the parent-child relationship. First, we investigate parent/caretaker and adolescent reports on the
parenting measures introduced in Chapter 4. We compare the responses of
the adolescents and parents/caretakers to adolescents and parents in two
samples of nonrunaway families from the same region of the Midwest. Second, we discuss parent/caretaker and adolescent reports on levels of neglect,
physical abuse, and sexual abuse of the adolescents by adult caretakers and
compare them to findings for other samples of homeless and runaway youth
and adolescents in the general population. We present reports from caretakers regarding violence directed toward them by the adolescents. Finally, we
extend the regression models presented in Chapter 3 to include parenting

and child maltreatment variables to examine their effects on age at first run, number of subsequent runs, and having ever spent time directly on the streets.

There is little or no systematic research that reports information directly from the parents and caretakers of runaway and homeless adolescents. Often the anecdotal information portrays beleaguered, frustrated parents of unmanageable and out-of control teenagers. These parents are seen testifying at legislative hearings or are reported in the press criticizing current laws or services. Although these anecdotal accounts may represent a small proportion of the families of runaway adolescents, it is apparent from research based on adolescent self-reports that all is not well in most of the homes that they leave. Our data provide the opportunity to systematically present the parents' side of the story.

## PARENTING:
## ADOLESCENT AND PARENT/CARETAKER REPORTS

The parents/caretakers of the adolescents and the adolescents themselves were asked to complete three basic parenting scales that assessed parental warmth and supportiveness, parental monitoring, and parental rejection (for a description of scale characteristics see Chapter 4). These measures were chosen for the study because they already were in use in the Iowa Youth and Families Project (Conger & Elder, 1994) and the Iowa Single Parent Project (Simons, 1996). The Iowa Youth and Families Project was a four-year panel study of 450 two-parent families in rural Iowa. The Iowa Single Parent Project was a related three-year panel study of divorced-mother-headed families in Iowa. These two samples of families with nonrunaway adolescents provided comparison groups from the same general geographic areas as the runaway adolescents. For comparison purposes we selected families from panels of the two studies where the target adolescents were the same average age as the adolescents in our study. In the two-parent families we used only mothers' reports of parenting for comparison with the divorced-mother-headed families and the parents/caretakers of the families of runaways.

The parents/caretakers of runaways scored themselves significantly lower on measures of parental monitoring than parents in two-parent and divorced-mother-headed households (Table 5.1). This meant that they were less apt to know who their child was with, less apt to know where the adolescent was, and less apt to have a set time to be in on weekend nights or to know whether the adolescent was in on time. Average scores for the measure of parental warmth and supportiveness were more similar than were those for parental monitoring. Still, the parents in two-parent families scored significantly higher on warmth and supportiveness than did the parents/care-

*Table 5.1.* Comparisons of Parent and Adolescent Reports

| Samples | Two-Parent | Single-Parent | Runaway |
|---|---|---|---|
| Monitoring | | | |
| Parent | 4.27 [a] | 4.11 [a,b] | 3.80 [a,c,d] |
| Adolescent | 3.87 | 3.68 [b] | 3.62 [d] |
| Warmth and Supportiveness | | | |
| Parent | 3.87 [a] | 3.82 [a] | 3.73 [a,d] |
| Adolescent | 3.56 | 3.53 | 3.05 [c,d] |
| Rejection | | | |
| Parent | 1.85 [a] | 2.18 [b] | 3.25 [a,c,d] |
| Adolescent | 1.78 | 2.13 [b] | 2.82 [c,d] |

[a] T-test indicates significant difference between parent and adolescent reports ($p < .05$).
[b] T-test indicates significant difference between two-parent and single-parent sample ($p < .05$).
[c] T-test indicates significant difference between runaway and single-parent sample ($p < .05$).
[d] T-test indicates significant difference between runaway and two-parent sample ($p < .05$).

takers of runaways. Mothers from the two-parent families were more likely to report that they let their adolescent children know that they cared about them, trusted them, and approved of them than the parents/caretakers of runaways. They were also more likely to discuss family matters and decisions they made about their adolescent with the adolescent than were the parents/caretakers of runaways.

It was on the measure of parental rejection that mean scores diverged most noticeably. Parents/caretakers of runaways scored much higher on average than did mothers in two-parent or mother-headed single-parent families. The parents/caretakers of runaways were more likely to report distrust, blame, lack of caring, unhappiness with what the adolescent does, and that the adolescent causes a lot of problems. Mothers in two-parent families scored the lowest on the measure. Mothers in the single-parent families scored significantly higher than did those in two-parent families, but lower than the parents/caretakers of runaways. Parents of nonrunaways scored lower on the rejection measures than those of runaways regardless of family structure.

Adolescents in all three family types completed the same measures as their parents. In all of the comparisons but one (the rejection measure for divorced-mother-headed families), adolescents' scores differed significantly from their parents. The adolescents tended to score their parents lower on measures of parental monitoring (i.e., they perceived less monitoring than did their parents), lower on parental warmth and supportiveness, and lower on the measure of rejection than did the parent generation. In general, the parent generation was a little more optimistic about monitoring and warmth than were their children and harder on themselves regarding the measure of rejection. The higher scores on the rejection measure were likely due to very real issues of trust and blame surrounding adolescent behaviors.

When we compared the runaway adolescents' reports on parenting measures to adolescents in nonrunaway families, the patterns were very similar to those of the adults. Runaway adolescents and adolescents in divorced mother-headed households did not differ significantly on their reports of parental monitoring. Both runaways and nonrunaway adolescents from mother-headed single-parent households rated parental monitoring significantly lower than adolescents from two-parent two-parent households. Runaway adolescents rated their parents/caretakers significantly lower on the measure of parental warmth and supportiveness and higher on the measure of parental rejection than did the nonrunaway adolescents regardless of family structure.

The most striking thing about our findings regarding parenting is the similar patterns of the parent/caretaker and the runaway adolescent reports. Regardless of reporter, the parents/caretakers of runaways were rated lower on measures of monitoring, lower on measures of warmth and supportiveness, and higher on our measure of parental rejection than parents of nonrunaway adolescents from two-parent families. They also scored lower on measures of warmth and supportiveness and higher on parental rejection than nonrunaways from divorced-mother-headed families. Parents/caretakers and their runaway adolescents are telling essentially the same story: the parents/caretakers of runaways were less effective parents than their counterparts in nonrunaway families.

## FAMILY NEGLECT, VIOLENCE, AND SEXUAL ABUSE: ADOLESCENT REPORTS

As noted in Chapter 1, most studies based on the self-reports of runaway and homeless adolescents report high levels of neglect and physical and sexual abuse. Our study was no exception. Two-thirds of the adolescent females and one- half of the adolescent males said they had felt neglected by a parent or caretaker (Table 5.2). About 12% reported that they had been made to go a day without food, water, clothing, or a toilet. Over one-fourth told us that they had been abandoned for at least 24 hours.

When asked to respond to items in the Conflict Tactics Scale (CTS; items 4–10, Table 5.2) (Straus & Gelles, 1990), they reported extraordinary rates of physical abuse. Two-thirds of them told us that an adult caretaker had thrown something at them in anger prior to their running away. Eighty-one percent had been pushed, shoved, or grabbed in anger, and 72% had been slapped in the face or head with an open hand. Two-thirds (64%) said that they had been hit with some object, and one-third (36%) had been beaten with fists

Table 5.2. Percentage of Adolescents Who Report Neglect or Abuse by an Adult Caretaker Prior to Running Away

| Caretaker Neglect or Abuse | Total % (N = 597) | Male % (N = 238) | Female % (N = 359) |
|---|---|---|---|
| Felt neglected | 58.9 | 51.3 | 63.9 |
| Made you go the day without food, water, clothing, or a toilet | 11.5 | 11.7 | 11.4 |
| Abandoned you for at least 24 hours | 27.6 | 23.0 | 30.6 |
| Threw something at you in anger | 66.2 | 61.3 | 69.4 |
| Pushed or grabbed you in anger | 80.8 | 75.9 | 84.1 |
| Slapped you | 72.0 | 64.6 | 77.0 |
| Hit you with an object | 63.8 | 59.2 | 66.9 |
| Beat you up | 36.2 | 30.7 | 39.8 |
| Threatened you with a knife or gun | 21.4 | 20.9 | 21.7 |
| Assaulted you with a knife or gun | 6.2 | 6.3 | 6.1 |
| Made a verbal request for sexual activity | 17.9 | 9.2 | 23.7 |
| Forced you to engage in sexual activity | 20.9 | 8.8 | 28.9 |

by an adult caretaker. Perhaps most surprising was that 21% alleged that they had been threatened with a weapon such as a gun or knife and 6% reported actual assault with a weapon by a parent or caretaker.

Some of the adolescents told graphic stories backing up their allegations of physical abuse. One young woman, aged 17 years, told us, "I can't remember the first time, both of our parents hit us a lot. I can remember . . . getting my dad's belt out and he'd just go nuts and hit with the belt, he wouldn't quit until he was tired." Sometimes there were cycles of violence. One 13-year-old told us "All my stepdads beat me and my sister." There had been five stepfathers in her life. The abuse started when she was very young. "My mom was like on and off with every . . . like all my stepdads. I mean, probably not until I was like three. And then she met some other guy and he beat us too, and she went back to this other guy but he beat us too. And it just kept going on and on and on." A 16-year-old male told us: "Besides physical abuse from my biological father, my stepfather used to . . . he had a 20 inch pump shotgun and some other assault rifle. And one of the times when he had a lot to drink, he threatened my life." Once family conflict escalated to violence, it could go in any direction.

[M]y father being drunk and high, some people believe that's what drove him to try to hit my mother, and drove him to hit me because I never let him close to hit my mother. If anything, I let him take it out on me. I'm going to do my damnedest to kill [him], still, I haven't succeeded, unfortunately. . . . Well, I don't want to kill him as much any more, but then, that's all I thought about doing. (Male, aged 15 years)

A significant number of the runaway adolescents reported an adult care-taker had sexually victimized them. The adolescents were asked two questions regarding sexual abuse. Twenty-four percent of the young women and 9% of the young men told us that an adult caretaker had made a verbal request for sexual activity prior to the time that they ran away from home. Twenty-nine percent of the young women had been forced to engage in sexual activity with an adult caretaker, as had 9% of the young men. A young woman, aged 16 years, told the interviewer that one of her mom's boyfriends had raped her. When she was returned home, he attempted to rape her again. A 15-year-old girl told us that her mother's live-in boyfriend had abused her beginning at about age 7 years: "It probably went on for like a year, or maybe almost a year, it seemed like. So probably until I was almost eight." We cautioned interviewers not to push for disclosure in this regard. One young woman who had been abused told the interviewer, "There are things I've tucked away in the back of my mind and don't want to look at. I am having lots of flashbacks right now." Follow-up services were offered all of the adolescents. Most were interviewed in shelters where these services were readily available.

## COMPARING ADOLESCENT AND PARENT/CARETAKER REPORTS ABOUT FAMILY VIOLENCE

We also asked the parents/caretakers to complete the CTS regarding their knowledge of maltreatment of their child by any adult caretaker (Matched sample, $N = 201$). Endorsement of the CTS items by the parents/caretakers did not indicate that the reporting adult was the perpetrator. Rather, it indicates knowledge that some caretaker adult engaged in maltreatment of the child. Of the 201 parents/caretakers reporting, 28% indicated an adult caretaker had thrown something at the child in anger prior to the young person's running away (Table 5.3, column 3); 80% said that the child had been pushed, shoved, or grabbed in anger; 62% reported that the child had been slapped in the face or head with an open hand; 37% reported that the young person had been hit with an object. Only 10% told us that the adolescent had been hit with a fist; 2% said the young person had been threatened with a weapon.

We matched adolescent and parent/caretaker reporters for the purpose of comparing their responses. The adolescent and parent/caretaker responses were most similar on reports of being pushed, shoved, or grabbed in anger, and of being slapped. As the severity of the maltreatment increased, the reports of adolescents and parents/caretakers diverged markedly. For example, fully one-third of the adolescents in the matched sample reported having been beaten with fists by a caretaker compared to 10% of the

*Table 5.3.*    Percentage of Caretakers and Adolescents Reporting Abuse (*N* = 201)

| Reporter: | Adolescent to Caretaker | Caretaker to Adolescent | |
|---|---|---|---|
| | Caretaker | Caretaker | Adolescent |
| Thrown something in anger | 32.3 | 28.4 | 68.2 |
| Pushed or shoved in anger | 45.3 | 79.9 | 84.0 |
| Slapped | 19.4 | 61.6 | 73.4 |
| Hit | 12.9 | 36.7 | 64.2 |
| Beat up | 12.4 | 9.5 | 34.3 |
| Threatened with a weapon | 9.5 | 2.0 | 17.9 |
| Assaulted with a weapon | 1.0 | 0.5 | 5.5 |
| Attempted to touch sexually | — | 17.5 | 18.5 |
| Forced sexual activity | — | 10.5 | 24.0 |

parents/caretakers. Adolescents were almost ten times more likely to report having been threatened with a weapon than their parents/caretakers (18% vs. 2%).

Many of the reporting adults were aware of sexual maltreatment of their children. Almost identical numbers of parents/caretakers and adolescents told us that an adult caretaker had attempt to touch the young person in a sexual manner (18% of parents/caretakers, 19% of adolescents). However, only about one-half as many of the parents/caretakers told us that a caretaker had forced their child into sexual activity than did the adolescents (11% parents/caretakers, 24% adolescents).

To more completely assess the degree and types of family violence, the parents/caretakers also responded to the CTS items regarding aggression directed toward them by the adolescent. Fully one-third (32%) of the parents/caretakers indicated that their adolescent child had thrown something at them in anger (Table 5.3, column 1). Almost one-half (45%) had been pushed, shoved, or grabbed in anger by the adolescent. Nineteen percent had been slapped with an open hand on the face or head; 13% said that the adolescent had hit them with a fist. Ten percent reported that their adolescent had threatened them with a weapon such as a gun or knife.

It was hard to determine the context of these reports of mutual violence. At least some of the time, it was the child striking back as he/she became old enough to counter physical abuse. One young woman, aged 17 years, who had been physically abused by both parents from the time she was very young graphically described the process:

> Last time either of them touched me was when my mom took a big old bread board—one of those with a handle—when I was in the 7th grade. That was the last time either of them touched me. She took it to me and I turned around and took it from her. . . . I mean she attacked me with her bare hands, you know,

she came after me after that and we got into some physical fights and I had the cops called on her and she had the cops called on me.

The picture that emerges is one of serious mutual violence between parents/caretakers and adolescents. Implicit in the data is the tendency for the generations to blame each other for more serious violent behaviors. Regardless, it is clear from our data that fists and weapons had been used in family confrontations. Who wielded the weapon or who was responsible for the violent altercations was a matter of perception. Whether adolescent or adult reporter, however, the data strongly suggest explosive and mutually harmful interactions among a significant number of reporting families. Even if we choose to ignore the adolescents' reports of maltreatment by caretakers, the adult generation is admitting to serious physical and sexual abuse within their families. Although we were unable to locate lifetime estimates of physical abuse based on the CTS, Straus and Gelles's (1990) national data indicate that only 7% of adolescents aged 15–17 years experienced severe violence in the past year (e.g., were slapped, spanked, or hit with an object). Sixty-two percent of the parents/caretakers in our study reported that their adolescent had been slapped at some point in their lives; 37% told us the child had been hit with an object. In the Straus and Gelles national sample, only 2.1% of 15–17 year old adolescents had been hit with a fist by an adult caretaker in the past year. In our sample, the caretakers reported 10% of the adolescents had been maltreated in this way.

Similarly, when we compare our findings regarding adolescent-to-parent violence to the Straus and Gelles sample, only about 10% of parents reported any violence directed toward them by adolescent children in the past year and just 3.5% had been hit with a fist by their adolescent child. Twelve percent of our caretaker adults say that their adolescent child at some point in their lives had hit them with a fist. Although the two samples are not strictly comparable, the Straus and Gelles data indicate the relative rarity of severe violence in families. Clearly, for the families we talked to, severe violence was not rare at all.


## THE PARENT/CARETAKER-ADOLESCENT RELATIONSHIP AND RUNNING AWAY

To investigate the extent parenting and maltreatment contribute to age at first runaway, the number of runs following the first runaway, and whether the adolescent ever spent time directly on the streets, we extended the regression models run in Chapter 3 by adding the parenting and child maltreatment variables. We have described the parenting variables (monitoring, warmth, and supportiveness, and rejection) in Chapter 4. The measure of *neglect prior to first runaway* was computed as a dichotomous measure with a value of 1 if the youth reported first being neglected by a parent or adult caretaker at an age younger than the age they first ran away. Youth who did not report neglect by a caretaker or reported first neglect at an age older than their first runaway were assigned a value of 0 to indicate no prior neglect. *Physical abuse prior to first runaway* and *sexual abuse prior to first run* were similarly dichotomized based on adolescents' reports of having experienced such abuse from caretakers prior to or subsequent to first runaway.

Our first regression models investigated the effects of parenting and care-taker maltreatment on the age at which the child first ran away (Table 5.4). Gender, family structure, and family geographic changes (see model in Chapter 3, Table 3.5) were included in the model as control variables. The parenting variables and the child maltreatment variables were then stepped into the models. The number of changes in family structure prior to first run-away was significantly negatively related to age at first run ($\beta = -.17$; Table 5.4, column 3). The more changes in family structure prior to first run, the younger the age at which the child first ran away. Of the parenting variables, only monitoring related to age at first run ($\beta = .09$). The greater the parental monitoring, the older the child was at the time he or she first ran away. Among the neglect and abuse variables, neglect was negatively related to age at first run ($\beta = -.21$) as was sexual abuse ($\beta = -.17$). Physical abuse was correlated with age at first run at the bivariate level ($r = -.22$, $p < .01$) but lost significance in the regression model due to multicollinearity with neglect and sexual abuse. For bivariate correlations, see Appendix Table 5A.1. The model explained 15% of the variance of age at first runaway.

We next regressed the variables on the number of runs subsequent to first runaway. The most significant indicator of subsequent runaways was age at

*Table 5.4.* Model Predicting Age at First Runaway (Standardized Coefficients)

| Predictor Variable | Step 1 | Step 2 | Step 3 |
|---|---|---|---|
| Gender | −.05 | −.03 | −.06 |
| Number of changes in family structure | −.20 *** | −.20 *** | −.17 *** |
| Number of family geographic changes | −.07 * | −.06 | −.04 |
| Parenting variables | | | |
| Monitoring | | .12 ** | .09 ** |
| Warmth | | .01 | .00 |
| Rejection | | .05 | .09 |
| Maltreatment variables | | | |
| Neglect | | | −.21 *** |
| Physical abuse | | | −.05 |
| Sexual abuse | | | −.17 *** |

* $p < .05$.    ** $p < .01$.    *** $p < .001$.

*Table 5.5.* Model Predicting Number of Runs Subsequent to First Runaway (Standardized Coefficients)

| Predictor Variable | Step 1 | Step 2 | Step 3 | Step 4 |
|---|---|---|---|---|
| Gender | −.02 | .00 | .02 | .01 |
| Number of changes in family structure | .05 | .03 | .01 | −.03 |
| Number of family geographic changes | .06 | .05 | .04 | .03 |
| Parenting variables | | | | |
| Monitoring | | −.09 * | −.08 * | −.06 |
| Warmth/support | | −.05 | −.05 | −.05 |
| Rejection | | .14 ** | .12 * | .14 ** |
| Maltreatment variables | | | | |
| Neglect | | | .02 | −.03 |
| Physical abuse | | | .06 | .05 |
| Sexual abuse | | | .15 *** | .11 ** |
| Age first time on own | | | | −.23 *** |

* $p < .05$.     ** $p < .01$.     *** $p < .001$.

first runaway ($\beta = -.23$; Table 5.5, column 4) as was the case in our analysis in Chapter 3 (Figure 3.5). The younger the age at first runaway, the greater was the likelihood of subsequent runs. Sexual abuse was positively associated with the number of runs subsequent to the first runaway ($\beta = .11$) as was parental rejection ($\beta = .14$). Again, it is noteworthy that sexual abuse correlated .33 with parental neglect and .30 with physical abuse. Multicollinearity reduced the other two variables to nonsignificance in the regression model. Bivariate correlations for the regression model are presented in Appendix Table 5A.2. The model explained 12% of the variance of number of runaways subsequent to the first run.

In a final regression model we investigated the effects of the family disorganization variables from Chapter 3, the parenting variables, and the child maltreatment variables on the adolescents having ever spent time directly on the streets (Table 5.6). As we found in Chapter 3, young men were almost twice as likely as young women to have spent time directly on the streets ($b = .58$; exp $b = 1.79$). Having been sexually abused increased the likelihood of having ever spent time on the streets over seven times ($b = 2.02$; exp $b = 7.56$). Finally, for every year the adolescent delayed running away, the likelihood of his/her spending time on the streets decreased by about 10% ($b = -.09$; exp $b = .91$).

## THE FAMILIES ADOLESCENTS LEAVE

The family portraits that emerge from our analyses are not encouraging. The young people we interviewed typically grew up in disorganized, highly

Table 5.6. Logistic Regression Predicting "Ever Spent Time on the Street"

| Predictor Variable | Step 1 | | Step 2 | | Step 3 | | Step 4 | |
|---|---|---|---|---|---|---|---|---|
| | B | exp b | B | exp b | B | exp | B | exp b |
| Gender | .53*** | 1.69 | .54*** | 1.71 | .60*** | 1.83 | .58*** | 1.79 |
| Number of changes in family structure | -.45 | 0.64 | -.60 | 0.55 | -.75 | 0.47 | -1.05 | 0.35 |
| Number of family geographic changes | -.28 | 0.75 | -.35 | 0.70 | -.49 | 0.62 | -.56 | 0.57 |
| Parenting variables | | | | | | | | |
| Monitoring | | | -.03 | 0.97 | -.03 | 0.97 | -.03 | 0.97 |
| Warmth | | | .00 | 1.00 | .00 | 1.00 | .00 | 1.00 |
| Rejection | | | .02 | 1.02 | .02 | 1.02 | .02 | 1.03 |
| Maltreatment variables | | | | | | | | |
| Neglect | | | | | 1.10 | 3.01 | .29 | 1.34 |
| Physical abuse | | | | | .09 | 1.09 | .01 | 1.01 |
| Sexual abuse | | | | | 2.60* | 13.52 | 2.02 | 7.56 |
| Age on own | | | | | | | -.09** | 0.91 |

* $p < .05$.    ** $p < .01$.    *** $p < .001$.

unstable family situations. Often there were substance abuse problems among their parents and stepparents. These problems sometimes were inter-generational, crossing into the grandparent generations. Where there were substance abuse problems, other types of family conflicts were typically present such as arguments, abuse, witnessing conflict, and violence. All of these family attributes culminated in less effective parenting. Parents/care-takers of runaways viewed themselves as less effective than parents of non-runaway adolescents. Both parents/caretakers and the runaway adolescents reported high levels of family violence. It is important to note that many of the current caretakers are struggling to remedy past harm and family disor-ganization in the lives of these young people. For others, the cycle of dis-ruptive change and conflict goes on and on.

Parents/caretakers and adolescents give remarkably similar descriptions of family life. The predominant pattern of runaway adolescent development is a history of weakening ties to family. The ties are eroded by a numerous changes in adult caretakers, caretakers and other adult family members with substance abuse problems, and high levels of family conflict that sometimes escalates to violence. Within the family, the children become increasingly self-sufficient. One young man (17 years old) told us:

> I mean, we really didn't have a place to stay, that was true, but, you know, we wasn't really getting neglected. I mean we had food to eat, you know what I'm saying? But you know, I was kind of like the person over the family, I was like the man of the family because, like, my father got locked up.

Precocious independence and early dependence on themselves rather than caretaker adults often occurred prior to running away. Leaving home became increasingly easy. It meant escaping conflict, and truly looking out for one's self.

Homelessness for young people doesn't happen all at once. Rather, there is a process of marginalization created by forced early maturation. The ear-lier the child leaves home, the more persistent and continuous this process is likely to become. The greater the family conflict and abuse the more the child separates from the family. The very process of leaving, if only for a lit-tle while at first, separates him/her even more. Once the adolescents experi-ence being on their own, their options change. New relationships and means of survival become apparent to them. As the adolescents transfer their alle-giance to nonadults, the separation process becomes more or less complete.

# III

## TAKING CHANCES
### *Adolescents on Their Own*

**6**

# Getting Along
## *The Social Networks of Runaway Adolescents*

*I didn't really have no adult that was important. I had like friends or people a little older than me or something like that.*
—Male, 16 years

Even for young people whose lives are progressing well, adolescence is a time of shifting social networks. As children move from the relatively supervised social environments of childhood into the greater independence of adolescent friendships, social networks become more complex and more compartmentalized. Prepubescent children depend primarily on parents for support, early and midadolescents turn to friends, and late adolescents depend most on romantic partners (Furman & Buhrmester, 1992). Adolescents not only spend most of their free time interacting with friends, they enjoy this time more than that spent with adults. They engage in more intimate self-disclosure with friends than adults (Larsen & Prescott, 1977).

Regardless of age, our sense of security derives in large part from our connectedness with social groups (Cotteral, 1994). Emotional distress deepens the need for supportive others. During the intense distress of leaving home at an early age, many of the conventional avenues for adult support are cut off. Leaving home precociously severs or, at minimum, weakens primary supportive ties to caretaker adults and hastens the developmental process of turning to same-aged friends. Runaway young people turn to peers for support, understanding, and sometimes aid. However, these similarly aged friends and new acquaintances most likely are troubled themselves, particularly those encountered on the streets and in shelters (Coie & Dodge, 1983;

69

Dodge, 1983). Although friends may be a source of personal support for adolescents, their influence may not encourage prosocial behaviors. As Cauce and Srebnik point out, "[I]t is crucial to keep in mind that support from peers occurs within the context of peer group values" (1989, p. 246). What adults may view as negative influence may be important social support to a distressed runaway. One young woman, aged 16 years, told us that friends were there for her when she was on her own. They helped out:

> By giving me places to stay, and giving me money, giving me cigarettes, giving me food, giving me drugs. I mean that's not really helping, but, I mean, to them it is. Yeah, I mean, they're mentally, that's helping, give her something to get by until she gets some of her own.

When adolescents strike out on their own, the developmental process takes a sharp turn. Conventional intergenerational sources of support and influence have been largely interrupted. In their place is an age-segregated, predominantly nonconventional support system made up of young people who, for the most part, are in similar circumstances.

This support system may be adaptive to the context. It provides aid, emotional support, and teaching of survival skills on the streets and in shelters. At the same time, it may be in constant flux and potentially exploitative. When adolescents are distressed and have no one to whom they can turn, they tend to invest in peripheral members of their social networks for social support needs that are usually reserved for more intimate members. Cotteral's (1994) work has shown that distressed adolescents listed more members of their social networks as very close than nondistressed adolescents. Some of the people distressed adolescents listed as close were actually those with whom they had weak ties. These relatively weak relationships were being called upon to meet support needs usually performed by those with much stronger ties. This is particularly evident for runaways. Their needs for support are very great as they move into unfamiliar and unsupervised environments and they must rely on relative strangers for information and support. There is a tendency to project greater intimacy on these new friendships or sexual relationships than would be anticipated by the relationship histories. Homeless adolescent social networks are often characterized by series of intense, but short-lived friendships and sexual relationships.

However, leaving home doesn't mean leaving everyone behind. Although it certainly suggests a serious breakdown in the adolescents' primary source of support, their relationship with their parents (Belle, 1989), it does not mean giving up all sources of family support. Parental ties may persist to some degree. Other relatives, such as aunts, uncles, and grandparents, may become important substitutes for biological parents. Extended family members may provide an alternative place to stay or someone in the family that the adolescent believes cares about him or her and who would give aid if needed.

## THE SOCIAL NETWORKS OF HOMELESS AND
## RUNAWAY ADOLESCENTS

The social networks of the adolescents in our study were primarily made up of similarly aged friends (Table 6.1). Eighty-two percent of the adolescents told us they had someone to whom they turned when they were sad or upset. Of these, 40% said they would turn to a friend. Less than 8% would turn to a biological parent. Similar percentages of adolescents listed other people in their extended families to whom they would turn when they needed emotional support. About 9% said a grandparent, 10% said siblings, 10% said aunts and uncles, and 5% said other relatives. Only about 4% mentioned adult professionals as a primary source of emotional support when they were sad or upset. When the young people were asked: "Who do you count on to care about you?" the shift to peer group as the primary source of emotional support was obvious. Although almost all of the young people (91%) told us that they had a person who cared about them, for the majority it was not an adult. Forty-four percent told us that they depended upon their friends to care about them. Only 13% designated a biological parent, fewer still specified extended family members (grandparents, 8%; siblings, 6%; aunts and uncles, 8%).

The percentages were comparable for instrumental support. Eighty-seven percent of the adolescents had someone they could count on for help or aid. Of these, 46% said they would turn to friends for help. Only about 9% said they could turn to a biological parent. Grandparents (8%) and aunts or uncles (10%) were viewed as sources of help at about the same level as biological parents.

However, when asked to whom they could turn for a place to stay if they wanted one, the percentages reversed. Only about one-half of the adolescents told us they had a place to stay if they wanted one, and, for these young people, relatives were much more likely to be designated as potential sources of shelter than were friends. Although only 12% of the runaways told us they could stay with a biological parent if they wanted, 26% said they could stay with a grandparent, and one-third reported they could stay with an aunt or uncle. Twelve percent said they could stay with "other relatives." Only 3% said they could stay with friends.

The patterns of social support clearly indicate that the runaway adolescents view friends as their primary source of emotional support. Biological parents particularly were reduced in significance. They were listed as persons the adolescents could turn to when sad or upset or as someone who

Table 6.1. Summary of Adolescent Reports of Social Networks among Homeless and Runaway Adolescents

| | Talk when sad or upset | | | Count on for help and aid | | | Care about you | | | Give you a place to stay | | |
|---|---|---|---|---|---|---|---|---|---|---|---|---|
| Relationship | Total % (N = 489) | Male % (N = 174) | Female % (N = 315) | Total % (N = 526) | Male % (N = 202) | Female % (N = 324) | Total % (N = 549) | Male % (N = 209) | Female % (N = 340) | Total % (N = 318) | Male % (N = 111) | Female % (N = 207) |
| Biological parents | 7.5 | 8.0 | 7.1 | 8.5 | 9.4 | 8.1 | 13.4 | 14.0 | 13.1 | 12.3 | 10.3 | 12.8* |
| Step/adopted parents | 2.3 | 2.2 | 2.5 | 2.0 | 2.1 | 2.3 | 2.3 | 2.5 | 2.2 | 2.0 | 1.3 | 1.8 |
| Grandparents | 8.7 | 10.1 | 8.2 | 8.1 | 7.3 | 8.5 | 7.7 | 7.9 | 7.7 | 25.7 | 25.6 | 24.8 |
| Biological siblings | 10.4 | 15.2 | 8.2 | 5.3 | 6.8 | 4.6 | 6.2 | 6.2 | 6.2 | 8.2 | 6.4 | 8.2 |
| Uncle/aunt | 10.4 | 12.3 | 9.2 | 10.1 | 11.1 | 9.6 | 8.1 | 9.1 | 7.7 | 33.0 | 33.3 | 33.0* |
| Other relatives | 5.2 | 5.1 | 5.1 | 4.0 | 5.1 | 3.5 | 3.5 | 4.5 | 2.9 | 12.4 | 17.9 | 10.1 |
| Friends | 39.9 | 35.5 | 41.8** | 45.7 | 43.6 | 46.5 | 43.8 | 40.9 | 45.3* | 3.1 | 2.6 | 2.8 |
| Professionals | 4.0 | 2.9 | 4.6* | 1.6 | 1.7 | 1.5 | 2.3 | 2.9 | 1.8 | 0.2 | 0.0 | 2.8 |
| Others | 11.6 | 8.7 | 13.3** | 14.6 | 12.8 | 15.4 | 12.7 | 12.0 | 13.1 | 3.1 | 2.6 | 3.7 |
| Total | 100 | 100 | 100 | 100 | 100 | 100 | 100 | 100 | 100 | 100 | 100 | 100 |

* Significant differences of mean between males and females at .05 level.
** Significant differences of mean between males and females at .01 level.

cared about them at about the same rates as extended family members. Friends also were viewed as the adolescents' primary source of help or aid. Only among the runaways who had a place to go if they wanted one did relatives exceed friends in perceived support. Grandparents were twice as likely as biological parents to be listed as providers of shelter; aunts and uncles were almost three times more likely than parents to be viewed as potential sources of shelter.

Cauce and colleagues (Cauce, Felner, & Primavera, 1982) have argued that social support networks among adolescents typically fall into three domains: family, formal, and informal support systems. Their findings indicate that the family is viewed by adolescents as the primary source of social support, followed by formal support providers (e.g., teachers, guidance counselors, clergy, social workers), followed by informal support sources such as friends. Among the adolescents we interviewed, this pattern was reversed. Friends were viewed as the primary providers of social support, followed by family and formal support providers. By running away, adolescents severed ties to the two most prominent sources of adult social support available to people of their age group: their parents and school. Very few of the adolescents listed adult professional helpers as sources of support.

Early separation from caretakers resulted in a shift to similarly aged peers for many of the support functions typically provided by caring adults. Although the street and shelter peer network may be adaptive for socializing the adolescent to street life, an essential element of conventional peer socialization is lost. During adolescence, peer relationships perform an important role in the acquisition of social skills and the rules for social relationships (Claes, 1992). Operating in an environment almost exclusively made up of young people with conduct problems, homeless and runway adolescents are at severe disadvantage in this crucial developmental process. Poor peer relationships during this developmental phase inhibit the learning of conventional behavioral strategies and encourage learning of maladaptive behavioral strategies and inadequate coping mechanisms (East, Hess, & Lerner, 1987; Parker & Asher, 1987). As we will show later in this volume, peer relationships not only act to socialize deviant behaviors (adaptive behaviors on the street), they are often the primary source of victimization and exploitation.

## CHARACTERISTICS OF PEER ASSOCIATIONS

The majority of the young people we talked to reported that they had close friends who had been involved in various delinquent behaviors (Table 6.2). Almost 80% had a close friend who had run away. Sixty-five percent had a close friend who sold drugs, 81% a close friend who used drugs. Most

*Table 6.2.* Summary of Adolescent Reports of Deviant Peers

| Have close friends ever | Total % | Males % | Females % |
|---|---|---|---|
| Run away | 79.3 | 75.5 | 81.8 |
| Sold drugs | 65.4 | 70.5 | 62.1* |
| Used drugs | 81.1 | 82.1 | 80.5 |
| Been suspended from school | 86.4 | 84.7 | 87.6 |
| Dropped out of school | 64.3 | 67.8 | 62.1 |
| Shoplifted | 75.3 | 78.4 | 73.2 |
| Broken and taken things from house | 43.9 | 53.2 | 37.3** |
| Taken money from someone | 64.7 | 71.5 | 60.1** |
| Sold sex for drugs or money | 18.8 | 15.9 | 20.7 |
| Sold sex for food or place to stay | 16.6 | 16.5 | 16.7 |
| Been arrested | 72.1 | 75.8 | 69.5 |
| Threatened someone with weapon | 55.1 | 63.5 | 49.4** |
| Assaulted someone with weapon | 41.5 | 49.1 | 36.2** |
| Tried to kill him/herself | 62.6 | 54.8 | 67.9** |
| Committed suicide | 32.9 | 30.3 | 34.6 |

* Significant differences of mean between males and females at .05 level.
** Significant differences of mean between males and females at .01 level.

of them had close friends who had school problems: 86% had a close friend who had been suspended from school; 64% a friend who had dropped out of school. One-half to two-thirds had friends who had shoplifted, burglarized, or stolen money. Fewer of the young people, between 15 and 20%, had friends who had sold sex for food, drugs, or a place to stay. Two-thirds of the young men and one-half of the young women had a close friend who had threatened someone with a weapon. One-half the young men and one-third of the young women had a close friend who had assaulted someone with a weapon. Two-thirds had a close friend who attempted suicide; one-third a close friend who committed suicide.

Gang activity is now part of the culture of most urban areas. Three-fourths of the adolescents we interviewed were aware of gangs in their area. One-half of the young men and one-third of the young women had been threatened or bothered by a gang (Table 6.3). Almost one-half (43%) of the adolescent males and one-fourth of the females said that they had participated in gang activity; about one-fourth reported that this activity took place during in the past 12 months. Over one-half of the young women (57%) and three-fourths of the young men (74%) had been asked to join a gang. One-half of the young men and 19% of the young women had gone through a gang initiation. One-third of the adolescent males and 14% of the females said that they currently belonged to a gang.

*Table 6.3.* Summary of Adolescent Reports of Gang Involvement

|  | Total % | Males % | Females % |
|---|---|---|---|
| Aware of gangs | 74.2 | 80.4 | 70.0** |
| Threatened or bothered by gang | 36.6 | 50.4 | 27.4** |
| Participated in gang activity | 32.6 | 42.9 | 25.7** |
| Participated in past 12 months | 27.5 | 34.7 | 22.6** |
| Asked to join a gang | 63.6 | 73.6 | 56.7** |
| Through a gang initiation | 31.9 | 50.6 | 19.0** |
| Belong to a gang | 21.9 | 33.1 | 14.2** |

* Significant differences of mean between males and females at .05 level.
** Significant differences of mean between males and females at .01 level.

Although we do not have exhaustive information regarding the characteristics of everyone in the adolescents' peer networks, it is clear that they have close friends who have been engaged in a variety of delinquent behaviors. In addition, a remarkable number have gang contacts and affiliations. The findings suggest that the shift from adult to peer influence is also a shift in the direction of nonconventional influences. Many of the young people described getting in trouble with their friends. As one 18-year-old male told us, "You don't even want to know . . . just trouble. Going to jail for shooting at people, for robbing people, for attempted murder, drugs, stealing cars, we do all kinds of stuff, stealing food and stuff out of stores, all kinds of stuff, because we be struggling." Another young man, aged 17 years, told us, "All my friends been locked up—not all of them, but the majority of them have been locked up. And they been in trouble for like drugs and possession, and assault charges. A lot of my friends got assault charges."

Although friendships are often made with other troubled young people, they are also important, perhaps sole, sources of emotional and instrumental support. One young man, aged 16 years, described his relationship with his best friend:

Since I left he's been the emotional support through the whole thing. I couldn't have made it as far as I have without him. . . . He started handling it worse than I did and we've just kind of grown together emotionally. . . . He was hurt very much by me getting thrown out, and I was hurt even worse, and he was just there for me to talk to, which is all I really needed—somebody at the time to talk to.

An 18-year-old woman told us that her friends "let me stay with them, they took me places I had to go, and they talked to me when I needed it and everything. It was very comforting." Friends were often counted on for direct aid. For example one young woman told us a friend gave her clothes and a place to stay: "When I ran away, I had no time to get no clothes and she let me borrow her clothes and her mother gave me a home and everything, food and stuff." There was also the perception that friends will be there should an emergency occur: "Like if I needed to, like get some help for like, go to the hospital or something, they'd do it. They'd take me there. They'd do anything for me" (female, aged 15 years). Friends were the primary source of information and socialization regarding street life. A young man aged 17 years told us that friends "give me places to stay, give me money, give me ideas, you know, of where I could go."

Peer relationships served a dual role for adolescent runaways. They were the primary source of emotional support, help, and aid when the young people were on their own. They provided comfort, someone who listened, as well as money, shelter, and other basic needs. At the same time, friends were also involved in deviant behaviors. They provided drugs and alcohol. They were partners and protectors when things got rough.

## CONTACTS WITH ADULTS

The world of runaway and homeless adolescents is not devoid of supportive adult contacts. Besides the ongoing contact with extended family members we have noted, there are professional helpers who may serve a variety of support roles. Almost all of the adolescents we talked to had had some contact with adult helping professionals. Ninety-six percent reported seeing a "professional counselor"; 79% told us that they had seen a mental health professional because of problems they were having. Eighty-two percent had spent time in a shelter; 55% had sought help from an agency that deals with runaways. Over 20% of the young men and 26% of the young women had been in a substance abuse treatment program. Almost one-half (43%) of the young men and one-third of the young women (30%) had spent time in juvenile detention. About one-fourth of the adolescents had been in foster care at some point, and over one-third had been in a residential group home. Only about 20% had ever called a runaway hotline for help. About one-fourth had sought help from a religious organization.

Not all experiences with adult professionals were positive. Many more of the young men said they had been hassled by the police (61%) than said they had been helped by them (42%). Almost equal numbers of young women reported being helped (43%) and hassled (42%) by police. The adolescents' stories ranged from rape to being pulled over and questioned. A young women, aged 17 years, told us she had been raped by three men, one of them a police officer. "He had smoked a joint with me and took me to a party, then he and his friends raped me." A 15-year-old woman reported,

"[W]e would be walking down the side of the road and they'd pull us over and say, you know, ask us what we were doing and just give us crap." Another young woman, aged 15 years, said, "[T]hey'd put you in the spotlight, they'd do that to me, that's about it." An adolescent male, aged 17 years, reported that the police would "make us lie on the ground, search our pockets and stuff." Sometimes, the officers would simply taunt the adolescents. A 16-year-old male told us that "they put us up against a car, told us to empty our pockets, and they sat around on their hoods and bullshitted for like a half an hour and then said 'you can get your things and go.'" For some, the day-to-day harassment took more serious forms. For example, a 17-year-old male reported that the police would "just pull you over and, you know, get you for something. Like you are out too late . . . put you in the back seat of the car and drive you to the wrong neighborhood and drop you off and make us walk home." Given the gang territoriality in the inner cities, the walk home could result in beatings or even worse. Although in many instances, police helped out by taking young people to shelters or referring them for help, the attitude of runaways was predominantly one of suspicion and distrust.

## SCHOOL EXPERIENCES

Almost all of the adolescents had attended school in the past 12 months (86% boys, 91% girls). However, very few were experiencing academic success. Forty-two percent of the boys and 32% of the girls had dropped out of school. Eighty percent of the boys and 66% of the girls had been suspended from school at some point. One-third of the boys and 17% of the girls had been expelled from school. A substantial minority reported they had learning problems. One-third of the boys and 22% of the girls had been told they had a learning disability; 39% of the boys and 28% of the girls had been in a special education class at some point. T-tests indicated there were statistically significant gender differences on all of these measures. Adolescent boys were more likely than girls to have dropped out, been suspended, and been expelled. They also were more likely to have been told they had a learning disability and to have been in a special education class. The adolescent girls were more likely to have attended school in the past 12 months than were the adolescent boys.

Running away almost automatically interrupts the educational process. A fifteen-year-old girl told us: "I haven't been to school in like three weeks, two to three weeks. . . . [I]f things get better a whole bunch, I plan to go to school every day. I mean, if things just stay the way they are, I'd probably skip a lot." Although most of the runaways we talked to were behind in school and currently not attending, many had plans that included completing high school

or their GED and going on to college. Many had done pretty well academi-
cally when they were younger. They blamed their drug use or poor attendance for failing grades when they were going to school. An 18-year-old
male told us that he was not in school right now, but when he had been "I
was smart. I was getting 3.0s and stuff. My last report card was bad. That's
because I started getting off into smoking marijuana, skipping class, girls,
gangs, and all of that." Another young man, aged 17 years told us: "I main-
tained good grades, I was, you know, I was about from C+ to A, you know, I
mean, at some points when I was out on the streets . . . up until I stopped
going to school, you know, my grades slumped. But when I was at home, you
know, in a comfortable environment, I made As and Bs." Although their
experiences in school were seldom positive, most told interviewers they
intended to return at some point or complete their GED.

## HEALTH NEEDS AND ACCESS TO HEALTH RESOURCES

Almost one-fifth (18%) of the adolescents we interviewed told us that they
had a current health concern for which they would like to see a doctor. Of
those reporting a physical or mental health condition that they were worried
about, about one-half indicated it was a physical problem or injury. Adolescent girls were more likely to report mental health problems than were boys
(40 vs. 20%). About one-fourth wanted to see a doctor about a sexual problem that was worrying them.

One-third of the adolescents had been hospitalized during the past twelve
months. (A complete list of reasons for hospitalization is presented in Table
6A.2 in the Appendix). For those hospitalized in the past year, 44% had been
in the hospital more than one time. Twenty-three percent had been hospitalized twice and 21% three or more times. Access to physicians was greater
than we had anticipated, probably because of the high percentage of shelter
interviews in the sample. Two-thirds (66%) of the adolescents had seen a
physician in the past year (54% males, 75% females). For 24% it had been a
year since they had seen a doctor; the remaining 10% had not seen a physician for two years or more. The adolescents were much less likely to have
had dental care. Only one-third (34%) told us that they had seen a dentist in
the past year. Twenty-nine percent said they had seen a dentist a year ago.
For the remaining 37% it had been two years or more.

Access to health care essentially ends while the adolescents are on the
street. Admission to hospitals automatically means contact with guardians or
social workers. The extent of health care received by the runaways we interviewed is reflective of the number of interviews that were conducted in shelters. Once in shelters, health needs may be attended to. Physical and dental
examinations may be scheduled.

## PREDICTORS OF SOCIAL NETWORK COMPOSITION

Support networks are crucial influences of adolescent behaviors. Conventional peer groups moderate deviant behaviors, nonconventional peer groups increase them. By running away, the adolescents in our study have separated themselves from most prosocial networks. Emotionally distressed and unsupervised in novel, perhaps threatening situations, they are seeking supportive others and may quickly invest in new relationships. They are particularly susceptible to influence in these situations. To better understand the factors that lead to affiliations with deviant peers and factors that perpetuate family contact, we investigated a model that included family of origin characteristics (parental warmth, family transitions, and family abuse) and adolescent experiences (adolescent-initiated transitions and the amount of time the adolescent had been on his/her own). Structural equation modeling allowed the simultaneous estimation of two dependent variables: continued support from the family network and affiliation with deviant peers.

All of the independent variables in the model (Figure 6.1) have been described in previous chapters except for *length of time on own*. This variable is the log transformation of the total number of days the adolescents reported having been on their own including all of the times they have run away. *Continued support from the family network* was measured with two

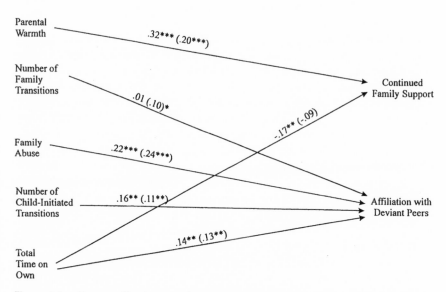

*Figure 6.1.* Factors affecting social networks of runaway and homeless adolescents. Standardized regression coefficients for males (females). N = 219 for males; N = 333 for females. *, p < 10; **, p < .05; ***, p < .01.

items that asked the adolescents whom they counted on to give them help or aid and whom they counted on to care about them. Response categories included both biological parents and members of their extended families (grandparents, aunts, uncles, siblings). *Affiliation with deviant peers* was the sum of a checklist in which the adolescent designated whether a close friend has participated in any of a number of deviant behaviors. The complete list is given in Table 6.2. Cronbach's alpha for the measure was .89. Bivariate correlations for the variables in the path model are provided in Appendix Table 6A.1.

Adolescents' perception of parental warmth was the only indicator positively associated with continued family support ($\beta = .32$ for males, $= .20$ for females). The number of family transitions was positively associated with deviant peer affiliations for adolescent females ($\beta = .10$; $p < .10$). The number of adolescent-initiated transitions was positively associated with association with deviant peers for both adolescent males ($\beta = .16$) and females ($\beta = .11$). Family abuse was positively associated with deviant peer associations for both the young men ($\beta = .22$) and women ($\beta = .24$) as was the length of time the adolescents had been on their own ($\beta = .14$ for males, $=.13$ for females). The length of time the adolescents had been on their own also was negatively associated with continued family support for adolescent males ($\beta = -.17$). The model explained 18% of the variance for continued family support for adolescent males and 9% for females. It explained 14% of the variance for affiliation with deviant peers for adolescent males and 17% for adolescent females.

Perceived parental warmth was the primary indicator of continued family contact for support. Family disorganization and a family history of abuse both contributed to adolescents' association with deviant peers. The more often the adolescents had chosen to leave home and the more time they had spent on their own decreased the likelihood of turning to family for support and increased affiliation with deviant peers. The processes that result in the adolescents leaving home (family disorganization and family abuse) also are those that result in affiliation with deviant peers (see Patterson, 1982; Moffitt, 1997). Similarly, the longer the adolescents are on their own the greater is the likelihood of having friends involved in deviant behaviors. Absent some positive perceptions of parents, the alienation process begun by leaving the family continues after separation.

## THE SOCIAL WORLDS OF RUNAWAYS

The adolescents we spoke with had largely left the sphere of influential adults behind them when they ran. They were more likely to view friends rather than family as caring for them, as someone they could to talk to, or as someone to turn to when in need of help. Most were out of school and beyond the reach of teachers and school counselors. Although almost all had been involved with helping professionals at some point in their lives, these professionals were rarely listed as sources of emotional support or help. Law enforcement officers were viewed more as threats than helpers.

The social worlds of the runaways were made up predominantly of same-aged friends, acquaintances, boyfriends, and girlfriends. Often, brothers or sisters of a girlfriend or boyfriend, or friends of friends, would be viewed as resources. The social networks were fleeting, forming and disappearing as living situations changed. The costs of these transitory same-aged social networks could sometimes be great. Emotional investments may not pay off. As we will see in later chapters, there was always the potential for exploitation, especially for the young women. On the other hand, the networks provided the adolescents with protection, people to talk to about their troubles, and information about how to get by.

Same-aged social networks have critical developmental consequences. First, these social networks are likely to be made up of young people with similar backgrounds. Young people on their own turn to other young people on their own to meet their needs for emotional and instrumental support. Second, the survival skills taught in age-segregated support systems are likely to be qualitatively different than those taught in conventional support systems made up of combinations of adults and same-aged friends. Young people with intergenerational support systems are more likely to be exposed to conventional expectations for behaviors and values both through the influence of adults and from peers with similar intergenerational support systems. There is a redundancy of expectations for prosocial values and behaviors that spills over generational boundaries. When social networks become age-segregated, behaviors become oriented toward early adult transitions. Adult perspectives are lost as are adult-initiated behavioral expectations and limits. In age-segregated social networks, when adolescents are troubled, hurt, or in need, they must turn to someone who may be in the same situation. Resources are fewer. There is less knowledge in emergencies or when serious decisions must be made. Fewer alternatives are available.

Moffitt (1997) and others (Caspi & Bem, 1990) have pointed out that across time behaviors develop inertia, that is, there are cumulative consequences of maladaptive behaviors that narrow available options. Precociously moving out of the sphere of adult influence provides freedom and self-direction, but it also eliminates access to adult resources. For example, there are few legitimate means of self-support for minors on their own. There are no formal support programs (e.g., welfare or food stamps) that do not involve adult supervision. As runaway and homeless adolescents move further away from adult control, they experience continually diminishing resources. Age-segregated social networks have no legitimate means of replacing these resources. To get by, adaptation often involves new survival skills. These may involve depending on friends and "borrowing" to get by. Or they may consist of minor risk behaviors such as learning to panhandle or shoplift. "Getting by" on your own, however, can mean taking very serious risks such as dealing drugs, survival sex, and theft. In the next chapter we will examine subsistence strategies and their consequences.

# 7

# Getting By
## *Survival Strategies of Runaway Adolescents*

*Like I got a big coat so I can go to the grocery store and steal something. Or if I see somebody and I got a knife or a BB gun or something, I'll rob them or whatever. Like I have a little bit of jewelry and I've pawned it, in fact it's in the pawn right now. And then like my stepdad who gets disability support and I get $150 a month and my mom tries to make sure I get it, so I have a little bit of money every month.*

—Male, 17 years

Leaving home means finding ways to get by on your own. For some of the adolescents, this is nothing new. They have been taking care of themselves to some extent prior to drifting out or choosing to leave and live on their own. For others, the situation requires learning new survival skills. Because formal financial programs are typically unavailable to minors, there are few legitimate means of self-support. Some of the adolescents work or were working just prior to leaving home. As is the case for homeless people regardless of age, maintaining a job without a permanent place to stay is very difficult. Furthermore, jobs available to people of this age and skill level are often part-time and low paying. They rarely pay enough to set up independent housekeeping.

The adolescents we talked to typically drew financial support simultaneously from a range of sources, some legitimate, some not. As an 18-year-old male told us:

It was mostly by selling drugs. Then, my sister is a stripper. Then one of my babies' mamas—she was doing it for a while. And I was getting money like that. And then—it was mostly selling drugs, though. I had a job for a while, but it was mainly selling drugs.

Getting by required considerable innovation and usually involved combinations of paid employment, borrowing money from friends and relatives, and various deviant subsistence strategies. For some, support from home continues even after they have left. As a 17-year-old male currently in a shelter for runaways told us: "I call my mama and she basically come to give me money or come see me so . . . [we] keep in contact that way sometimes." Sometimes it just meant panhandling and drifting from place to place:

> I'd ask people, or friends if I could borrow like a couple of dollars for the day or so. And for like, extra money in my pocket or just like eat over at a friend's house and stuff. Take showers and stuff like that over at friends' houses. (Female, 15 years)

Subsistence strategies often were opportunistic. As one young man, aged 15 years, put it: "Selling drugs, hustling, robbing, whatever works." In the situations that these young people find themselves, getting by usually came down to "whatever works."

The adolescents we interviewed reported multiple sources of income. Table 7.1 provides a duplicated count of their strategies for obtaining money. Almost one-third (29%) reported that they had no money at the time of interview. About one-half (47%) told us that they would ask parents or other relatives for money at times; 50% said they would borrow from others to get

*Table 7.1.* Adolescent Reports of Ways of Getting Money While on His/Her Own

| Means for Getting Money | Total (N = 602) | Male (N = 241) | Female (N = 361) |
|---|---|---|---|
| Allowance | 28.2 | 25.3 | 30.2 |
| Asking parents, relatives, or caretakers | 46.7 | 47.7 | 46.0 |
| Borrowing | 49.0 | 50.6 | 47.9 |
| Regular employment | 29.2 | 30.7 | 28.3 |
| Chores/odd jobs | 46.0 | 53.5 | 41.0 |
| Welfare or public assistance | 9.5 | 7.5 | 10.8 |
| State vouchers | 5.5 | 7.1 | 4.4 |
| Social Security | 5.5 | 6.2 | 5.0 |
| Panhandling or spainging* | 16.4 | 23.2 | 11.9 |
| Took money or something else from someone* | 22.6 | 32.8 | 15.8 |
| Broke in and took things from a store, house, etc.* | 14.0 | 25.3 | 6.4 |
| Prostitution | 2.3 | 2.5 | 2.2 |
| Ever sold drugs to get money* | 30.4 | 48.1 | 18.6 |

* Proportions significantly different for males versus females ($p < .05$ for Chi-Square Contingency Table Test).

money when they needed it. Thirty percent of the adolescent girls and 25% of the boys told us that they had allowances at the time they left home. About one-third (31% males, 28% females) had regular employment of some kind. Almost 50% reported having done odd jobs for money. A few of the older homeless young people reported selling blood, a strategy often used by adult homeless people (Whitbeck & Simons, 1993). About 20% reported that they had some sort of formal governmental assistance such as welfare, social security payments, or state vouchers. Adolescent boys (23%) were twice as likely as girls (12%) to report panhandling or "spainging" (i.e., "spare-chang-ing"). They also were more likely to engage in theft (32% boys, 16% girls) and burglary (25% boys, 6% girls). Almost half of the young men (48%) told us that they had sold drugs to obtain money compared to 19% of the young women. Among those who told us they sold drugs, more than 85% had done this more than one time. Very few reported engaging in prostitution (2%); the percentages for both sexes were nearly equal.

Because the economy of the street is often barter, or simply sharing avail-able resources, we also asked the young people about their primary sources of food when on their own (Table 7.2). Again, a range of strategies was given. Over two-thirds said they purchased their own food; three-fourths said they ate with friends. More than one-half told us that parents or other relatives provided them with food. Adolescent boys (34%) were more likely to report shoplifting for food than were girls (16%). One-fourth of the young men and 17% of the young women had obtained food through social services agen-cies such as shelters or drop-in centers. A few had resources from state vouchers, fewer still engaged in "dumpster diving." Males were much more likely to report this (5%) than females (1%).

Although much has been written about "survival sex" among runaway and homeless adolescents, relatively few reported trading sexual favors for money,

*Table 7.2.* Adolescent Reports of Ways of Getting Food While on His/Her Own

| Means for Getting Food | Total (N = 602) | Male (N = 241) | Female (N = 361) |
|---|---|---|---|
| Buy food | 68.6 | 71.4 | 66.8 |
| Parents, relatives, or caretakers | 54.3 | 55.6 | 53.5 |
| Friends | 71.1 | 74.3 | 69.0 |
| Panhandling or spainging* | 12.5 | 17.4 | 9.1 |
| Stealing or shoplifting* | 23.3 | 34.0 | 16.1 |
| Social services (drop-in centers)* | 19.8 | 24.5 | 16.6 |
| State vouchers | 7.1 | 6.2 | 7.8 |
| Dumpsters* | 2.8 | 5.0 | 1.4 |

* Proportions significantly different for males versus females (*p* < .05 for Chi-Square Contin-gency Table Test).

drugs, food, or shelter. This may be due, in part, to varying perceptions of situations. Although the sexual encounter may be transient and superficial in the eyes of adults, runaway adolescents may view the encounter as a "relationship," or as the beginning of a potential relationship rather than outright exchange. For example, a couple may get high together, have sex, and part. The encounter would not be interpreted as a direct exchange of sex for drugs. It is striking that although few adolescents reported sexual exchanges themselves, many more reported knowing someone who did (39% males, 44% females). Also, the adolescents were two to three times more likely to report considering sexual exchanges than actually doing so. For example, 11% of the young women and 12% of the young men reported having thought about trading sex for food or shelter, but only 6% of the young men and 3% of the young women had ever done so.

## PREDICTORS OF CONVENTIONAL AND DEVIANT
## SUBSISTENCE STRATEGIES

Housed adolescents of the ages we interviewed typically would still be dependent on parents at this stage of life. However, for runaways, parents and relatives were one of many sources of support. To better understand factors affecting choice of subsistence strategies, we extended the social network model examined in Chapter 6 to predict three basic strategies for getting by: (1) depending on family and other relatives for food and money; (2) employment; and (3) deviant subsistence strategies as a source of food and money. *Depending upon family and relatives* was measured by two items, "asking parents, relatives, or caretakers" for food and for money (see Tables 7.1 and 7.2). *Employment* was assessed by summing the items "regular employment" and "chores/odd jobs" for reports of ways of getting money and getting food. Finally, *deviant subsistence strategies* was measured with seven items regarding nonconventional sources of food or money: panhandling, stealing, burglary, shoplifting, selling drugs, dumpster diving, and prostitution. Cronbach's alpha for the scale was .73 for males and .68 for females.

We found that the three subsistence strategies were uncorrelated with one another at the bivariate level (for correlation matrix see Table 7A.1 in the Appendix). Further, there were separate trajectories into the three subsistence strategies (Figure 7.1). When family ties remained, adolescents were more likely to depend on kin for money and food ($\beta = .17$ for males, $= .20$ for females). However, when adolescents could not depend on family members for aid and support, they were more likely to depend on self-employment for food and money ($\beta = -.16$ for males, NS for females) or deviant subsistence strategies ($\beta = -.15$ for males, $= -.10$ females). The length of time the adolescents had been on their own was positively associated with the likelihood of employment for both young men (β = .18) and young women (β = .12). The longer the young people had been on their own, the more likely they were employed. Length of time on own also was negatively associated with deviant subsistence strategies for the young men (β = –.20). However, it was positively associated with association with deviant peers (β = .14 for males, = .12 for females) and, in turn, deviant peer affiliation was strongly positively associated with deviant subsistence strategies for both males (β = .51) and females (β = .35). Among adolescent males who did not associate with deviant peers, the amount of time on own did not increase the likelihood of deviant behaviors.

The model explained 7% of the variance of obtaining money and food from family for young men and 8% for young women. It explained 7% of the variance of employment for young men and 3% for young women. The model did a much better job explaining the trajectory into deviant subsistence strategies than more conventional ones. It explained 29% of the variance for deviant subsistence strategies for young men and 17% for young women.

Although we expected that better parental relationships and closer family ties would be associated with conventional subsistence strategies, this was

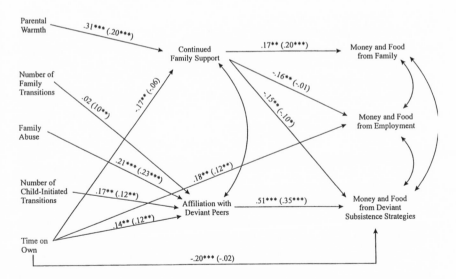

*Figure 7.1.* Factors affecting subsistence strategies for runaway and homeless adolescents. Standardized regression coefficients for males (females). *N* = 215 for males; *N* = 323 for females. *, *p* < .10; **, *p* < .05; ***, *p* < .01.

not the case. Rather, continued family contact was associated only with turn-ing to the family for money and food. The absence of continuing family con-tact increased the likelihood of both conventional and nonconventional independent subsistence strategies. There were three distinct trajectories for getting by independently. For those with continued family connections, who perceived their parents as warm and supporting and who came from less dis-organized families, there was food and monetary support from relatives. For those with more troubled family backgrounds, there was a greater likelihood of affiliating with deviant peers and, through them, becoming involved in deviant subsistence strategies. Young people who have been independent for longer periods of time and who do not report friends who were engaging in delinquent acts were more likely to be employed and less likely to support themselves through deviant subsistence strategies.

## PATHS TO DEVIANCE

Much has been written about deviant and criminal behaviors among run-away and homeless adolescents (Hagen & McCarthy, 1997). It is apparent from our data, however, that runaway adolescents are engaging in a range of survival strategies and that some severely deviant behaviors (e.g., prostitu-tion) are relatively infrequent. Although deviant behaviors among young people are known to be highly correlated (Donovan & Jessor, 1985; Rowe, Rodgers, Meseck-Bushey, & St. John, 1989; Whitbeck, Conger, Simons, & Kao, 1993), selection into various deviant survival strategies may be due to factors such as family background, gender, and peer affiliations. To better understand factors that contribute to various deviant subsistence strategies we investigated three path models that predicted victimizing behaviors, sur-vival sex, and drug dealing as ways of getting by on the streets.

## DEALING DRUGS

The model for drug dealing (Figure 7.2) included three family background variables described previously in this volume (adolescent report of serious crime by a biological parent, family abuse, and adolescent report of alcohol and drug abuse by a biological parent). It included two variables relating to time away from home (total time on own and number of child-initiated tran-sitions), and two street behaviors (alcohol and drug use and association with deviant peers).

Two of the exogenous family background variables had direct effects on drug dealing as a survival strategy. Having a biological parent who had a sub-stance abuse problem with alcohol or drugs was directly positively associ-

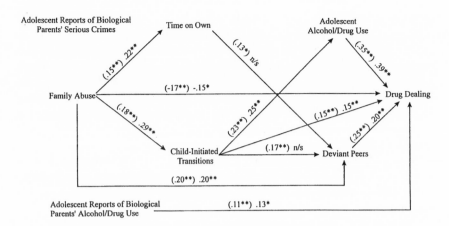

*Figure 7.2.* Predictors of drug dealing as a subsistence strategy. Standardized co-efficients for females (*N* = 330) shown in parentheses; males (*N* = 220). **, *p* < .01; *, *p* < .05; n/s, nonsignificant path.

ated with adolescent drug dealing (β = .11 for males, = .13 for females). However, we were puzzled to find that family abuse was negatively associated with drug dealing when controlling for all other variables in the model (β = −.17 for females, = −.15 for males). Bivariate correlations between drug dealing and family abuse were positive but nonsignificant for males and .23 for females (for correlation matrix see Table 7A.1 in the Appendix). Decomposition of effects indicated that indirect effects of family abuse were significantly positively correlated with drug dealing for both males and females, while the direct effects were significantly negatively associated with drug dealing. This indicates that when all of the negative behavioral effects associated with family abuse (indirect effects via child-initiated transitions, time on own, and affiliation with deviant peers) were controlled, victims of family abuse were less likely to deal drugs. Family abuse was positively related to total time on own (β = .15 for females, = .22 for males) and child-initiated transitions (β = .18 for females =.29 for males). It also was positively associated with affiliation with deviant peers (β = .20 for both males and females).

The total amount of time on own (β = .13) and the number of child-initiated transitions (β = .17) were positively associated with deviant peer affiliations for females but not males. The number of child-initiated transitions also was positively associated with alcohol and drug use (β = .23 for females, = .25 for males) and drug dealing (β = 15 for males and females). Adolescent alcohol and drug use was strongly related to drug dealing (β = .35 for females, = .39 for males). Deviant peer affiliations also was positively related to drug dealing ($\beta = .25$ for females, $= .20$ for males). The path model explained 33% of the variance for drug dealing by adolescent males and 36% of the variance for adolescence females.

The path model tells an interesting story. Drug dealing was more likely among adolescents who had biological parents who abused alcohol and/or drugs. Young people with family histories that were positive for substance abuse experienced the concomitant disorganization associated with such families (see Chapter 4) including earlier and more independent transitions. They were likely to be substance abusers themselves and to hang out with delinquent friends. It also appears that the effects of maltreatment are indirect via their influence on exposure variables such as the amount of time on own, child-initiated transitions, and association with deviant peers rather than direct.

## VICTIMIZING BEHAVIORS

The model for victimizing behaviors (e.g., theft, burglary, shoplifting) was similar to that of drug dealing (Figure 7.3). Family abuse was consistently associated with early independence behaviors. It was positively related to total time on own ($\beta = .22$ for both males and females) and child-initiated transitions ($\beta = .31$ for females, $= .29$ for males). It also had positive direct effects on association with deviant peers ($\beta = .20$ for both males and females). Having a biological parent who had committed a serious crime (e.g., crimes against persons or property; see Chapter 4) had mixed effects. For adolescent women, the main effect was negative ($\beta = -.11$). Young women who had a biological parent who had committed a serious crime were less likely to engage in victimizing behaviors themselves. On the other hand, having parents who had been involved in serious crime was positively related to deviant peer affiliations for young women ($\beta = .12$). Decomposition of effects indicated that the influence of parental histories was split. Direct effects were negative and statistically significant; indirect effects were positive and statistically significant. When all of the exposure and behavioral variables are considered, a parental history of serious crime reduced the likelihood that daughters would be victimizers. Rather, the effects were indirect through the effects of parental history on deviant peer affiliations.

The total amount of time on own was negatively associated with victimizing behaviors for adolescent males ($\beta = -.23$). When controlling for all other variables such as drug and alcohol use and deviant peers, the length of time on own actually suppressed victimizing behaviors. If a young man is living independently and not engaging in other deviant behaviors or hanging out with deviant peers, he is less likely to engage in victimizing subsistence strategies. Total time on own significantly increased the likelihood that young

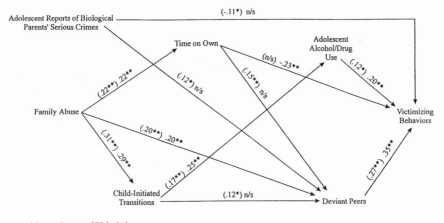

*Figure 7.3.* Predictors of victimizing behaviors as a subsistence strategy. Standardized coefficients for females (*N* = 330) shown in parentheses; males (*N* = 220). Only significant paths shown. \*\*, *p* < .01; \*, *p* < .05; n/s, nonsignificant path.

women would associate with deviant peers (β = .15) as did the number of child-initiated transitions (β = .12). Child-initiated transitions increased the likelihood of alcohol and drug use (β = .17 for females, = .25 for males). In turn, alcohol and drug use (β = .12 for females, = .20 for males) and affiliation with deviant peers (β = .27 for females, = .35 for males) were positively associated with victimizing behaviors. The model explained 17% of the variance for victimizing behaviors of adolescent females and 25% of the variance for adolescent males.

The path to victimizing behaviors is similar to that of drug dealing. It begins with a dysfunctional family history that results in early independence. Early independence and the effects of family history contribute to relationships with friends who are involved in deviant behaviors and to alcohol and drug use. These behaviors and friendships are highly related to victimizing behaviors. When controlling for family abuse, the early independence variables, and the street behavior variables, young women with biological parents who had been involved in criminal activity were less likely to engage in such behaviors themselves. That is, if the young woman is able to avoid negative associations and other deviant behaviors, she is less likely to become a victimizer. However, such family histories contributed indirectly to criminal activities through the behavioral variables.

## SURVIVAL SEX

Our results indicated that engaging in survival sex is really about having been sexually abused. Of all of the models we investigated regarding predictors of survival sex, the most powerful begin with early sexual abuse by an adult caretaker (Figure 7.4). Early sexual abuse resulted in leaving home at an earlier age ($\beta = -.17$ for females, $= .16$ for males) and the adolescents having spent more time on own ($\beta = .14$ for females, $= .41$ for males). In turn, the older the adolescents were when first on their own the more likely they had engaged in survival sex ($\beta = .16$ for females, $= .26$ for males). The younger they were when first on their own, however, the more likely they were to become involved in deviant peer groups ($\beta = -.13$ for females, $= -.17$ for males). The total amount of time on own was positively associated with drug and alcohol use among adolescent women ($\beta = .11$). Affiliation with deviant peers had a direct positive effect on survival sex. ($\beta = .20$ for females, $= .38$ for males). As noted in our discussion of sexuality, many more of the adolescents told us they knew someone who was engaging in survival sex than admitted to doing so themselves. Having deviant friends also was positively related to alcohol and drug use ($\beta = .47$ for females, $= .49$ for males) and having had multiple sexual partners in the past year ($\beta = .20$ for females, $= .21$ for males). Having had multiple sex partners was positively associated with survival sex for young women ($\beta = .19$). Alcohol and drug use was positively associated with survival sex ($\beta = .30$ for females, $\beta = .15$ males).

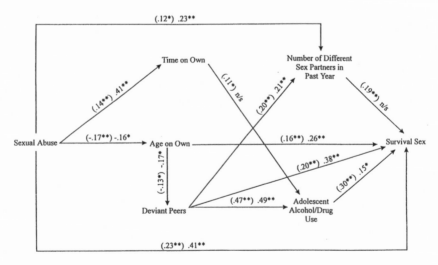

*Figure 7.4.* Predictors of survival sex as a subsistence strategy. Standardized coefficients for females ($N = 330$) shown in parentheses; males ($N = 220$). Only significant paths shown. **, $p < .01$; *, $p < .05$; n/s, nonsignificant path.

The most interesting aspect of the model, however, is that even when accounting for all of the behavioral variables that would lead to survival sex, early sexual abuse by an adult caretaker retained a very powerful direct effect ($\beta$ = .23 females, = .41 for males). It also directly affected having had multiple sex partners during the past year ($\beta$ = .12 for females, = .23 for males). Clearly, early sexual misuse by caretakers is a major factor in self-destructive sexual behaviors while on the streets. The model explained 38% of the variance for survival sex among adolescent women and 41% of the variance for adolescent men.

## UNDERSTANDING DEVIANT PATHWAYS

Although adolescent deviant behaviors are highly intercorrelated, these results suggest significant variance in ways young people selected into deviant subsistence strategies. Adolescents who turned to drug dealing as a survival strategy were more likely to have biological parents who were substance abusers. Those who engaged in survival sex were much more like to have been sexually victimized by an adult caretaker. For young women, a biological parent who had a history of criminal activity had modest indirect effects on victimizing behaviors. The commonality in all of the developmental trajectories was the role of family abuse in contributing to total time on own, child-initiated transitions, and directly and indirectly to deviant peer affiliations and deviant street behaviors.

These results suggest that the adolescents carried what they knew into early independence. When leaving a home where alcohol and drug abuse was common, they carried that behavior into independent living and perhaps even used it to generate income. When sexually misused, this conception of self and sexuality was projected onto situations encountered in early independence. Sex was more likely to be used as a commodity to barter for day-to-day survival. When treated aggressively by parents, they would, in turn, treat others aggressively and to associate with others who did likewise. These developmental trajectories suggest that maladaptive behaviors and styles of interaction learned at home are those adapted to situations in precocious independence. These early experiences guide interpersonal relationships and provide information regarding strategies for getting by on their own.

# 8

## Getting It On
### Sexuality, Risky Sex, and Pregnancy

*This is my second pregnancy. My first one. . . . I had to terminate it because I was fourteen and this is my second pregnancy. But this is the first one I'm going through with.*

—Female, aged 18 years

Recent reports from the Youth Risk Behavior Surveillance System sponsored by the Center for Disease Control (1996) indicate that 53% of high school students in grades 9–12 have experienced sexual intercourse. In comparison, almost all (84%) of the adolescents we talked to were sexually experienced, the same percentage as that found by Rotherum-Borus and colleagues (Rotherum-Borus et al., 1992). The young men and young women were equally likely to have been sexually active. The great majority was heterosexual in orientation (94% of males, 95% of females). About 2% of the young men reported that they were gay, and 3% said they were bisexual. Among the young women, 3.6% told us they were bisexual and only 0.8% reported that they were lesbian. Regardless of sexual orientation, 20% of the young women and 10% of the young men reported that they had left home or had been kicked out because of a conflict with parents/caretakers about sexuality or sexual behaviors.

According to the CDC (1996), 13% of male high school students and 5% of female high school students in grades 9–12 had experienced coitus prior to age 13 years. Among the adolescents we interviewed, the median age of first sexual intercourse was 13 years for young men and 14 years for young women. Reports of first sex began with sexual molestation at under 5 years

(2% of males, 1% of females). Sixteen percent of the young men and 3% of young women reported first intercourse between the ages of 6 and 10 years. The modal category for first sex was age 14 years for males (20%). Modal categories for females were ages 13 years (27%) and 14 years (24%).

Reports of the number of lifetime sexual partners ranged dramatically from 1 to 300 for young women and 1 to 160 for young men. These ranges of behaviors are misleading. Although a very few of the adolescents had been highly sexually active, the majority had not. The median was 5 lifetime sexual partners for young men and 4 for young women. In contrast, the CDC (1996) study of 9th- to 12th-grade students indicated that about 18% reported 4 or more partners during their lifetimes. Among the adolescents we spoke with, 9% of the young men and 8% of the young women had had more than 16 partners. The modal category was 6–10 sexual partners (24% of males, 20% of females). Eleven percent of the young men and 17% of the young women had had only one sexual partner in their lives. Fifty-nine percent of the young men and 65% of the young women reported 5 or less sexual partners.

When asked about sexual behavior in the past 12 months, the numbers dropped considerably. About one-third (29% of boys, 35% of girls) reported only one sexual partner in the past year, one-fourth (25% of boys, 23% of girls) reported two sexual partners. Fifteen percent of the young men and 12% of the young women reported 3 sexual partners in the past 12 months. Only 22% of the adolescents reported having 4 or more sexual partners in the past year. The median number of sexual partners during the past 12 months was 2.0 for both adolescent boys and girls. The range was 0–50 partners.

## CONTEXTS OF SEXUAL RELATIONSHIPS

When we asked the adolescents about the contexts of their sexual relationships during the past year most told us that they were sexually active with a "steady" boyfriend or girlfriend. In about equal proportions, the adolescent men and women reported one (45%), two (26%), or three (12%) "steady" relationships that involved sexual intercourse in the past year. Although most of their sexual expression was in the context of steady relationships, 19% of the young men and 13% of the young women reported at least one sexual encounter with an "acquaintance" or "stranger." Twelve percent of the young men and 8% of the young women reported two such encounters; 14% of the young men and 10% of the young women told us that they had had three or more sexual encounters with strangers or acquaintances. In response to our question regarding "one-time partners" during the past year, 24% reported one, 10% reported two; only 9% reported three or more "one night stands."

## CONDOM USE

Forty-one percent of the young men and 32% of the young women reported using a condom "all of the time" when having vaginal sex during the last 12 months. Sixteen percent of the young men and 19% of the young women said they had never used a condom when they had vaginal intercourse. About one-third of the adolescents (29% of males, 37% of females) used condoms less than half the times they had vaginal sex. Koopman and colleagues reported that about one-third of the runaways in their study used condoms regularly (Koopman, Rosario, & Rotherum-Borus, 1994). Rotherum-Borus and her research team reported that only 18% of runaway females and 14% of males consistently used condoms in heterosexual sex. Almost 40% of the runaway adolescents they interviewed never or rarely used condoms (Rotherum-Borus et al., 1992). According to the Center for Disease Control (1996), 54.4% of high school students used a condom at last sexual intercourse.

Few of the adolescents had engaged in anal intercourse in the past year (20% of males; 7% of females), and fewer still engaged in it with any frequency. Of those who had anal sex during the last 12 months, one-third of the young men (35%) and more than one-half of the young women (52%) had not used a condom. Fifty-six percent of the males and 71% of the females used a condom less than half the time that they had anal sex during the past year. Oral sex was much more common among the adolescents. Only about one-third of the males (37%) said that they had not experienced oral sex during the past 12 months. Young women (57%) were much more likely than the men to report no oral sex in the past year. Of those who engaged in oral sex, two-thirds of the young men (66%) and three-fourths of the young women (78%) had not used a condom.

## PREDICTORS OF CONDOM USE

To better understand condom use by the adolescents, we created a regression model consisting of factors known to affect consistent use. The model included measures of alcohol and drug use, having friends who prostituted themselves, a history of sexual victimization, multiple sex partners in the past year, concern about the AIDS virus, age at first sex, sexual orientation, having engaged in HIV risk behaviors, having ever had a sexually transmitted disease (STD), and having ever been or made someone pregnant.

*Alcohol/marijuana* use was measured with 3 items that asked the respondent, "During the past 12 months, how often have you used beer, hard liquor, or marijuana?" Response categories were 0 = never to 6 = daily. The three items were summed and coded so that the higher the score, the higher the usage. Cronbach's alpha was .85.

Similarly, *hard drug* use was assessed with 8 items in which the adolescent was asked about use of drugs such as crack, amphetamines, cocaine, hallucinogens, and opiates during the past 12 months. The 8 items were dichotomized and then summed such that the higher the score, the higher the hard drug use. Cronbach's alpha for this measure was .82.

Having a *close friend who sold sex* was a 2-item measure in which the respondent was asked if any of his or her close friends had ever traded or sold sexual favors for drugs or money or whether a close friend had ever traded sexual favors for food or shelter. These items have an alpha reliability of .86. The two items were summed and then dichotomized into 0 = close friend has never traded sex and 1 = close friend has traded sex.

*Sexual victimization* was a 2-item indicator that asked the adolescents how often their caretaker or parent asked them to do something sexual and how often their caretaker or parent forced them to do something sexual. Response categories ranged from 0 = never to 3 = many times. The 2 items were summed and coded so that the higher the score, the more frequent the victimization. Cronbach's alpha was .91.

*Number of sex partners* was assessed by a single-item indicator asking the adolescents the number of different people with whom they had had sex in the past 12 months.

*Concern about HIV infection* was a single-item indicator in which the adolescent was asked, "Are you worried about the possibility that you might get AIDS?" Responses ranged from 1 = very worried to 4 = not at all worried. Items were reverse coded so that the higher the score, the more worried about the possibility of getting AIDS.

*Early sexual initiation* was a dichotomized variable with 1 indicating those who initiated sex at age 13 years of age or younger and 0 indicating those who initiated sex after age 13 years or who had never engaged in sexual intercourse.

*Adolescents' sexual orientation* was a single-item coded 0 = those who considered themselves heterosexual and 1 = those who saw themselves as gay, lesbian, or bisexual.

*HIV risk behaviors* were assessed by 4 items in which the adolescents were asked whether they had traded sex for money or drugs, traded sex for food or shelter, engaged in prostitution, or used IV drugs. The four items were summed, then dichotomized into 0 = no HIV risk behaviors and 1 = one or more HIV risk behaviors. Cronbach's alpha was .67.

Whether the adolescent had ever had a *sexually transmitted disease* was assessed by a single dichotomous item that asked the adolescent if he or she had ever had been diagnosed with a STD. The response categories were 0 = no, 1 = yes.

*Pregnancy* was assessed by a single dichotomous item in which 1 indicated the adolescent had ever been pregnant or indicated whether a male had made someone pregnant; 0 indicated no pregnancies.

*Condom use* consisted of 3 items in which the adolescents were asked how often they wore condoms when engaging in vaginal, oral, and anal sex in the past 12 months. A count procedure was used for all 3 items and then the items were coded so that those who used condoms only some of the time or never were coded as 0 and those who used condoms all of the time were coded as 1. Cronbach's alpha was .72.

The regression model investigating condom use controlled for age, gender, and race. *Gender* was coded 0 = males and 1 = females. Race was dichotomized into two variables. European-American was dichotomized into 0 = nonwhite and 1 = white, and African-American was coded 0 = nonblack and 1 = black.

Alcohol and marijuana use, early sexual initiation, having ever been pregnant, and age were negatively associated with regular condom use for young women (Table 8.1). Use of alcohol and/or marijuana was negatively related to regular condom use ($b = -.13$) decreasing the likelihood of regular use by about 13%. Becoming sexually active prior to age 13 years decreased the likelihood of consistent condom use by 58% ($b = -.86$; exp $b = .42$). Ever having been pregnant also was negatively related to condom use ($b = -.94$; exp $b = .39$) and decreased the likelihood of regular use by 61%. Younger women were almost one-third ($b = -.37$; exp $b = .69$) less likely to regularly use condoms as were older adolescent women. Finally, there was a weak effect for number of sexual partners in the past year ($b = -.11$; $p = .10$).

*Table 8.1.* Predictors of Condom Use for Male and Female Homeless and Runaway Adolescents (Logistic Regression Coefficients)

| Independent Variables | Male | | Female | |
|---|---|---|---|---|
| | B | exp b | B | exp b |
| Alcohol/marijuana use | −.08* | .92 | −.13** | .87 |
| Hard drug use | −.27* | .76 | .02 | 1.02 |
| Close friends engaged in survival sex | −.83 | .44 | .23 | 1.26 |
| Adult caretaker sexual victimization | .01 | 1.01 | −.10 | .90 |
| Number of different sex partners in past year | −.10 | .90 | −.11 | .90 |
| AIDS concern | .25 | 1.28 | −.03 | .97 |
| Early coitus | −.62 | .54 | −.86** | .42 |
| Sexual orientation | −8.05 | .00 | −.37 | .69 |
| HIV risk behaviors | 1.08 | 2.94 | −.38 | .68 |
| STD | −.30 | .74 | −.46 | .63 |
| Pregnant | −1.43* | .24 | −.94** | .39 |
| Age | −.22* | .81 | −.37** | .69 |
| European-American | −.52 | .59 | .05 | 1.05 |
| African-American | .10 | 1.10 | −.02 | .98 |

*$p < .05$.  **$p < .01$.

Number of sexual partners decreased the likelihood of regular condom use among the adolescent women by about 10%.

Among the young men, alcohol and marijuana use decreased the likelihood of regular condom use by about 8% ($b = -.08$; exp $b = .92$). Hard drug use had a much stronger negative effect ($b = -.27$; exp $b = .76$), decreasing the likelihood of consistent condom use by 24%. Having ever made someone pregnant was negatively associated with regular condom use ($b = -1.43$; exp $b = .24$). It decreased the likelihood of regular use by 76%. Age also was negatively related to condom use ($b = -.22$), with younger adolescent males almost 20% less likely to regularly use a condom than their older counterparts.

It is noteworthy that HIV risk behaviors had no significant effect on regular condom use for either adolescent women or men. Those in the highest risk categories were not more likely to use condoms than those whose behaviors put them at less risk. It is also noteworthy that concern about HIV infection had no significant effect on preventive behaviors.

## SURVIVAL SEX

Even though much has been written about homeless and runaway adolescents' sexuality in the popular media (see Hersch, 1988), survival sex is relatively uncommon. Instead, adolescents move from "relationship" to "relationship." These transient relationships often involve sharing what they have, but the adolescents seldom articulate a direct exchange of sex for resources. This results in the underestimation of the degree of actual survival sex that occurs when adolescents find themselves in tough situations. Rotherum-Borus and colleagues (1992) reported survival sex rates of 13% for males and 7% for females from their sample of New York City street youth. Pennbridge and associates (Pennbridge, Freese, & Mackenzie, 1992) found that 28% of the adolescent homeless males in their Hollywood sample had engaged in survival sex in the last three months. Twenty-six percent of runaways were reported to engage in survival sex compared 0.2% of nonrunaways in Los Angeles (Yates et al., 1988)

Many of the young people we talked with were acquainted with people who had engaged in survival sex (Table 8.2), but more had considered it when in desperate circumstances than actually reported doing so. Almost one-half of the adolescents (39% of males, 44% of females) told us that they knew someone who had engaged in trading sexual favors for food, shelter, drugs, or money. About one-fifth (19%) had considered trading sex for resources; however, only 7% of the males and 6% of the females admitted to doing so.

*Table 8.2.* Survival Sex

| | Total (N = 599) | | Male (N = 240) | | Females (N = 359) | |
|---|---|---|---|---|---|---|
| | N | % | N | % | N | % |
| Know anyone who does trade sex for food, shelter, money, or drugs | 250 | 41.7 | 94 | 39.2 | 156 | 43.5 |
| Thought about trading sex for food, shelter, money, or drugs | 113 | 18.9 | 45 | 18.8 | 68 | 18.9 |
| Traded sex for food, shelter, money, or drugs | 40 | 6.7 | 17 | 7.1 | 23 | 6.4 |

## SEXUALLY TRANSMITTED DISEASES AND HIV RISK BEHAVIORS

The lifestyles and environments of runaway young people put them at particular risk for contracting STD. Estimates have been as high as 50–71% infection rate among street youths (Shalwitz, Goulart, Dunnigan, & Flannery, 1990). In our sample, 23% of the young women and 12% of the young men had contracted a STD at some point in their lives. Among the young women who reported having had a STD, 33% had been diagnosed with chlamydia, 25%, gonorrhea, and 17% pubic lice. Six percent had been diagnosed with pelvic inflammatory disease and 5% had genital herpes. The young men who had ever been had a STD primarily reported pubic lice (48%) and gonorrhea (16%). Only one person in our sample reported being HIV positive.

Because of their high-risk sexual behaviors, runaway adolescents also are especially susceptible to HIV infection. Although only about 4% are currently estimated to be HIV infected (Stricof, Novick, & Kennedy, 1990), there is fear that higher rates will emerge as the adolescents become young adults. Regional estimates of HIV infection among street youth range from 5.3% in New York to a high of 12% in San Francisco (Rotherum-Borus, Koopman, & Ehrhardt, 1991).

Multiple factors contribute to HIV risk. Runaway adolescents are sexually precocious, initiating coitus much younger than nonrunaways and hence are at risk for more of their adolescence. As we have shown, they are more likely to engage in unprotected intercourse and to have multiple sexual partners than are nonrunaways. Their sexual partners are more likely to be HIV positive. Runaways also are more likely than nonrunaways to have engaged in IV drug use or be exposed to HIV drug users in the street environment. Kipke and associates (Kipke, Montgomery, Simon, Unger, & Johnson, 1997) reported that 29% of the adolescents in their study had had intercourse with an IV drug user. Young women are particularly at risk from sexual partners who are IV drug users in that they are likely to engage in sexual activity with older men who have higher IV drug use rates (Athey, 1991).

## PREDICTORS OF HIV RISK BEHAVIORS

Although only one of the adolescents we interviewed had been diagnosed as HIV positive, 18% had been exposed to other STDs, and 59% of the young men and 68% of the young women had not used condoms consistently when engaging in vaginal sex during the last 12 months. All of the major risk factors were present in the young people we spoke with. Based on the same variables from the condom use regression model, we examined a second model using the variable HIV risk behaviors as the dependent variable. *HIV risk behaviors* was operationalized as having ever traded sex for food or shelter, traded sex for drugs or money, engaged in prostitution, or injected drugs.

Among the young men (Table 8.3), hard drug use ($b = .53$) and having friends who engaged in survival sex ($b = 1.54$) were the primary predictors of HIV risk behaviors. Having friends who engaged in survival sex increased the likelihood of HIV risk behaviors 5 times (exp $b = 4.7$). Hard drug use almost doubled (exp $b = 1.7$) the likelihood of risky behaviors. Initiating

*Table 8.3.*  Predictors of HIV Risk Behaviors for Male and Female Homeless and Runaway Adolescents

|                                                | Male | | Female | |
|------------------------------------------------|------|-------|--------|-------|
| *Independent Variables*                        | B    | *exp* b | B    | *exp* b |
| Alcohol/marijuana use                          | .13  | 1.14  | .10    | 1.10  |
| Hard drug use                                  | .53** | 1.70  | .29    | 1.33  |
| Close friends engaged in survival sex          | 1.54* | 4.68  | 2.05** | 7.75  |
| Adult caretaker sexual victimization           | .38  | 1.46  | .30*   | 1.36  |
| Number of different sex partners in past year  | .06  | 1.07  | .07    | 1.08  |
| AIDS concern                                   | −.06 | .94   | .17    | 1.19  |
| Early coitus                                   | 1.33 | 3.78  | 2.45** | 11.61 |
| Sexual orientation                             | 1.65 | 5.23  | −.46   | .63   |
| Condom use                                     | .55  | 1.74  | .03    | 1.03  |
| Age                                            | .33  | 1.39  | .17    | 1.19  |
| European-Americans                             | 1.08 | 2.93  | .52    | 1.69  |
| African-American                               | 1.51 | 4.53  | −.39   | .68   |

*$p < .05$.     **$p < .01$.

coitus at age 13 years or before was marginally significant ($b$ = 1.33; $p$ = .07) and increased the likelihood of HIV risk behaviors almost four times (exp $b$ = 3.8). Sexual victimization by an adult caretaker also was marginally significant ($b$ = .38; $p$ = .08) and increased HIV risk behaviors 1.5 times.

Among young women, having a close friend who engaged in survival sex ($b$ = 2.05) increased the likelihood of HIV risk behaviors almost 8 times (exp $b$ = 7.8). Having been sexually victimized by an adult caretaker was positively related to HIV risk behaviors among the young women ($b$ = .30) and increased the likelihood of such behaviors 1.4 times. Precocious sexual initiation at age 13 years or earlier ($b$ = 2.45) increased the likelihood of HIV risk behaviors by a factor of 12 (exp $b$ = 11.6). Use of hard drugs was marginally significant ($b$ = .29; $p$ = .07) and increased risk 1.3 times.

It is noteworthy that concern about HIV infection was nonsignificant for both adolescent males and females in decreasing HIV risk behaviors. The adolescents perceive little risk and are behaving accordingly. Regardless of low rates of condom use and high rates of STDs, the young people who talked to us were relatively unconcerned about HIV infection. Only 16% of the adolescent males and 13% of the females said that they were very worried about getting AIDS. More than half (57 of males, 61% of females) told us that they were either not very worried or not at all worried about getting AIDS.


## PREGNANCY AND PREGNANCY OUTCOMES

Although very little has been written about pregnancy among homeless and runaway adolescents, it is extremely prevalent. The combined pregnancy rates among the runaway adolescent males and females we interviewed were 3 times the rate reported for 9th- to 12th-graders in the CDC study (1996) (22 vs. 7%). Over one-fourth (26%) of the young women we interviewed had been pregnant. Of the young women who had ever been pregnant two-thirds (67%) had been pregnant only once, 22% had been pregnant twice and the remaining 11% had been pregnant three or more times. The range was 1–6 pregnancies. The modal age category for first pregnancy was 15 years (32%). Two-thirds (69%) of the young women who became pregnant were aged 15 years or younger. Among the young men, 16% told us they had gotten someone pregnant. Of these, 61% had been responsible for one pregnancy, 26% for two pregnancies, and the remaining 13% for three or more pregnancies. The median age at first getting someone pregnant was 15 years. Eighty-two percent of the young men who were responsible for a pregnancy were 16 years or younger.

The great majority of young women told us that their first pregnancy ended in a miscarriage (63%). Only 8% told us that they had terminated their first pregnancy. Eighteen percent of the pregnancies ended in live births. The remaining 11% were either still pregnant at the time of interview, or their infants had been still born or died at birth.

Of those who delivered their babies, 38% told us that they had the child with them at the shelter, 31% said the child was with relatives, the remaining 31% were in foster homes, shelters, the hospital, or had been adopted.

Young men were about one-half as likely as the young women to report that the pregnancy had ended in miscarriage (26 vs. 63%). Thirteen percent said the pregnancy was terminated, 9% said the baby was stillborn or died at birth: 8% said the women was pregnant at the time of the interview; 8% did not know what happened in the pregnancy. Of those whose children had been carried to term, 13% did not know the whereabouts of the child; 40% said the child was with the father's family or relatives; 20% said that the child was with the mother or her relatives; and 20% said the child had been adopted.

## PREDICTORS OF PREGNANCIES AMONG HOMELESS AND RUNAWAY ADOLESCENTS

We investigated a regression model to assess the relative impact of factors known to be associated with early pregnancy among homeless and runaway adolescents. The model included all of the variables previously described in this chapter and used in our examination of factors associated with regular condom use and HIV risk behaviors. For the young women (Table 8.4), number of sex partners in the past year ($b = .12$), becoming sexually active at age 13 years or younger ($b = .68$), condom use ($b = -1.01$), ever having been diagnosed with a STD ($b = .78$), and age ($b = .53$) were associated with becoming pregnant. Becoming sexually active at age 13 years or younger increased the likelihood of pregnancy among the young women twofold, as did ever having been diagnosed with a STD. Inconsistent condom use increased the likelihood of pregnancy by 64%.

Among the young men only condom use ($b = -1.42$) and age ($b = .38$) were significantly associated with making someone pregnant. Inconsistent condom use increased the likelihood of making a partner pregnant by 76%. Becoming sexually active at age 13 years or before was marginally significant ($b = .87$; $p = .07$) and increased the likelihood of making someone pregnant two times. Engaging in HIV risk behaviors also was marginally significant ($b = 1.15$; $p = .09$) and increased the likelihood of getting a sexual partner pregnant threefold.

## SUMMARY AND CONCLUSIONS

In summary, although the adolescents in our sample were as sexually experienced as those from larger metropolitan areas (e.g., Rotherum-Borus

*Table 8.4.* Predictors of Homeless and Runaway Males Ever Gotten Someone Pregnant and Females Ever Having Been Pregnant

| Independent Variables | Male | | Female | |
|---|---|---|---|---|
| | B | *exp* b | B | *exp* b |
| Alcohol/marijuana use | .00 | 1.00 | −.02 | .98 |
| Hard drug use | −.04 | .97 | −.24 | .79 |
| Close friends engaged in survival sex | −1.09 | .34 | −.27 | .76 |
| Adult caretaker sexual victimization | .03 | 1.03 | .03 | 1.03 |
| Number of different sex partners in past year | −.01 | 1.00 | .12* | 1.13 |
| AIDS concern | .14 | 1.15 | −.07 | .93 |
| Early coitus | .87 | 2.38 | .68* | 1.97 |
| Sexual orientation | .66 | 1.93 | −1.28 | .28 |
| Condom use | −1.42* | .24 | −1.01** | .36 |
| HIV risk behaviors | 1.15 | 3.17 | −.02 | .98 |
| STD | .43 | 1.53 | .78* | 2.18 |
| Age | .38** | 1.46 | .53** | 1.69 |
| European-American | .64 | 1.89 | .46 | 1.58 |
| African-American | .70 | 1.07 | .08 | 1.08 |

* $p < .05$.    ** $p < .01$.

et al., 1992), they may have been a little less sexually active. Rotherum-Borus and colleagues reported 47% of the males and 16% of the females in their New York study had 10 or more sexual partners. The modal category for our Midwest sample was 6–10 partners (24% of males, 20% of females). However, a small percentage had been very active. Nine percent of the young men and 8% of the young women had had 16 or more sexual partners. Most of the differences in lifetime sexual activity may be attributable to our low percentages of street intercepts.

Condom use among the adolescents in our sample was very similar to that reported in other studies of runaways. Pregnancy rates were also similar to those found in other samples of runaway adolescents (Rotherum-Borus et al., 1991). Among the predictors of condom use, HIV risk behaviors, and pregnancy, early initiation of coitus stood out as a consistent predictor of maladaptive sexual behaviors. As with other negative outcomes we have discussed in this volume, the earlier the transition to adultlike behaviors, the more developmental risk the child is exposed to.

Finally, it is important to note that from the adolescents' perspective their sexual activity is largely in the context of "steady" relationships. Although these relationships may appear transitory to others, they may be viewed as instrumentally and emotionally supportive to the adolescent. As with other perceived supportive relationships (see Chapter 7), homeless adolescents may "overinvest" sexually in short-term, tangential relationships. This serves multiple purposes. Most importantly, it negates perceptions of bartering sexual favors for resources. Rather, the young person views herself or himself as having been in a relationship that turned out badly or, at least, not as he or she would have hoped. These relationships provide mutual support, protection, and caring in the short run. Finally, these behaviors are an extension of normal adolescent heterosexual experimentation where young people move in and out of affectionate, supportive relationships. The difference is that these relationships are more often sexual and may become sexual more quickly in the unsupervised environment of runaways. Too often, however, overinvesting in others when on the streets results in disappointment, exploitation, and even worse. We turn next to victimization of runaways when they are on their own.

# 9

# Getting Hurt
## Victimization and Trauma on the Streets

*He was raped by three men. He got very emotional as he described this and hung his head very low when he spoke. This was difficult for me. I was near tears because I felt so awful that such a great kid had to have such a terrible thing happen to him. Of all the surveys I've done so far this one has touched me the most.*

—Interviewer comment regarding a 17-year-old male

However self-sufficient adolescents may have become at home, being alone and on the streets is frightening. Goodman and her colleagues make the case that experiencing homelessness is traumatic even for adults. These traumatic effects are magnified when they occur during a developmental period when young people may still expect and need caretaking adults. Based on trauma theory, Goodman and associates chronicle the psychological stress experienced by adults who become homeless (Goodman et al., 1991). They argue that experiencing homelessness is traumatic for adults in three ways. First, the process of becoming homeless may produce symptoms of psychological distress. Becoming homeless means the loss of familiar routines, loss of day-to-day contacts with friends, relatives, and neighbors, and the loss of a safe and private space. All of these losses are associated with factors that contribute to a sense of security in children and adolescents.

Second, the condition of homelessness is psychologically alarming. It results in a heightened sense of vulnerability, hypervigilance, anxiety, and fear. This hyperalert state may be adaptive to street life, but it is stress producing nonetheless. Finally, if the individual is already experiencing psychological distress when he or she becomes homeless, the stress associated with the experience of homelessness will almost certainly exacerbate existing symptoms. All of the adolescents who leave home are experiencing psychological stress or family turmoil or they would not be on the streets. What they find there only adds to their distress.

Sadly, the stress of homelessness goes well beyond anxiety and vulnerability. Too often, especially among the young, fears of being harmed become reality. More than 50% of Kipke's sample of Hollywood street youth feared being shot or stabbed and almost 50% feared being sexually assaulted or beaten up (Kipke, Simon, Montgomery, Unger, & Iverson, 1997). Fifty-one percent actually had been beaten up since being on the streets, 45% had been chased, and 26% had been shot at. Nineteen percent had been stabbed while living on the streets, 15% sexually assaulted, and 7% wounded by gunfire. Rotheram-Borus and associates (Rotherum-Borus et al., 1991) reported that in a New York sample of runaways, 20% were physically assaulted, 20% sexually assaulted, and 20% robbed in the three months prior to seeking shelter.

The adolescents we spoke with had similar stories of threats and actual harm, often on multiple occasions (Table 9.1). One-third (34%) of the young men and 22% of the young women had been beaten up at least one time when on their own. One-fourth of the young men and 16% of the young women had been robbed at some point when on the streets or in shelters. One-third of the women and 22% of the men had been asked to do sexual things they did not want to when on their own; 12% of the women had been raped one time; 7% had been raped more than once. Seven percent of the young men reported having been sexually assaulted at least one time.

Physical fighting and assaults were more common among the young men. Adolescent males (47%) were more than twice as likely to have been threatened with a weapon than young women (21%). They were also more than twice as likely to report having been assaulted with a weapon (25% of males vs. 9% of females).

Percentages mask the trauma of victimizing events. Consider a 13-year-old whose friend dies of a drug overdose when sleeping under a porch in a large city. She said she "woke up next to his body. I had been high the previous night." We had the interviewers ask the young people about their most traumatic event while on their own as part of the posttraumatic stress disorder screener. One young woman told an interviewer that when she was aged 15 years her friend died in her arms of an IV drug overdose. Young women were at particular risk for sexual victimization, sometimes when prostituting themselves, but more often when alone and in circumstances that made them vulnerable. One girl who was prostituting herself at age 14 years was sent to an apartment through an escort service where she was to meet one man. "When she went to meet the guy, four more guys came out, they took

Table 9.1. Victimization While Out on Their Own

| | Total % (N = 597) | | Male % (N = 239) | | Female % (N = 358) | |
|---|---|---|---|---|---|---|
| | Once | More than once | Once | More than once | Once | More than once |
| Beaten up | 12.4 | 14.4 | 16.3 | 17.6 | 9.8 | 12.3 |
| Robbed | 11.2 | 8.5 | 14.2 | 10.9 | 9.2 | 7.0 |
| Asked to do sexual acts you did not want to do | 11.4 | 17.3 | 9.2 | 12.6 | 12.8 | 20.4 |
| Sexually assaulted or raped | 9.2 | 4.5 | 5.9 | 1.3 | 11.5 | 6.7 |
| Threatened with a weapon | 14.9 | 16.6 | 21.8 | 25.5 | 10.3 | 10.6 |
| Assaulted and wounded with a weapon | 8.9 | 6.7 | 13.8 | 11.3 | 5.6 | 3.6 |
| Forced to go the day without eating because you could not get food | 9.2 | 27.9 | 7.5 | 30.4 | 10.3 | 26.3 |

turns raping her. It lasted all night long. They had a gun and told her if she tried to leave they would kill her" (interviewer summary).

More often, rapes were by acquaintances or friends of acquaintances. An interviewer summarized a 15-year-old women's sexual victimization by several young men:

> She was raped when she was 15 by four or five guys she didn't know. She was over at a friend's house hanging out and talking with these guys—friends of friends—and they tried to pressure her into having sex. They offered her a place to stay and drugs in exchange for sex. She agreed to have sex with them once, but they repeatedly forced her to do it over and over again.

Sometimes the attacker was someone she knew. An interviewer summary of the trauma history of a 17-year-old respondent reads as follows:

> A man she was seeing forced her to do cocaine and got her really drunk and forced her to do sexual things. He held a knife to her throat and split her lip open by biting her and bruised her by punching her.

While the young women were more at risk for sexual victimization, the young men were at greater risk for serious assaults through attacks, fights, and gang activities.

Almost all of the young men had a "fight story" to tell. Some were very serious. A 15-year-old male was assaulted with a weapon during a gang encounter in which he said a girl was killed. In his words:

> My brother—gang brother—got a couple of bucks [shotgun pellets] in his shoulder, my other brother got a couple in the ankle. Me I got one right here in my thigh and another one went through the same spot and cut my thigh open. . . . She caught every buckshot from both those barrels through her back. All I remember is falling by her side crying, then my brothers dragged me away.

Often there was a "macho," almost "Old West" quality to the violent stories the young men told. For example:

> [H]e pulled a knife, and then I said, "Hey, hey," something like that. I held up my hands like I surrender, you know. I started backing up and I was like, here, you can have my jacket and I pulled up my jacket and pulled out my gun and said, "You better run now." And he ran and I fired at his feet and he just kept running. (17-year-old male)

Fighting, backing others down, and knowing how to avoid confrontations are an every day part of street life for the young men. Sometimes fighting was necessary just to keep what you owned or to protect yourself. For some, being tough was just part of daily living on the streets. When asked about reasons for fighting, one young man aged 17 years told us:

> Like some reasons was because, you know, trying to get robbed or rob some-body, you know what I'm saying? So, and just any of your normal day things, you know, somebody bump up against you . . . you know, it's just one of them things.

Often fighting was associated with gang membership or gang encounters. The ever-present threat of gang violence was a common concern. There was talk of avoiding gang colors and signs in efforts to be left alone. Strategies for avoiding contact included knowing areas to avoid and taking care not to dress in gang colors. It is noteworthy that although predatory adults were a part of the runaway scene, the greatest threats encountered by the adolescent young men and women were from peers.

## PREDICTORS OF STREET VICTIMIZATION

We used logistic regression models to calculate odds for physical and sexual victimization based on various street experiences and behaviors. *Physical victimization* was measured by 6 items in which the adolescents were asked whether they had been beaten up, robbed, threatened with a weapon, assaulted with a weapon, asked to break the law such as shoplift-ing or selling drugs, or forced to go a whole day without food because they couldn't get food. For the logistic regression, the items were dichotomized and summed so that $0 =$ never occurred when on their own and $1 =$ occurred at least one time when on their own. *Sexual victimization* was assessed by 2 items to which the adolescents responded whether they had ever been forced to do something sexual they did not want to do, or had been sexually assaulted or raped. The items were summed and dichotomized for the logistic regression models so that $0 =$ these things had never occurred when they were on their own and $1 =$ these things had occurred at least one time when on their own.

Initially we ran a full regression model controlling for gender (not shown). Gender was a highly significant predictor of both physical and sexual vic-timization. Adolescent females were almost 20% less likely to be physically victimized than were adolescent males ($b = -.20$; exp $b = .82$) and almost four times more likely than males to be sexually victimized on the streets ($b = 1.35$; exp $b = 3.85$). After checking for gender effects in the full sample, separate models were run for males and females.

Only the physical victimization model is reported for adolescent males because of small cell sizes for male sexual victimization (Table 9.2). Having

Table 9.2. Logistic Regression for Victimization of Runaway Adolescents

| | Male | | Female | | | |
| | Physical Victimization (N = 216) | | Physical Victimization (N = 329) | | Sexual Victimization (N = 325) | |
| | B | exp b | B | exp b | B | exp b |
|---|---|---|---|---|---|---|
| Age on own | .03 | 1.03 | -.02 | .98 | -.03 | .97 |
| Time on own | .11 | 1.11 | .27** | 1.31 | .15 | 1.16 |
| Ever on the street | -.04 | .96 | .04 | 1.04 | -.12 | .89 |
| Family support | -.22* | .81 | -.06 | .94 | -.25** | .78 |
| Friend support | -.01 | .99 | .04 | 1.04 | -.03 | .98 |
| Deviant peers | 3.84** | 46.33 | 2.02** | 7.55 | 2.49** | 12.02 |
| Alcohol/marijuana | -.09 | .91 | -.01 | .99 | .22 | 1.25 |
| Hard drugs | .34* | 1.40 | .05 | 1.05 | .07 | 1.08 |
| Nonvictimizing behavior | .04 | 1.04 | .30 | 1.36 | .18 | 1.20 |
| Victimizing behavior | .56* | 1.74 | .48 | 1.61 | -.20 | .82 |
| Survival sex | — | — | — | — | 1.09** | 2.96 |

* $p < .05$.    ** $p < .01$.

continued contact with family members reduced the likelihood of physical victimization among adolescent males almost 20% ($b = -.22$; exp $b = .81$). Associating with deviant peers increased the likelihood of physical victimization among adolescent males 46 times ($b = 3.84$; exp $b = 46.33$). It is apparent from the magnitude of the coefficient that most physical victimization occurred in the context of same-age relationships. Use of hard drugs further increased the likelihood of physical victimization almost one and one-half times ($b = .34$; exp $b = 1.40$). Engaging in victimizing behaviors almost doubled the odds of the adolescent males becoming victims themselves ($b = .56$; exp $b = 1.74$)

We examined both physical and sexual victimization logistic regression models for adolescent females (Table 9.2). For young women the amount of time they had spent on their own was significantly related to physical victimization, although the effect was relatively modest ($b = .27$; exp $b = 1.31$). As was the case with the adolescent males, affiliation with deviant peers dramatically increased the odds of physical victimization. For the females, deviant peer associations increased the likelihood of physical harm almost eight times ($b = 2.02$; exp $b = 7.55$). Also similar to the adolescent males, engaging in victimizing behaviors increased the odds of physical victimization ($b = .48$; exp $b = 1.61$; one-tailed test).

In terms of female sexual victimization, continued family contact decreased the odds of sexual assault when the girls were on their own more than 20% ($b = -.25$; exp $b = .78$). Again, deviant peers were the primary risk factor for sexual assault for adolescent females on their own. Such associations increased the odds of sexual victimization 12 times ($b = 2.49$; exp $b = 12.02$). Survival sex increased the risk of sexual victimization three times ($b = 1.09$; exp $b = 2.96$).

As we have seen throughout this volume, the trajectory of runaway adolescents is away from adult influences to that of peers. However, it is in this context of deviant peers that they are most at risk for further harm. The dramatic effects of deviant peer affiliations are evidence of this. Physical harm is 46 times more likely for adolescent males who affiliate with deviant peers and 7 times more likely for females. Deviant peer associations increased the risk of sexual victimization among adolescent females 12 times.

## TRAUMATIC SEXUAL VICTIMIZATION AMONG YOUNG WOMEN

As we have noted, adolescent girls were twice as likely to be sexually victimized than were adolescent boys. Although 18% of the young women we interviewed had been sexually assaulted when on their own on at least one occasion, the percentages do not tell the whole story. To better assess risk, we created an event history file analyzing the risk of sexual victimization by age, years since the girl was first on her own, and whether the girl had ever been sexually abused by an adult caretaker prior to leaving home. The probability of sexual victimization varied dramatically. There was a natural progression for sexual victimization of young women on their own by age, a function of increased years at risk. For example, compared to 13-year-old females: those aged 15 were 3.41 times more likely to be sexually victimized, those aged 16 years were 2.16 times more likely, and those aged 17 years were 5.05 times more likely. When age and gender were controlled, adolescent females who had been sexually abused at home by an adult caretaker were two times more likely to be revictimized when they were on their own. As Figure 9.1 illustrates, young women, aged 17 years who had been sexually abused by an adult caretaker and who were in their first year on their own had more than a 30% probability of being sexually victimized. Under the same circumstances, the odds were more than 20% for 15-year-olds and about 14% for 16-year-olds. Young women who were least likely to be sexually victimized were those younger than aged 17 years who had not been sexually abused by an adult caretaker prior to leaving home and who had been on their own for a longer period of time. It appears that if a young woman successfully navigates the early period of independence unscathed, her chances of being sexually victimized are somewhat diminished.

The odds for an independent young woman (out of home less than one year) who had been sexually abused at home exceeded 1 in 5 for 15- and

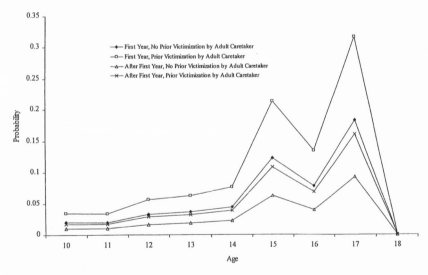

*Figure 9.1.* Traumatic sexual victimization of adolescent females when on their own.

16-year-old adolescent females and for 17-year-old women the odds climb to one in three. These are probably conservative estimates in that many of these young women may have experienced forced or coerced sex and may not perceive it as forced or as an "assault." Some situations involving survival sex may clearly constitute acquaintance rape for housed females, but may not be viewed as such by runaways. Having sex may be a means to being housed for the night or beyond.

## LIVING WITH FEAR

Physical harm or the fear of it characterized the lives of many of the runaways we spoke with. Witnessing violence, avoiding it, and occasionally being caught up in it were part of everyday life when on the streets. The runaways frequented areas of cities that adults avoid at night for fear of harm. From their qualitative reports and from the quantitative analyses it is apparent that their primary victimizers were people their own ages or close to it. The strongest predictor of physical or sexual victimization regardless of gender was deviant peer affiliations. Runaway adolescents leave family situations where they were subject to physical and/or sexual abuse for situations where similar incidents occur between peers.

The developmental harm from repeated victimization and the fear of it should not be underestimated. Perceptions of relationships are forming that may involve expectations of aggression or exploitation from others. Perceptions of self are also developing that may involve a sense that they are not worth caring about, or that they don't want or need such care. Sexual scripts are being formed. Those most damaged by the families they have left are at greatest risk for revictimization. We believe that this is due to the effects their early lives have on basic behaviors and interpersonal relationships. Patterson and colleagues (Patterson, Dishion, & Bank, 1984) have made the case that coercive/abusive caretakers train their offspring for poor peer relationships and antisocial behaviors. These are the young people who are more likely to hang out with friends who are engaging in risky behaviors and who are more likely to engage in such behaviors themselves. This makes them extremely vulnerable to serious revictimization, first through the hazardous situations in which their friendships and associations may place them, and second through their own high-risk and aggressive behaviors. The process is cumulative. The children who are most severely hurt physically and emotionally at the point they find themselves on their own are those who are most likely to be further harmed. In Part IV, we present findings regarding predictors of internalization and externalization among the runaways we talked to. These chapters hinge on the harm experienced inside the families the runaways left and the harm experienced since they opted to be on their own.

# IV

## NOWHERE TO GROW
*The Developmental Consequences of
Running Away*

# 10

## Internalization Problems among Runaway and Homeless Adolescents

*[B]ack in May, I took an overdose and they like pumped my stomach. And I was still depressed because they didn't hospitalize me, but in August they seen that I was still depressed and they hospitalized me.*

—Female, aged 18 years

Runaway and homeless adolescents fall into nearly all of the risk categories for internalization symptoms enumerated in the adolescent depression literature. As we have shown thus far, runaways experience high rates of family disorganization, ineffective parenting, and physical and or sexual abuse. Research on nonrunaways indicates that adolescents are at risk for depressive symptoms when they have parents who are rejecting or emotionally unavailable (Burge & Hammen, 1991) and when they live in families where there is high conflict (Burbach & Borduin, 1986; Carlton-Ford, Paikoff, & Brooks-Gunn, 1991; Forehand, Brody, Slotkin, Fauber, McCombs, & Long, 1988). Children with histories of maltreatment are also at risk for depressive symptoms (Downey & Walker, 1992; Finkelhor, 1984) as are those who report negative life events in their own lives and those of family members (Compas, Howell, Phares, Williams, & Ledoux, 1989; Ge, Lorenz, Conger, Elder, & Simons, 1994). Depressed adolescents report lower levels of social support available to them to help cope with stressful events (Armsden, McCauley, Greenburg, Burke, & Mitchell, 1990; Daniels & Moos, 1990). They often view themselves as unpopular with others their own age and report having poor peer relationships (Jacobsen, Lahey, & Strauss, 1983).

Given the numerous risk factors associated with precocious independence, there is a surprisingly lack of systematic research on the mental health status of runaway and homeless adolescents (Mundy et al. 1990). The small number of studies that exist indicate that homeless and runaway adolescents score higher on measures of behavioral and emotional disorders than do nonrunaway youth. Most studies document depressive symptoms, suicidal behavior, and substance abuse among runaway and homeless adolescents (Smart & Walsh, 1993; Yates et al., 1988). Schweitzer and Hier (1993) found that over 53.7% of their sample of Australian homeless adolescents scored within the clinical range on the externalizing and/or internalizing Youth Self-Report (YSR; Achenbach, 1991) subscales compared to 5.2% of the control group adolescents. The few studies that use diagnostic protocols are based on small samples at single centers or in a single metropolitan area. Feital and colleagues (Feital et al., 1992) using the Diagnostic Interview for Children and Adolescents—Revised (DISC-R) with a sample of 150 shelter adolescents reported that 49.3% met criteria for major affective disorder, 37.3% for dysthymic disorder, and 31.8% for posttraumatic stress disorder (PTSD). Mundy and associates (Mundy et al., 1990) reported that 20% of their sample of 97 Los Angeles street youth exceeded the cutoff for a clinical level of mood disturbance. DISC-R evaluations of 296 runaway and homeless adolescents in Seattle (Cauce et al., 1997) indicated that one-third met criteria for major depressive disorder or dysthymia.

To assess depressive symptoms among the adolescents in our sample, we administered the 20 items from the Center for Epidemiologic Studies Depression (CES-D) Scale (Radloff, 1977). The adolescents responded to questions regarding feeling low in energy, thoughts of ending one's life, crying easily, and feeling helpless by rating the number of days in the past week that they had experienced the symptoms: 0, 1–2, 2–4, or 5–7 days. Cronbach's alpha for the measure was .87 for the adolescent males and .90 for females. To assess clinical levels of depression, we used a very conservative cutoff score of 28. This cutoff represents those adults who scored in the 95th percentile on the Community Mental Health Assessment study (see Radloff, 1991). Almost 90% of the acutely depressed adults in Radloff's sample scored at or above this cutoff score, as did 13% of junior high school students and 18% of high school students. In our sample of runaway and homeless adolescents, 23% of the adolescent males and 39% of the females met this stringent clinical criterion for depression.

## PREDICTORS OF DEPRESSIVE SYMPTOMS AND DEPRESSION

To better understand factors contributing to depressive symptoms and depression scores above the CES-D clinical cutoff score of 28, we constructed panel regression models that included all of the potential risk factors addressed thus far in this volume (see Table 10.1). Separate panels were run for variables measuring family disorganization, parental characteristics, parental behaviors, family abuse and neglect, early independence, social networks of runaways, risky behaviors on the streets, subsistence activities on the streets, and street victimization. Gender was controlled for in all of the models and potential interactions with gender were assessed for all of the variables. Statistically significant predictors and interactions from each of the panels were then included in a full model assessing the most potent predictors of depressive symptoms and depression scores above the clinical cutoff. Bivariate correlations for the regression models are presented in Appendix Table 10A.1.

### Family Disorganization

Two family disorganization variables were considered: changes in family structure and number of changes in family residence while the child was still living at home. The model controlled for gender. As was the case in all of the panels, gender was highly significant in both the ordinary least squares regression model for depressive symptoms and the logistic model for CES-D scores above the clinical cutoff of 28. Adolescent females were about twice as likely to meet clinical criteria than were males ($b = -.71$; exp $b = .49$). Neither of the family disorganization variables achieved statistical significance, but the interaction of gender and changes in family residence was associated with depressive symptoms. For young women, changes in family residence contributed to depressive symptoms when controlling only for other family disorganization variables.

### Parental Characteristics

When considering only gender of adolescent and parental characteristics such as parental alcohol and/or drug use, serious crime by a biological parent, and parental depression, only parental depression increased the likelihood of adolescent depressive symptoms ($\beta = .12$) and exceeding the CES-D clinical cutoff score ($b = .47$) when controlling for gender of adolescent. Having a biological parent who was depressed increased the likelihood of child depression 1.6 times.

### Parenting Behaviors

Three parenting behaviors were assessed for their impact on depression and depressive symptoms when controlling only for gender of adolescent: parental warmth and supportiveness, monitoring, and parental rejection. Of these, only parental rejection had a statistically significant effect on depressive symptoms ($\beta = .21$) and depression ($b = .09$). Gender interacted with

Table 10.1. Standardized Regression Coefficients of Depression and Depressive Symptoms

| Variable | Symp | Depression | | Symp | Depression | | Symp | Depression | | Symp | Depression | | Full Model Symp | Full Model Depression | |
|---|---|---|---|---|---|---|---|---|---|---|---|---|---|---|---|
| | β | B | exp B | β | B | exp B | β | B | exp B | β | B | exp B | β | B | exp B |
| Family disorganization | | | | | | | | | | | | | | | |
| Gender | -.18** | -.71** | .49 | | | | | | | | | | -.22** | -.78** | .46 |
| Change in family structure | .06 | .04 | 1.04 | | | | | | | | | | | | |
| Change in family residence | .00 | .02 | 1.02 | | | | | | | | | | | | |
| Gender * family residence | -.12* | -.18 | .84 | | | | | | | | | | -.07 | | |
| Parental characteristics | | | | | | | | | | | | | | | |
| Gender | | | | -.17** | -.71** | .49 | | | | | | | | | |
| Parental alcohol/drug use | | | | .04 | .07 | 1.07 | | | | | | | | | |
| Parental serious crime | | | | .07 | .18 | 1.19 | | | | | | | | | |
| Parental depression | | | | .12** | .47* | 1.61 | | | | | | | .06 | .17 | 1.19 |
| Parenting behavior | | | | | | | | | | | | | | | |
| Gender | | | | | | | -.17** | -.70** | .50 | | | | | | |
| Warm/Support | | | | | | | .08 | .02 | 1.02 | | | | | | |
| Monitoring | | | | | | | -.01 | -.02 | .98 | | | | | | |
| Rejection | | | | | | | .21** | .09** | 1.09 | | | | -.01 | .02 | 1.02 |
| Gender * rejection | | | | | | | .10* | .07 | 1.07 | | | | .05 | | |
| Family abuse/neglect | | | | | | | | | | | | | | | |
| Gender | | | | | | | | | | -.14** | -.55** | .58 | | | |
| Neglect | | | | | | | | | | .04 | .11 | 1.12 | | | |
| Physical abuse | | | | | | | | | | .20** | .06** | 1.06 | .10* | .03 | 1.03 |
| Sexual abuse | | | | | | | | | | .04 | .36 | 1.43 | | | |

| | b | β | Exp(b) | b | β | Exp(b) |
|---|---|---|---|---|---|---|
| **Early independence** | | | | | | |
| Gender | -.20** | -.82** | .44 | | | |
| Age at first run | .01 | .03 | 1.03 | | | |
| Time on own | .00 | -.01 | .99 | | | |
| Ever on street | .13** | .60** | 1.82 | -.03 | .21 | 1.24 |
| Gender * ever on street | .14* | .50 | 1.65 | .11 | | |
| **Street networks** | | | | | | |
| Gender | -.18** | -.73** | .48 | | | |
| Family support | -.20** | -.19** | .82 | -.11** | -.09 | .92 |
| Friend support | -.09* | -.05 | .95 | -.07 | -.53 | .59 |
| Deviant peers | .19** | 1.02** | 2.76 | .02 | | |
| **Street risk behavior** | | | | | | |
| Gender | -.20** | -.72** | .49 | | | |
| Alcohol/marijuana use | -.07 | -.03 | .97 | | | |
| Hard drug use | .16** | .13* | 1.14 | .04 | .03 | 1.03 |
| Different sexual partners | .03 | .07 | 1.07 | | | |
| **Subsistence activity** | | | | | | |
| Gender | -.23** | -.97** | .38 | | | |
| Nonvictimizing strategy | .05 | .10 | 1.11 | | | |
| Trade sex | .13** | 1.10** | 3.00 | .00 | .39 | 1.47 |
| Victimizing strategy | .11* | .20* | 1.22 | .01 | .06 | 1.06 |
| **Street victimization** | | | | | | |
| Gender | -.22** | -.94** | .39 | | | |
| Physical victimization | .26** | .16** | 1.18 | .15** | .10* | 1.11 |
| Sexual victimization | .13** | .66** | 1.93 | .13** | .86** | 2.36 |

* $p < .05$.   ** $p < .01$.

parental rejection such that the effect was greater for adolescent boys than for girls.

## Maltreatment

Three measures of adult caretaker abuse and neglect were regressed in a panel controlling only for gender of adolescent: neglect, physical abuse, and sexual abuse. Of these, physical abuse had the strongest effects ($\beta = .20$ for depressive symptoms; $b = .06$ for depression). Sexual abuse was marginally significant for the cutoff depression score ($b = .36$; one-tailed test; exp $b = 1.43$). It increased the likelihood of scoring above 28 one and one-half times. There were no significant interactions with gender.

## Early Independence

We assessed the effects of the three early independence variables: age at first run, total amount of time the adolescent had been on his/her own, and whether the adolescent had ever spent time directly on the streets. Having ever spent time on the streets was the most powerful predictor of depressive symptoms ($\beta = .13$) and depression ($b = .60$; exp $b = 1.82$). It increased the likelihood of scoring above the cutoff for depression almost twofold. Having ever spent time on the streets interacted significantly with gender such that the effects on depressive symptoms were greater for males than females.

## Street Networks

Three types of social networks were regressed on depressive symptoms and all but one of the coefficients were significant. Support from family members was negatively related to depressive symptoms ($\beta = -.20$) and depression ($b = -.19$; exp $b = .82$). Continued support from family reduced the likelihood of scoring above the cutoff for depression by almost 20%. Support from friends was negatively associated with depressive symptoms ($\beta = -.09$), but did not significantly affect scoring above the CES-D cutoff. Association with deviant peers was positively related to depressive symptoms ($\beta = .19$) and scoring above the cutoff for depression ($b = 1.02$; exp $b = 2.76$). Deviant peer affiliations increased the likelihood of scoring above the cutoff almost 3 times when controlling only for gender and other social networks.

## Risk Behaviors When on the Streets

We assessed the effects of three high-risk street behaviors on depressive symptoms and depression: alcohol/marijuana use, hard drug use, and risky sexual encounters. Of these, hard drug use was positively related to depressive symptoms ($\beta = .16$) and to scoring above the cutoff of 28 for depression ($b = .13$; exp $b = 1.14$).

### Subsistence Activities

We examined three types of subsistence activities: nonvictimizing strategies (e.g., panhandling, borrowing from friends and family, employment), trading sex for food, shelter, drugs, or money, and victimizing behaviors (e.g., theft, shoplifting, burglary). Of these, sexual and victimizing subsistence strategies were uniformly associated with depressive symptoms and scores above the cutoff for depression, while nonvictimizing subsistence strategies were not. Trading sex to get by was positively associated with depressive symptoms ($\beta = .13$) and depression scores ($b = 1.10$; exp $b = 3.00$). Survival sex increased the likelihood of scoring above the cutoff for depression threefold. Victimizing behaviors also were positively associated with depressive symptoms ($\beta = .11$) and scoring above the cutoff for depression ($b = .20$; exp $b = 1.22$).

### Street Victimization

Two types of victimization when the adolescents were on their own were evaluated for their effects on depressive symptoms and depression scores above the cutoff score of 28 on the CES-D: physical victimization (e.g., beaten, robbed, threatened or assaulted with a weapon) and sexual victimization (e.g., sexual coercion and assault). Physical victimization was positively related to depressive symptoms ($\beta = .26$) and depression ($b = .16$; exp $b = 1.18$). Sexual victimization also was positively related to both depressive symptoms ($\beta = .13$) and depression ($b = .66$; exp $b = 1.93$), increasing the likelihood of scores above the cutoff of the CES-D 2 times when controlling only for gender and physical victimization.

### The Full Model

After examining the effects of each panel of variables controlling only for gender of adolescent, the significant variables and interactions with gender were combined into a full model to determine relative strengths of significant effects when controlling for all others. Gender remained strongly significant in the full model. Young women were about 2 times more likely than young men to score above the cutoff for the CES-D. Of the parenting and maltreatment variables, only physical abuse ($\beta = .10$) remained in the full model for depressive symptoms. Of the early independence variables, only the interaction between gender and having ever spent time on the streets was marginally significant for depressive symptoms ($\beta = .11$; one-tailed test). The effects of time on the street on depressive symptoms were greater for adolescent females than males. Among the social networks variables, however, family support continued to exert a negative effect on depressive symptoms ($\beta = -.11$) and scoring above the cutoff for depression ($b = -.09$; one-tailed test; exp $b = .92$). Support from friends continued to have a weak negative effect ($\beta = -.07$; one-tailed test) on depressive symptoms. All of the high-risk street behavior indicators and subsistence activities variables became non-significant in the full model. The street victimization variables, however, remained statistically significant in the full model. Physical victimization was positively related to depressive symptoms ($\beta = .15$) and cutoff depression scores ($b = .10$; exp $b = 1.11$). Similarly, sexual victimization was positively associated with depressive symptoms ($\beta = .13$) and depression scores above the cutoff score of 28 on the CES-D ($b = .86$; exp $b = 2.36$). Sexual victimization increased the likelihood of scoring in the clinical range for depression 2.4 times.

These results suggest that although numerous factors contribute to depressive symptoms and depression among adolescent runaways, the primary factor is the harm they come to when on their own. Similar results have been found for path-analytic models examining these same variables (Whitbeck et al., 1997; Whitbeck, Hoyt, and Bao, under review). Using longitudinal data from a Seattle study of runaways, we have also shown that the effects of street victimization on depressive symptoms are significant when controlling for earlier depressive symptoms (Hoyt, Whitbeck, & Cauce, under review). To fully address the issue of the internalization effects of precocious independence we need longitudinal data. However, it is becoming evident from the consistent cross-sectional effects that street experiences have profound mental health effects on young people.

## POST-TRAUMATIC STRESS DISORDER

To understand the consequences of victimization when adolescents are on their own, we did a diagnostic screening for post-traumatic stress disorder (PTSD). DSM-IV lifetime prevalence rates for PTSD based on community studies range from 1 to 14%. Prevalences of 3 to 58% have been reported among at-risk adults depending on severity and nature of the traumatic incident (American Psychiatric Association, 1994). Studies of traumatized children and adolescents based on DSM-III criteria have reported PTSD rates ranging from 0 (Sirles, Smith, & Kusama, 1989) to 90% (Kiser et al., 1988). As these prevalence rates suggest, there is considerable disagreement regarding the extent of PTSD among at-risk young people (McNally, 1996). Children respond very differently to traumatic events depending on the nature and severity of the event, the psychological health of parent, and their support systems. Trauma that occurs to children within families has been particularly difficult to assess (Boney-McCoy & Finkelhor, 1996). However, most researchers agree that familial sexual abuse is related to PTSD in children and adolescents (Deblinger, McLeer, Atkins, Ralphe, & Foa, 1989: Godwin, 1985; McLeer, Callaghan, Henry, & Wallen, 1994). Recent evidence suggests that physical abuse alone is not related (Pelcovitz, Kaplan, Goldenberg, Mandel, Lehane, & Guarrera, 1994). Physical abuse from caretakers may be viewed by the recipient as neither unusually traumatic nor unpredictable. Pelcovitz and colleagues (1994) point out that young people with histories of traumatic incidents may be less at risk for PTSD symptoms than their more protected counterparts. There is evidence that positive assumptions about fairness, predictability, and benevolence of the world may magnify the effect of sudden negative life events (Janoff-Bulman, 1992). Pelcovitz and colleagues (1994) also note that their lack of findings for physical abuse may reflect delayed onset of PTSD symptoms similar to that found among concentration camp victims. The symptoms may emerge when the chronic victimization abates.

Our own findings also indicate that precursors of PTSD symptoms are not straightforward. Among the adolescents we interviewed, two-thirds had experienced serious trauma such as rape, being beaten, or witnessing a death or serious injury. Of those who experienced a traumatic event, almost one-half (46%) met diagnostic criteria for PTSD. However, almost one-fourth of the adolescents screened positive for PTSD even though they reported no experiences that were coded as traumatic. For many of these young people the cumulative trauma ranging from maltreatment at home to multiple victimization when on their own may create a sense of "normalcy" regarding situations that others would view as traumatic. For example, one young woman aged 15 years told us:

> One of my friends has a boyfriend. Me and him got into an argument and he hit me in the jaw and I had to go to the hospital because of my jaw. . . . It was real swelled and it was bleeding on the inside of it. If you want to call that beaten up, then, yeah.

We believe that although some of the young people who screened positive for PTSD did not specify a particular traumatic event, there probably had been significant trauma in their recent lives that they simply did not identify as exceptionally traumatic. An alternative explanation would be that of Pelcovitz and colleagues (1994). Symptomatic responses to earlier trauma may occur when the adolescents escape chronic abusive situations at home. This could account for the proportion of runaways screening positive for PTSD but reporting no precipitating traumatic event. A third explanation is that the very experience of finding oneself alone at this age may create PTSD symptoms in some of the adolescents.

There is evidence that the likelihood and severity of PTSD symptoms are a function of the harshness of the traumatic incident (March, 1990). This was true among the adolescents we interviewed. Sexual assault was the most common traumatic event resulting in screening positive for PTSD. Seventy-seven percent of those who reported a rape as their traumatic event screen positive for PTSD. Many of these sexual assaults involved gang rapes. Forty-one percent of those who had been physically assaulted screened positive for PTSD as did 48% of those who witnessed a serious injury or killing. The latter included drive-by shootings, witnessing suicides, and drug deals that ended in shootings (for a complete listing of traumatic events reported by the adolescents, see Table 10A.2 in the Appendix).

## PREDICTORS OF POST-TRAUMATIC STRESS DISORDER

To better determine the relationship of the adolescents' early history and more recent traumatic events we investigated a series of panel regressions using the same predictor variables as in the depression panel. Post-traumatic stress disorder was estimated using questions from the PTSD module of the University of Michigan–Composite International Diagnostic Interview (UM-CIDI). The protocol for the PTSD module is to first screen for lifetime experiences of a number of potentially traumatic events and, if one or more are identified, then select the most traumatic of these events to use as a referent for the subsequent symptom questions. Each youth was asked to recall his or her "single most terrible or traumatic" experience since being on his or her own. This experience was then used as the referent point for administering the PTSD questions to all of the adolescents who identified some type of negative experience. The PTSD symptom measure is a simple summation of the affirmative responses to these questions. The PTSD diagnostic estimate was generated using the recommended scoring procedures for the UM-CIDI.

As in the depression panels, we first ran each panel controlling only for gender of runaway and checking for interactions between gender and the independent variables in each panel. A final model, consisting of all significant variables and interactions from the individual panels, was then examined (Table 10.2).

### Family Disorganization

Neither of the two family disorganization variables (number of changes in residence, number of changes in family structure) was significantly associated with meeting diagnostic criteria for PTSD when controlling only for gender. The interaction between gender and changes in residence was marginally significant ($p < .05$, one-tailed test) indicating that multiple changes in residence when still with their families made adolescent girls more susceptible to later symptoms of PTSD. Gender was highly significant ($b = -.69$; exp $b = .50$), indicating that adolescent females were twice as likely to meet criteria for PTSD than were adolescent males when controlling only for family disorganization.

### Parent Characteristics

We ran three parent characteristics as indicators of susceptibility for PTSD: parental alcohol and drug use, parent involvement in serious crime, and parental history of depression. Of these, when controlling only for gender, parental history of depression was positively related to child PTSD ($b =$ .46; exp $b = 1.58$), increasing the likelihood 1.6 times.

### Parenting Behaviors

Of the three indicators of parenting—warmth and supportiveness, monitoring, and parental rejection—only monitoring was weakly (one-tailed test) negatively associated with later symptoms of PTSD when controlling only for gender. Adolescents who reported that they were monitored by their parents were very slightly less susceptible to PTSD symptoms.

### Family Abuse and Neglect

We examined three indicators of child maltreatment: neglect, physical abuse, and sexual abuse. Of these only the adolescents' sense of having been neglected by their caretakers was significantly associated with PTSD ($b =$ .52; exp $b = 1.69$), increasing the likelihood of such symptoms 1.7 times. Both adolescent reports of physical abuse (one-tailed test) and sexual abuse interacted with gender of child. In both cases, adolescent males were more likely to meet criteria for PTSD if they had been physically or sexually abused than were females.

### Early Independence

We assessed three indicators of early independence: age at first run, the total amount of time the adolescent had been on his or her own including all runs, and whether the adolescent had ever spent time directly on the streets. Of these, the total amount of time the adolescent had been on his or her own was positively related to PTSD ($b = .14$; exp $b = 1.15$). The interaction of gender and the total amount of time on own was also statistically significant ($b = -.22$; exp $b = .80$). The effects of time on own for risk of PTSD were much greater for adolescent females than for males.

### Street Networks

The effects of three types of social support networks were examined: continued contact with family members, support from friends, and association with deviant peers when on the streets. All of these support networks were significantly associated with PTSD when controlling only for gender of adolescent. Family support was negatively associated with PTSD ($b = -.17$; exp $b = .84$) as was support from friends ($b = -.10$; exp $b = .90$). Association with

Table 10.2.  Standardized Regression Coefficients of PTSD

| Variable | B | exp B | B | exp B | B | exp B | B | exp B | Full Model B | exp B |
|---|---|---|---|---|---|---|---|---|---|---|
| Family disorganization | | | | | | | | | | |
| Gender | -.69** | .50 | | | | | | | -1.01** | .36 |
| Change in family structure | .00 | 1.00 | | | | | | | | |
| Change in family residence | -.07 | .94 | | | | | | | | |
| Gender * family residence | -.20 | .81 | | | | | | | | |
| Parental characteristics | | | | | | | | | | |
| Gender | | | -.64** | .53 | | | | | | |
| Parental alcohol/drug use | | | -.01 | .99 | | | | | | |
| Parental serious crime | | | .04 | 1.04 | | | | | | |
| Parental depression | | | .46* | 1.58 | | | | | .10 | 1.10 |
| Parenting behavior | | | | | | | | | | |
| Gender | | | | | -.65** | .52 | | | | |
| Warmth/support | | | | | .00 | 1.00 | | | | |
| Monitoring | | | | | -.04 | .96 | | | | |
| Rejection | | | | | .00 | 1.00 | | | | |
| Family abuse/neglect | | | | | | | | | | |
| Gender | | | | | | | -.59** | .56 | | |
| Neglect | | | | | | | .52** | 1.69 | .15 | 1.16 |
| Physical abuse | | | | | | | .01 | 1.01 | | |
| Sexual abuse | | | | | | | .10 | 1.10 | | |
| Gender * physical abuse | | | | | | | .06 | 1.06 | | |
| Gender * sexual abuse | | | | | | | .96* | 2.62 | .85 | 2.34 |

| | b | Exp(b) | b | Exp(b) |
|---|---|---|---|---|
| **Early independence** | | | | |
| Gender | -.77** | .46 | | |
| Age at first run | -.02 | .98 | | |
| Time on own | .14** | 1.15 | .13 | 1.14 |
| Ever on street | .26 | 1.30 | | |
| Gender * on own | -.22* | .80 | -.23* | .79 |
| **Street networks** | | | | |
| Gender | -.80** | .45 | | |
| Family support | -.17** | .84 | -.12* | .89 |
| Friend support | -.10** | .90 | -.12** | .89 |
| Deviant peers | 1.56** | 4.75 | .58 | 1.78 |
| **Street risk behavior** | | | | |
| Gender | -.80** | .45 | | |
| Alcohol/marijuana use | .01 | 1.01 | | |
| Hard drug use | .07 | 1.07 | | |
| Number of different sexual partners | -.06 | .94 | | |
| **Subsistence activity** | | | | |
| Gender | -.90** | .41 | | |
| Nonvictimizing strategy | .40** | 1.49 | .16 | 1.18 |
| Survival sex | .65 | 1.92 | | |
| Victimizing strategy | -.02 | .98 | | |
| **Street victimization** | | | | |
| Gender | -.83** | .44 | | |
| Physical victimization | .14** | 1.16 | .10* | 1.10 |
| Sexual victimization | 1.05** | 2.86 | .79** | 2.21 |

* $p < .05.$   ** $p < .01.$

deviant peers was strongly positively associated with PTSD ($b = 1.56$; exp $b$ = 4.75), increasing the likelihood of meeting diagnostic criteria almost 5 times when controlling only for gender other types of social networks.

### Risk Behaviors When on the Streets

None of the three types of risky behaviors we examined were significantly associated with meeting criteria for PTSD when controlling only for gender. Alcohol and/or marijuana use, hard drug use, or number of different sexual partners did not place the adolescent at special risk for PTSD.

### Subsistence Strategies

Two of the three subsistence strategies we examined contributed to risk for PTSD. Nonvictimizing subsistence strategies such as panhandling, dumpster diving, and living off friends was significantly positively associated with meeting criteria for PTSD ($b = .40$; exp $b = 1.49$). Nonvictimizing survival strategies increased PTSD risk 1.5 times. Survival sex was marginally significant (one-tailed test) and increased the likelihood of such symptoms almost 2 times when controlling only for gender and other subsistence strategies ($b$ = 65; exp $b = 1.92$). Victimizing behaviors were unrelated to PTSD.

### Street Victimization

Experiencing a traumatic incident is a necessary criterion for establishing the diagnosis of PTSD. Among the adolescents we interviewed, both physical victimization and sexual victimization when they were on their own were statistically significant indicators. Physical victimization was the weaker of the two predictors ($b = .14$; exp $b = 1.16$). Sexual victimization was highly significant ($b = 1.05$; exp $b = 2.86$) and increased the likelihood of meeting criteria for PTSD threefold when controlling only for gender and physical victimization.

### The Full Model

When we combined all of the significant indicators from the individual panel models into a full model, the most significant predictor was gender ($b$ = –1.01; exp $b = .36$). Adolescent females were 3 times as likely to meet criteria for PTSD than adolescent males. The gender by sexual abuse interaction remained significant in the full model ($b = .85$; exp $b = 2.34$) indicating that young men who were sexually abused by a caretaker adult were more likely to meet criteria for PTSD than were adolescent females who were similarly abused. The total amount of time the adolescents had been on their own remained in the full model (one-tailed test), increasing risk of meeting PTSD criteria ($b = .13$; exp $b = 1.14$), as did the gender by time on own interaction ($b = -.23$; exp $b = .79$). The effect of total time on own on the likelihood of meeting diagnostic criteria for PTSD was greater for adolescent females than for males. Two of the support variables remained in the full model. Both remaining in contact with family members and having supportive friends reduced the likelihood of PTSD. The effects of deviant peer affiliation did not remain significant in the full model. Both physical and sexual victimization when the adolescents were on their own remained in the full model. The effect for sexual victimization ($b = .79$; exp $b = 2.21$) was twice that of physical victimization ($b = .10$; exp $b = 1.10$) and increased the likelihood of meeting diagnostic criteria twofold.

Experiencing a traumatic event is a necessary precondition for PTSD. In the regression model just examined, sexual victimization was a stronger predictor of PTSD than was physical victimization, perhaps because of the everyday nature of living on the streets. Bullying and protecting oneself from being bullied are part of everyday interactions. Being female increased the likelihood of meeting PTSD diagnostic criteria 3 times. Family risk and protective factors from the panel models provide some interesting insights into at-risk adolescents. Having a parent judged by the adolescent to be depressed increased the likelihood in the panel model, but lost significance in the full model. A sense of having been neglected and having been sexually abused by a caretaker were significant in the panel model. Sexual abuse remained marginally significant in the full model and increased the likelihood of meeting PTSD criteria 2 times. Time at risk was a stronger factor for adolescent females than for males. It is noteworthy that support variables when the adolescents are on their own (e.g., family contact and friendship supports) reduced the likelihood of meeting criteria for PTSD among the runaway adolescents. Any type of support appears to have a positive effect on dealing with traumatic events, even that of same-aged street friends.

A straightforward analysis of factors predicting PTSD doesn't tell the whole story. PTSD is highly likely to coexist with other disorders in adults and adolescents. Among the adolescents in our sample 18% met criteria for PTSD and also exceeded the conservative cutoff score of 28 for the CES-D, indicating comorbidity for PTSD and depression (Table 10.3). Twenty-five percent of the adolescent females who scored in the clinical range of the

*Table 10.3.* Comorbidity of PTSD with Other Disorders

|  | Total | Male | Female |
|---|---|---|---|
| PTSD and depression | 17.8 | 13.4 | 20.6 |
| PTSD and externalization | 25.3 | 15.1 | 24.9 |
| PTSD | 37.7 | 28.6 | 43.8 |
| PTSD and substance abuse | 12.3 | 12.0 | 12.5 |

externalization scale of the YSR also met criteria for PTSD. Twelve percent of the adolescents who met diagnostic criteria for PTSD also reported that they used alcohol, marijuana, or hard drugs on a daily or almost daily basis.

## INTERNALIZATION PROBLEMS AMONG RUNAWAY AND HOMELESS ADOLESCENTS

The emergent risk profile for internalizing symptoms among runaway and adolescents is that of a female who has spent significant time on her own and has a history of being sexually abused by a caretaker adult. She is also likely to have been sexually victimized on the streets. Runaway and homeless adolescents are in double jeopardy for internalization problems. Many would meet criteria for depression and PTSD had they never been on their own. However, it is evident from our analyses that current, rather than historical factors are the primary precursors of internalization symptoms. Although the extent to which this is true cannot be resolved without longitudinal data, the vulnerability, stress, and actual trauma experienced by these adolescents when they are on their own must take a psychological toll. Our cross-sectional analyses certainly reflect this. Early family developmental factors may have resulted in precocious independence, but "too-early adulthood" exacts a heavy development price above and beyond the negative family experiences.

# 11

## Substance Use and Externalization Problems among Runaway Adolescents

*Umm, alcohol, weed, crystal meth, acid, shrooms, and then opium and that's about it, probably and huffing, it's the first thing I started doing was huffing. . . . Um, whatever drugs I'm doing, um, when I was doing crystal I lost a bunch of weight and it caused me to have my first miscarriage, doing crystal.*
—Female aged 17 years

Alcohol and drugs are woven through the life experiences of many homeless and runaway adolescents. As we have seen, substance abuse by caretakers and other family members often contributes to poor parenting, family fights, and maltreatment. A significant number of runaway adolescents abused substances prior to leaving home and their own or their caretakers' substance use contributed directly or indirectly to their current homelessness. Once on their own, runaway adolescents often find themselves in environments where drugs and alcohol are readily available and there is pressure to join in. Relationships may be initiated on the basis of getting high together or going to someone's place where there will be drugs.

Studies of drug and alcohol use among runaway and homeless young people indicate that it is very prevalent. Yates and colleagues reported rates of drug abuse 4 times higher among runaway adolescents than nonrunaways who were treated in a Hollywood outpatient clinic (Yates et al., 1988). A more recent study of street youth in Hollywood reports that 93% have used marijuana, 66% speed, 61% LSD, and 50% cocaine. Eighty-nine percent had used alcohol, 45% mushrooms, 44% inhalants, and 41% crack cocaine (Kipke, Montgomery, & MacKenzie, 1997). Windle (1989) using data from the National Longitudinal Survey of Youth reported that repeat runaways had positive drug histories 7–12 times the rate of nonrunaways and those who had run away on only one occasion. Nineteen percent of runaways surveyed in New York City reported crack cocaine use, 43% marijuana, and 71% alcohol (Koopman et al., 1994).

Alcohol and marijuana were the most-used substances among the runaways we interviewed (Table 11.1). Three-fourths of the males and two-thirds of the females had used marijuana during the past year. The next most popular drugs were hallucinogens (35% of males, 20% of females), inhalants (23% of males, 13% of females), and amphetamines (32% of males, 22% of females). About 10% of the males had tried opiates, 19% of the males and 13% of the females had used crack during the past year; 18% of the males and 13% of the females had used cocaine. Only 7% of the adolescent males and 4% of the females had taken drugs intravenously at some point in their lives (not shown). Of these, 25% of the males and 46% of the females had shared needles at least some of the time when taking IV drugs.

## FACTORS ASSOCIATED WITH DAILY OR ALMOST DAILY USE OF ALCOHOL AND/OR DRUGS

Thirty percent of the young men and 19% of the young women told us that they used marijuana daily or almost daily during the past year. Five percent of the males were daily or almost daily crack users. Similarly, 5% of the males said they used amphetamines daily or almost daily. Of the users of hard drugs, most reported that they used once or a few times during the past year, although 9% of the males said that they had used hallucinogens about once per month, almost the same rate as had used marijuana once per month in the past year.

Essentially the same panel regressions as those used in Chapter 10 were run using daily or almost daily use of alcohol, marijuana, or hard drugs as the dependent variable. As in the internalization models, separate panels were run for variables measuring family disorganization, parental characteristics, parental behaviors, family abuse and neglect, early independence, social networks of runways, risky behaviors on the streets, subsistence activities on the streets, and street victimization. We controlled for gender of adolescent in all of the panels and ran interactions with gender for all of the variables. Statistically significant predictors and interactions were then included in a full model to evaluate the most important predictors of daily or almost daily substance abuse.

### Family Disorganization

This panel examined two predictors of family disorganization: changes in family structure and changes in residence when the adolescent was in the

Table 11.1. Drug and Alcohol Use in the Past Year: Percentages of Males and Females

| Frequency of use | Alcohol | | | Marijuana | | | Crank | | | Amphetamines | | | Cocaine | | |
|---|---|---|---|---|---|---|---|---|---|---|---|---|---|---|---|
| | Males (N = 240) | Females (N = 357) | Total (N = 597) | Males (N = 239) | Females (N = 355) | Total (N = 594) | Males (N = 240) | Females (N = 357) | Total (N = 597) | Males (N = 238) | Females (N = 357) | Total (N = 595) | Males (N = 240) | Females (N = 357) | Total (N = 597) |
| Never | 19.6 | 19.9 | 19.8 | 26.8 | 34.9 | 31.6 | 81.7 | 87.1 | 84.9 | 68.1 | 77.6 | 73.8 | 82.5 | 87.1 | 85.3 |
| Once | 4.6 | 10.4 | 8.0 | 4.2 | 8.5 | 6.7 | 4.6 | 3.6 | 4.0 | 8.4 | 6.2 | 7.1 | 9.2 | 5.6 | 7.0 |
| A few times | 27.1 | 32.8 | 30.5 | 20.1 | 21.4 | 20.9 | 5.0 | 5.9 | 5.5 | 11.3 | 10.9 | 11.1 | 5.0 | 3.6 | 4.2 |
| About monthly | 12.1 | 14.3 | 13.4 | 8.4 | 6.5 | 7.2 | 1.7 | 0.6 | 1.0 | 3.8 | 1.7 | 2.5 | 0.8 | 1.1 | 1.0 |
| About weekly | 20.8 | 16.0 | 17.9 | 10.9 | 9.6 | 10.1 | 2.5 | 2.0 | 2.2 | 4.6 | 1.4 | 2.7 | 1.7 | 0.8 | 1.2 |
| Almost daily | 9.2 | 3.6 | 5.9 | 13.8 | 12.1 | 12.8 | 2.9 | 0.6 | 1.5 | 2.5 | 1.4 | 1.8 | 0.4 | 0.6 | 0.5 |
| Daily | 6.7 | 3.1 | 4.5 | 15.9 | 7.0 | 10.6 | 1.7 | 0.3 | 0.8 | 1.3 | 0.8 | 1.0 | 0.4 | 1.1 | 0.8 |

| Frequency of use | Opiates | | | Hallucinogens | | | Tranquilizers | | | Barbiturates | | | Inhalants | | |
|---|---|---|---|---|---|---|---|---|---|---|---|---|---|---|---|
| | Males (N = 240) | Females (N = 357) | Total (N = 597) | Males (N = 240) | Females (N = 357) | Total (N = 597) | Males (N = 240) | Females (N = 357) | Total (N = 597) | Males (N = 239) | Females (N = 357) | Total (N = 596) | Males (N = 240) | Females (N = 357) | Total (N = 597) |
| Never | 90.4 | 95.8 | 93.6 | 65.0 | 80.4 | 74.2 | 92.9 | 93.3 | 93.1 | 87.0 | 93.3 | 90.8 | 77.1 | 87.4 | 83.2 |
| Once | 2.5 | 2.0 | 2.2 | 9.2 | 5.6 | 7.0 | 2.1 | 2.0 | 2.0 | 4.2 | 2.0 | 2.9 | 9.2 | 2.5 | 5.2 |
| A few times | 4.6 | 1.1 | 2.5 | 10.4 | 9.8 | 10.1 | 2.9 | 2.5 | 2.7 | 2.5 | 3.1 | 2.9 | 10.8 | 6.2 | 8.0 |
| About monthly | 1.3 | 0.3 | 0.7 | 9.2 | 2.0 | 4.9 | 0.8 | 0.6 | 0.7 | 2.5 | 1.1 | 1.7 | 0.4 | 0.8 | 0.7 |
| About weekly | 0.8 | 0.6 | 0.7 | 3.8 | 2.0 | 2.7 | 0.8 | 0.8 | 0.8 | 1.7 | — | 0.7 | 1.7 | 1.1 | 1.3 |
| Almost daily | 0.4 | — | 0.2 | 1.7 | 0.3 | 0.8 | 0.4 | 0.3 | 0.3 | 1.7 | — | 0.7 | 0.4 | 1.1 | 0.8 |
| Daily | — | 0.3 | 0.2 | 0.8 | — | 0.3 | — | 0.6 | 0.3 | 0.4 | 0.6 | 0.5 | 0.4 | 0.8 | 0.7 |

family, while controlling for gender of adolescent (Table 11.2). Adolescent males were about twice as likely to be substance abusers than were females (exp $b$ = 1.88). The only significant coefficient in the family disorganization panel was the interaction of gender and changes in family structure (one-tailed test). Adolescent females were slightly more likely to be affected by such changes than were males. Young women from families that experienced numerous changes in family configuration were more likely to become substance abusers.

### Parental Characteristics

There were strong effects for parent characteristics on adolescent substance abuse. Having a biological parent who abused substances (adolescent reports) was positively associated with the adolescents' own substance abuse, increasing the likelihood 1.5 times (exp $b$ = 1.46). Having a parent who the adolescent believed was depressed increased the odds of adolescent substance abuse problems 1.7 times. Parent criminality was nonsignificant.

### Parenting Behaviors

Among the parenting variables we examined (warmth and supportiveness, monitoring, and parental rejection) only monitoring was statistically significant. Parental monitoring had a modest effect, decreasing the likelihood of serious substance abuse by adolescents about 6%.

### Maltreatment

Of the three measures of parental maltreatment—neglect, physical abuse, and sexual abuse—only physical abuse achieved statistical significance for serious substance abuse among the adolescent runaways. There was a modest positive association between physical abuse by a parent or caretaker and adolescent substance abuse ($b$ = .05) when controlling only for sexual abuse, caretaker neglect, and gender.

### Early Independence

We assessed three early independence variables with regard to their effect on substance abuse: age at first run, total time on own, and having ever spent time directly on the streets. Of these, the amount of time on own was statistically significant ($b$ = .20) as was the interaction of gender and time on own. The gender interaction indicated that the effects of the total time on own were stronger for adolescent females than males. Also, the interaction of having ever spent time directly on the street and gender was strongly significant

*Table 11.2.* Standardized Regression Coefficients of Substance Abuse

| | | | | | | | | | Full Model | |
|---|---|---|---|---|---|---|---|---|---|---|
| *Variable* | B | *exp* B | B | *exp* B | B | *exp* B | B | *exp* B | B | *exp* B |
| Family disorganization | | | | | | | | | | |
| Gender | .63** | 1.88 | | | | | | | .57* | 1.76 |
| Change in family structure | .06 | 1.06 | | | | | | | | |
| Change in family residence | −.01 | .99 | | | | | | | | |
| Gender * family structure | −.16 | .86 | | | | | | | | |
| Parental characteristics | | | | | | | | | | |
| Gender | | | .70** | 2.01 | | | | | | |
| Parental alcohol/ drug use | | | .38** | 1.46 | | | | | .22 | 1.24 |
| Parental serious crime | | | −.10 | .91 | | | | | | |
| Parental depression | | | .54** | 1.71 | | | | | .31 | 1.36 |
| Parenting behavior | | | | | | | | | | |
| Gender | | | | | .62** | 1.85 | | | | |
| Warmth/support | | | | | −.01 | .99 | | | | |
| Monitoring | | | | | -.06** | .94 | | | −.05 | .95 |
| Rejection | | | | | .04 | 1.04 | | | | |
| Family abuse/ neglect | | | | | | | | | | |
| Gender | | | | | | | .69** | 2.00 | | |
| Neglect | | | | | | | .15 | 1.16 | | |
| Physical abuse | | | | | | | .05** | 1.05 | −.05 | .95 |
| Sexual abuse | | | | | | | .03 | 1.03 | | |
| Early independence | | | | | | | | | | |
| Gender | .54** | 1.71 | | | | | | | | |
| Age at first run | −.02 | .98 | | | | | | | | |
| Time on own | .20** | 1.22 | | | | | | | .12 | 1.12 |
| Ever on street | .06 | 1.06 | | | | | | | | |
| Gender * time on own | −.18 | .84 | | | | | | | | |
| Gender * ever on street | −.70* | .50 | | | | | | | −.39 | .68 |

*(Continued)*

*Table 11.2.* Standardized Regression Coefficients of Substance Abuse *(continued)*

| | b | exp b | b | exp b | b | exp b | b | exp b | b | exp b |
|---|---|---|---|---|---|---|---|---|---|---|
| **Street networks** | | | | | | | | | | |
| Gender | | | .76** | 2.15 | | | | | | |
| Family support | | | .01 | 1.01 | | | | | | |
| Friend support | | | .04 | 1.04 | | | | | | |
| Deviant peers | | | 3.46** | 31.70 | | | | | 1.82** | 6.16 |
| Gender * deviant peers | | | 1.33 | 3.79 | | | | | | |
| **Street risk behavior** | | | | | | | | | | |
| Gender | | | | | .74** | 2.10 | | | | |
| Different sexual partners | | | | | .35** | 1.42 | | | .25** | 1.29 |
| **Subsistence activity** | | | | | | | | | | |
| Gender | | | | | | | .29 | 1.34 | | |
| Nonvictimizing strategy | | | | | | | .04 | 1.04 | | |
| Survival sex | | | | | | | 1.04** | 2.82 | −.13 | .88 |
| Victimizing strategy | | | | | | | .61** | 1.83 | .46** | 1.59 |
| **Street victimization** | | | | | | | | | | |
| Gender | .31 | 1.37 | | | | | | | | |
| Physical victimization | .26** | 1.30 | | | | | | | .06 | 1.06 |
| Sexual victimization | −.28 | .76 | | | | | | | | |

* $p < .05$.    ** $p < .01$.

($b = -.70$; exp $b = .50$), indicating that the effect of ever having spent time on the street was much greater for females than for males.

### Street Networks

Three kinds of social networks available to runaways were assessed: continued contact with family members, having supportive friendships, and associating with deviant peers. Of these, affiliation with deviant peers had a dramatic effect on daily or almost daily substance use. Deviant peer associations increased the likelihood of serious substance abuse almost 32 times ($b = 3.46$; exp $b = 31.70$) when controlling only for other social networks and gender of adolescent. In addition, the interaction of gender and deviant peers was marginally significant (one-tailed test), indicating that the effect of deviant peers on daily or almost daily substance use was stronger for males than it was for females.

### Risk Behaviors When on the Streets

Only one high-risk street behavior was considered in this panel because the other indicators had to do with substance use on the streets. The number of different sexual partners in the past year was significantly related to daily or almost daily substance abuse ($b = .35$; exp $b = 1.42$) and increased the likelihood of such substance abuse behaviors 1.5 times.

### Subsistence Activities

Three street subsistence activities were considered in this panel. Nonvictimizing strategies referred to panhandling, borrowing money from friends or family, employment, and the like. Victimizing strategies involved theft, burglary, and shoplifting. Trading sex involved survival sexual strategies such as trading sex for food, money, shelter, or drugs. Both of the more deviant survival strategies were positively associated with substance abuse. Trading sex increased the likelihood of daily or almost daily alcohol and/or drug use 3 times ($b = 1.04$; exp $b = 2.82$). Victimizing strategies increased the likelihood almost 2 times ($b = .61$; exp $b = .183$).

### Street Victimization

The effects of physical and/or sexual victimization when on the streets were evaluated in the final panel. Physical victimization was statistically significant and increased the likelihood of serious substance abuse by the runaways 1.3 times.

### The Full Model

After examining the effects of each panel of variables on daily or almost daily substance use among runaway adolescents when controlling only for gender of adolescent, we combined all the significant variables and interactions with gender into a single model. As noted, young men were almost 2 times more likely to engage in serious substance abuse than were young women (exp $b = 1.76$). Parental monitoring had a weak negative effect on substance use ($b = -.05$; $p < .05$, one-tailed test). Physical abuse also was significant when using a one-tailed test ($b = -.05$). Total amount of time on own also was weakly associated (one-tailed test) with daily or almost daily use ($b = .12$; (exp $b = 1.12$). Affiliation with deviant peers remained strongly significant ($b = 1.82$; exp $b = 6.16$) and increased the likelihood of daily or almost daily substance use by 6 times. The number of sexual partners in the past year also remained statistically significant in the full model ($b = .25$; exp

$b = 1.29$). Victimizing subsistence strategies continued to be significant in the full model ($b = .46$; exp $b = 1.59$) and increased the likelihood of daily or almost daily substance use 1.6 times.

## SUMMARY OF THE SUBSTANCE ABUSE MODELS

The picture that emerges from our analysis of substance abuse is quite different from that of internalizing symptoms. Where victimization at home and on the streets were the most important predictors of internalization symptoms, deviant peer affiliations was the most important predictor of daily or almost daily substance use. Our results suggest that daily or almost daily substance abuse by runaway adolescents is largely a function of the company they keep. Association with deviant peers increased the likelihood of regular use sixfold. Frequent substance abuse is a social activity that involves drug or alcohol procurement, sharing resources, and getting high together. Also, congruent with research on problem behavior syndrome (Jessor & Jessor, 1977), daily or almost daily substance use was associated with multiple sexual partners in the past year and subsistence strategies involving victimizing behaviors. Both of these behaviors, in turn, are strongly associated with deviant peer affiliations. Substance abuse is group behavior on the streets. With it comes risky sex and antisocial behaviors.

## EXTERNALIZATION SYMPTOMS AMONG HOMELESS AND RUNAWAY ADOLESCENTS

Running away from home "overnight at least twice while living in a parental or parental surrogate home (or once without returning for a lengthy period of time)" is one of the diagnostic criteria for conduct disorder (DSM IV; APA, 1994, p. 90). Community studies indicate that prevalence rates for conduct disorder vary widely based on community characteristics. According to the DSM IV, prevalence rates for males range from 6 to 16%; prevalence rates for females range from 2 to 9%. In diagnostic studies of runaways, conduct disorder is the most common diagnosis. Feital and colleagues (Feital et al., 1992) reported that 59% of the 150 adolescents who were interviewed in shelters met DSM IV criteria for conduct disorder. Using DISC-R evaluations of 296 street kids in Seattle, Cauce and associates (Cauce, Paradise, Embry, Lohr, & Wagner, 1997) found that almost one-half (48%) met criteria for conduct disorder.

Symptoms inventories also show high rates of externalizing behaviors among homeless and runaway adolescents. Schweitzer and Hier (1993) reported that 41% of their sample of 54 homeless runaway adolescents scored within the clinical range for externalization on the Youth Self-Report (Achenbach, 1991). In our sample, the adolescent females were more likely to exceed the Youth Self-Report (YSR) clinical cutoffs for externalization than were the adolescent males. Fifty-five percent of the adolescent girls scored within the clinical range compared to 44% of the adolescent boys. Regardless of gender differences, it is noteworthy that about one-half of our sample fell into the clinical range of the YSR. This is very similar to others' findings regarding conduct problems among runaway adolescents.

## FACTORS PREDICTING EXCEEDING YSR CLINICAL CUTOFFS FOR EXTERNALIZATION

Panel regression models using the same variables as in the substance abuse panels were used to investigate the likelihood of exceeding the clinical cutoffs for externalization (23 for males, 20 for females) on the YSR (see Table 11.3). As was the case with the other panel regression models, gender was controlled and interactions with gender were checked. A full model was run consisting of the statistically significant variables and interactions from the panels.

### Family Disorganization

Neither of the family disorganization variables was related to externalization symptoms among the runaways. Gender, however, was highly significant and indicated that adolescent females were more likely than adolescent males to exceed the YSR clinical cutoff for externalization ($b = -.41$; exp $b = .66$).

### Parental Characteristics

Of the characteristics of biological parents, only having a parent who had engaged in serious criminal activity (adolescent report) was significantly related to adolescent externalizing symptoms ($b = .48$; exp $b = 1.61$). Having a parent who had been involved in serious crime increased the likelihood of adolescent externalizing symptoms 1.6 times. The interaction of gender and criminal activity of a parent was also statistically significant (one-tailed test), indicating that the effect was stronger for adolescent females than for males.

### Parent Behaviors

Of the parenting variables, parental monitoring ($b = -.05$; exp $b = .95$) and parental rejection ($b = .07$; exp $b = 1.07$) were modestly associated with externalizing symptoms in the expected directions. Parental monitoring had a weak negative effect on externalization when controlling for only gender

*Table 11.3.*  Standardized Regression Coefficients of Externalization

| | | | | | | | | | Full Model | |
| Variable | B | exp B | B | exp B | B | exp B | B | exp B | B | exp B |
|---|---|---|---|---|---|---|---|---|---|---|
| Family disorganization | | | | | | | | | | |
| Gender | -.41** | .66 | | | | | | | -1.08** | .34 |
| Change in family structure | .05 | 1.05 | | | | | | | | |
| Change in family residence | .03 | 1.03 | | | | | | | | |
| Parental characteristics | | | | | | | | | | |
| Gender | | | -.44** | .65 | | | | | | |
| Parental alcohol/drug use | | | .05 | 1.05 | | | | | | |
| Parental serious crime | | | .48* | 1.61 | | | | | .59** | 1.80 |
| Parental depression | | | .18 | 1.20 | | | | | | |
| Gender * parental crime | | | -.45 | .64 | | | | | | |
| Parenting behavior | | | | | | | | | | |
| Gender | | | | | -.49** | .61 | | | | |
| Warmth/support | | | | | .01 | 1.01 | | | | |
| Monitoring | | | | | -.05* | .95 | | | .01 | 1.01 |
| Rejection | | | | | .07* | 1.07 | | | .03 | 1.03 |
| Family abuse/ neglect | | | | | | | | | | |
| Gender | | | | | | | -.30 | .74 | | |
| Neglect | | | | | | | -.03 | .97 | | |
| Physical abuse | | | | | | | .07** | 1.07 | -.01 | .99 |
| Sexual abuse | | | | | | | .29 | 1.33 | | |
| Early independence | | | | | | | | | | |
| Gender | -.46** | .63 | | | | | | | | |
| Age at first run | -.07* | .93 | | | | | | | -.05 | .95 |
| Time on own | -.01 | .99 | | | | | | | | |
| Ever on street | .13 | 1.14 | | | | | | | | |

*(Continued)*

Table 11.3. Standardized Regression Coefficients of Externalization *(continued)*

| | b | Exp(b) | b | Exp(b) | b | Exp(b) | b | Exp(b) |
|---|---|---|---|---|---|---|---|---|
| Street networks | | | | | | | | |
| Gender | -.47** | .63 | | | | | | |
| Family support | .06 | 1.06 | | | | | | |
| Friend support | .05 | 1.05 | | | | | | |
| Deviant peers | 2.45** | 11.64 | | | | | .61 | 1.84 |
| Street risk behavior | | | | | | | | |
| Gender | | | -.65** | .52 | | | | |
| Alcohol/ | | | | | | | .03 | 1.03 |
| marijuana use | | | .07** | 1.08 | | | | |
| Hard drugs | | | .12* | 1.13 | | | .08 | 1.08 |
| Number of different sexual partners | | | .18** | 1.20 | | | .12 | 1.13 |
| Subsistence activity | | | | | | | | |
| Gender | | | | | -1.00** | .37 | | |
| Non-victimizing strategy | | | | | -.17 | .85 | | |
| Survival sex | | | | | .21 | 1.24 | | |
| Victimizing strategy | | | | | .77** | 2.16 | .57** | 1.77 |
| Street victimization | | | | | | | | |
| Gender | -.71** | .49 | | | | | | |
| Physical victimization | .18** | 1.19 | | | | | -.02 | .98 |
| Sexual victimization | .04 | 1.04 | | | | | | |

* *p* < .05.  ** *p* < .01.

and other parenting variables. Parental rejection had a weak positive effect on externalization.

### Maltreatment

Of the three parental maltreatment variables, only physical abuse achieved statistical significance (*b* = .07; exp *b* = 1.07). All of these variables were highly correlated with one another at the bivariate level (see Table 11A.1 in the Appendix) and therefore may have weakened individual effects when included in the same model.

### Early Independence

Only age at first run was significantly associated with externalizing symptoms among the early independence variables ($b = -.07$; exp $b = .93$) The effect was modest and negative, indicating that the younger the adolescents were at the point they left home, the more likely they exceeded YSR clinical cutoffs for externalization.

### Street Networks

Among the social network variables, association with deviant peers was strongly and positively associated with externalizing symptoms ($b = 2.45$; exp $b = 11.64$). Deviant peer affiliations increased the likelihood of exceeding YSR clinical cutoffs almost 12 times when controlling only for other social network variables and gender.

### Risk Behaviors When on the Streets

It is not surprising that every one of the risky behavior variables was significantly related to externalization. Alcohol and marijuana use ($b = .07$; exp $b =1.08$), hard drug use ($b = .12$; exp $b = 1.13$), and the number of different sexual partners in the past year ($b = .18$; exp $b = 1.20$) were positively associated with externalization scores in the clinical range.

### Subsistence Activities

Among the subsistence variables, only victimizing behaviors was associated with externalization symptoms among the adolescents ($b = .77$; exp $b = 2.16$). Using such strategies to get by increased the likelihood of exceeding the YSR cutoffs twofold when controlling only for gender and other subsistence activities.

### Street Victimization

Although the magnitude of the effect was very modest in comparison to internalization models, physical victimization was positively associated with externalizing symptoms among homeless and runaway young people ($b = .18$; exp $b = 1.19$).

### The Full Model

When all of the statistically significant variables and interactions with gender were combined into a full model, a very few powerful indicators predominated. Gender was highly significant. In our sample, the adolescent females were 3 times more likely to exceed clinical cutoff scores on the YSR then were males ($b = -1.08$; exp $b = .34$). Having a parent who had engaged in serious crime increased the likelihood of externalization among adolescent offspring almost 2 times ($b = .59$; exp $b = 1.80$). Deviant peer associations, although strongly significant in the panel of social network indicators, lost significance in the full model. Multiple sexual partners in the past year remained in the full model, although the association was modest and significant only for a one-tailed test ($b = .12$; exp $b = 1.13$). Engaging in victimizing subsistence strategies was highly significant ($b = .57$; exp $b = 1.77$), increasing the likelihood of exceeding the YSR clinical cutoffs almost 2 times.

## SUMMARY OF THE EXTERNALIZATION MODELS

When controlling for all of the statistically significant predictors from the panel models, three indicators of adolescent externalization stood out in the full model: (1) gender, (2) having a biological parent who had engaged in serious criminal activity, and (3) engaging in victimizing survival strategies. The fact that adolescent females were more likely than males to exceed the YSR clinical cutoffs for externalization may have been a sampling artifact. That is, because our sample is predominantly shelter youth, we may have undersampled more externalizing males, who may be found on the streets rather than in shelters. A second interpretation may be that for girls to run away, they must be higher on externalizing symptoms than boys. Because girls tend to be socialized more to stay close to home (Ruble & Martin, 1998), it may be that a greater degree of externalizing symptoms must be present for them to strike out on their own.

The persistent strong effect of having a biological parent who had engaged in serious crime is congruent with several other of our findings regarding parental histories, the multiple reporter model of intergenerational criminal activity (Chapter 4), and the effects of biological parent characteristics in the subsistence activities models (Chapter 7). Among the runaways we interviewed, substance abuse and antisocial behaviors appear to run in families. There was some indication in the panel analysis that the effect of having a biological parent who engaged in serious crime exerted a stronger influence on the antisocial behaviors of adolescent girls than for boys. This weak interaction effect did not remain significant in the full model.

Finally, the adolescents who are most antisocial are those who are victimizers rather than those who are victims. A clear distinction in the role of victimization on internalizing vs. externalizing symptoms emerged in our analyses. Street victimization was a strong predictor of internalizing symptoms among the adolescents. Street victimizing was a strong predictor of externalizing symptoms.

Modeling externalizing behaviors with runaway adolescents is extremely difficult because the very behavior of running away is an indication of externalization. The process is complicated further because running away narrows the opportunities for prosocial choices. As North and colleagues point out (North et al., 1993), individual histories prior to becoming homeless create serious difficulties in diagnosing antisocial personality among homeless adults. The same is true for diagnosing onset of clinical externalization problems among runway youth. It is highly likely that symptoms of externalization were present prior to running away and almost certain that they were present prior to becoming a chronic runaway. Whatever tendencies toward antisocial behaviors runaway adolescents may have had prior to leaving home will be exacerbated by situations they encounter and the people they meet when on the streets. As we have seen, just getting by on the streets often requires antisocial options.

## SUBSTANCE ABUSE AND EXTERNALIZATION AMONG HOMELESS AND RUNAWAY ADOLESCENTS

Whatever was going on with adolescents with regard to substance use and externalizing behaviors prior to running away, there is very little that will happen to them on the street that will suppress these behaviors. Rather, our data suggest that there is much that will act to increase these behaviors in intensity and frequency. As we have shown throughout this volume, the street environment is replete with antisocial options and solutions to problems posed by day-to-day life. Substance use is a social behavior and, perhaps, a way of getting by via sharing resources or selling drugs. Aggressive behaviors may be necessary for self-protection, or as a means of supporting oneself. Multiple sexual partners may be a way to connect with a support network, and a way to connect to needed resources.

Substance abuse, deviant subsistence activities, and externalizing behaviors are highly interrelated. They are part of the social environment in which the runaways move. Although there is much to encourage the learning or continuation of such behaviors in early independence, there is little outside shelters and the youth services system that will substantially reduce antisocial options or make them less attractive.

# 12

# A Risk-Amplification Developmental Model for Runaway and Homeless Adolescents

*I feel like, you know, I think I read this somewhere, but like you're on a plane, you know, and everybody's got a parachute on and everybody's been through parachuting lessons, but you never had. The plane is crashing and everybody's jumping out of the plane and pulling their parachutes . . . you have to jump out yourself and you know, pull it on the way down, but you don't know when to do it, you don't know how to stop yourself from . . . you just keep spiraling down.*

—Seventeen-year-old male

The consequences of early independence on later life have received very little attention. Historically, the effects on development have been largely underestimated, perhaps because the individualist mythology of American society has romanticized striking out on one's own. Cowboys, new immigrants, and depression hobos sought ways out of hard times by using their wits and initiative even though they were often underage and without education. However, later generations of runaways have no frontiers to conquer or new worlds in which to start over. There are no jobs just down the road or in the next state. Whatever societal niches existed for "too early adults" have disappeared. Contemporary runaways enter into an underworld of shelters, drifting from "friend" to "friend" or, at times, making their own way directly on the streets.

149

All of the findings we have reported thus far converge into a single developmental theme: psychologically harmed children run away from home and the process of running away further harms them. The risks are multiple and cumulative. Negative developmental trajectories gain momentum across time. The disorganized, often volatile families from which runaways typically emerge have influenced behaviors long before the young people leave. There is plentiful evidence that disorganized family situations and coercive/abusive parenting characterized by harsh and inconsistent discipline provide "basic training" for antisocial behavior (Patterson et al., 1984). Aggressive, antisocial behavior is reinforced in such families in two ways. First, parental aggression elicits aggressive responses from the child. The parent responds in turn. Coercive interaction chains develop that often escalate to the use of physical force (Patterson, 1982). The "loser" is forced to back down. The child learns aggressive behaviors directly through the rewards of forcing the parent to back down in response to his or her escalating behaviors. Second, the child learns indirectly when the parent "wins" by force. The person who is most coercive gets his or her way. By running away, the child "wins" the coercive struggle. He or she is revoking adult controls and asserting adult status.

The victory is an empty one. Already at great disadvantage for learning interaction skills needed for conventional success, asserting adult status prior to developing adult skills narrows prosocial options. The most important consequence of asserting adult status is that the adolescent substitutes the influence of caretaker adults for the influence of other adultlike adolescents. The process takes on momentum as the runaway further separates from adult controls. Getting by on the streets may involve delinquent or other high-risk behaviors. Establishing social networks is often associated with alcohol, drug use, and risky sexual encounters. All of these factors converge to increase risk for serious harm.

## A RISK AMPLIFICATION DEVELOPMENTAL MODEL

To illustrate this process we constructed a theoretical model containing the elements of cumulative risk we have examined thus far. Variations of the risk amplification model have been tested elsewhere with different cross-sectional samples (Whitbeck & Simons, 1990; Whitbeck, Hoyt, & Ackley, 1997). A one-year longitudinal analysis of a similar model has shown that the amplification process holds up over time when internalization symptoms are controlled at time 1 (Hoyt, Whitbeck, & Cauce, in press). The current analysis ties together constructs previously examined in this volume into a single developmental model.

The model (Figure 12.1) begins with biological parents who are perceived by their adolescent offspring as having problems with alcohol and/or drug

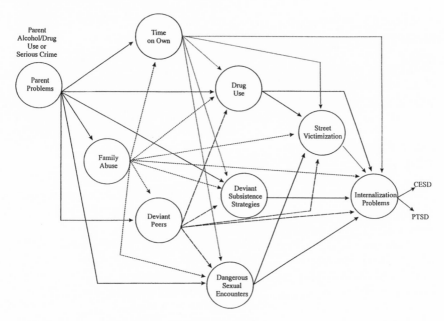

*Figure 12.1.* A risk-amplification model.

use or serious criminal behaviors. In Chapter 4 we found evidence for inter-generational transmission of substance abuse and serious criminal behaviors across three generations (Figures 4.1 and 4.2). Many of the effects of parental substance abuse and serious crime were transmitted by increasing the likelihood of exposing the adolescent to physical and/or sexual abuse within the family. It was therefore predicted that parental problems of substance abuse and serious criminal activity would be strongly associated with adolescent reports of physical and/or sexual abuse by an adult caretaker.

As we found in Chapter 5, family abuse was a robust predictor of age at first run (Table 5.4). In general, the more abusive the family background, the earlier the age the child left home and the greater the time the adolescent will have spent away from home. Family abuse was also a strong predictor of the types of social networks in which runaways moved (Chapter 6, Figure 6.1). Adolescents from abusive families were more likely to affiliate with deviant peers than were those who had not suffered from serious abuse at home. We have also found that histories of family abuse are associated with deviant survival strategies (Chapter 7), street victimization (Whitbeck, Hoyt, & Ackley, 1997), and internalization symptoms (Chapter 10). Family abuse therefore was predicted to be associated with the total amount of time the adolescent had spent on his or her own, affiliations with deviant peers, and various high-risk behaviors (i.e., drug/alcohol use, risky sex, and deviant subsistence strategies). We also predicted that family abuse would be directly associated with street victimization and internalization symptoms.

As noted in Chapter 11, the most important single predictor of substance abuse by runaway adolescents was affiliation with deviant peers (Table 11.2). Deviant peer associations also were highly predictive of physical and sexual victimization when on the streets (Chapter 9, Table 9.2). Because of the strength of this variable in our previous analyses, associations were predicted between deviant peer affiliations and all of the subsequent variables in the model. In turn, we found in Chapter 10 and elsewhere (Whitbeck, Hoyt, & Ackley, in press) that street victimization was a major contributor to symptoms of internalization. A positive association between victimization when the adolescents were on their own and symptoms of internalization was therefore predicted.

Measures for the model are those used elsewhere in this volume and are provided in Tables 12A.1–12A.3 in the Appendix. The only new measure introduced in this model is the combined *internalization symptoms* latent construct, which is made up of CES-D depression scores and those meeting criteria for PTSD. Separate structural equation models were run for males and females and the models were then compared path by path for statistically significant differences (Joreskog & Sorbom, 1993). Bivariate correlations for the structural equation models for males and females are provided in Appendix Table 12A.1.

## RESULTS FOR ADOLESCENT FEMALES

The model for adolescent females (Figure 12.2) fit the data very well (chi-square = 13.61; df = 9; $p$ = .14; GFI = .99; AGFI = .97). Adolescent girls who reported that their biological parents had drug/alcohol problems and/or had engaged in serious criminal activity (e.g., crimes against persons or property) were highly likely to report that they had suffered physical and/or sexual abuse from an adult caretaker ($\Gamma$ = .46). Parent alcohol/drug and criminal activity also was directly positively associated with adolescent females' drug/alcohol use ($\Gamma$ = .17). Family abuse was positively associated with the total amount of time that the adolescent had spent on her own ($\beta$ = .28) and affiliation with deviant peers ($\beta$ = .32). Family abuse was also directly and positively related to street victimization ($\beta$ = .21). Those victimized prior to leaving home were more likely to be revictimized when on the streets.

The amount of time the adolescent females had spent on their own related only to street victimization ($\beta$ = .17). The longer on their own, the more likely the young women were to be victimized. Affiliation with deviant peers, however, was strongly associated with all of the deviant street behaviors and

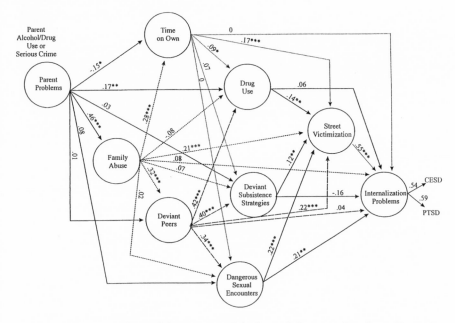

*Figure 12.2.* A risk-amplification model for adolescent females (*N* = 311).
*,.10 *p* ≤ .05; **, .05 *p* ≤ .01; ***, *p* ≤ .01.

street victimization. Affiliation with deviant peers was positively related to drug/alcohol use (β = .42), dangerous sexual encounters (β = .34), and deviant subsistence strategies (β = .40). It was also directly related to street victimization even when controlling for effects on high-risk deviant behaviors (β = .22), indicating perhaps that deviant peers were important direct sources of victimization. There was no direct effect on internalization problems.

Adolescent drug/alcohol use was positively associated with street victimization (β = .14). Dangerous sexual encounters was positively associated with street victimization (β = .22) and with internalization problems (β = .21). Adolescent girls who participated in survival sex or had a high number of sexual partners in the past year were more likely to be victimized on the streets and were more likely to experience internalization symptoms. Deviant subsistence strategies (e.g., taking money by force, burglary) was positively associated with victimization of adolescent females (β = .12). Street victimization was strongly associated with internalization symptoms (depression and PTSD scores) (β = .55). The model explained 46% of the variance for internalization symptoms for adolescent females and 45% of the variance for their victimization when on the streets.

When we examined the decomposition of effects for the girls' model, several important themes emerged (see Table 12A.2 in the Appendix). First, the effects of parental problem behaviors (alcohol/drug use and serious crime) and family abuse on internalization symptoms for girls were all indirect through the other components of the model. All of the effects of family abuse on internalization symptoms were mediated by the effects of intervening variables in the model such as affiliation with deviant peers, risky street behaviors, and victimization. The effects of family abuse on street victimization were almost evenly split between direct effects and indirect effects. Second, the effects of deviant peer affiliation on internalization symptoms for adolescent girls were mediated by its effects on risky street behaviors and street victimization. The effects of deviant peer affiliations on street victimization were almost equally divided between direct and indirect effects. Third, all of the effects of family abuse on risky street behaviors (drug/alcohol use, deviant subsistence strategies, risky sex) were indirect through affiliation with deviant peers.

Decomposition of effects indicates that a history of abuse within the family puts in motion a series of behavioral and social consequences for runaway girls that increases their likelihood of further victimization and emotional distress. The psychological harm from early family experiences is exacerbated by its social and behavioral consequences when the child strikes out on her own.

## RESULTS FOR ADOLESCENT MALES

As was the case with the model for adolescent girls, the model for adolescent boys fit the data very well (Figure 12.3) (chi-square = 5.01; df = 9; $p$ = .83; GFI = 1.0; AGFI = .99). Parent alcohol/drug problem and/or serious criminal activity behaved very differently in the model for adolescent males than it did in the model for females. Parental problem behaviors were positively associated with family abuse ($\Gamma$ = .33) as in the model for adolescent females. However, parental problem behaviors were negatively associated with the total amount of time adolescent males had spent on their own ($\Gamma$ = –.20) and negatively associated with dangerous sexual encounters by adolescent males such as survival sex and the number of sexual partners in the past year ($\Gamma$ = –.27). Having experienced physical and/or sexual abuse from an adult caretaker, however, was positively associated with dangerous sexual encounters for boys ($\beta$ = .23). Family abuse was also positively associated with the total amount of time the adolescent had spent on his own ($\beta$ = .25) and association with deviant peers ($\beta$ = .24). As in the model for adolescent females, there was a direct effect between family abuse and victimization on the streets ($\beta$ = .14). Unlike the girl's model there was a direct

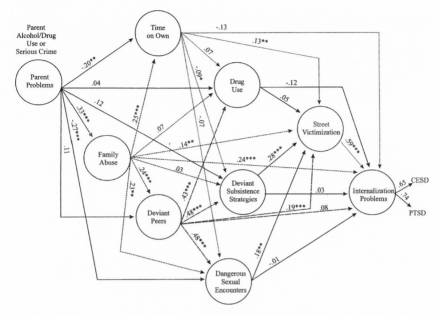

*Figure 12.3.* A risk-amplification model for adolescent males (*N* = 208). *,.10 *p* ≤ .05; **, .05 *p* ≤ .01; ***, *p* ≤ .01.

effect for family abuse on internalization problems for adolescent boys (β = .24).

Similar to the model for adolescent females, affiliation with deviant peers was strongly associated with all of the deviant behavioral variables. It was positively associated with drug/alcohol use (β = .43), deviant subsistence strategies (β = .48) and dangerous sexual encounters (β = .48). As in the model for females, there was a positive direct effect for street victimization (β = .19). In turn, participation in deviant subsistence strategies (e.g., taking money by force, burglarizing) was positively related to street victimization (β = .28). Dangerous sexual encounters also was positively related to street victimization (β = .18). Street victimization was strongly associated with internalization symptoms among adolescent males (β = .59). The model explained 49% of the variance for internalization symptoms for adolescent boys and 40% of the variance for street victimization.

Decomposition of effects for the adolescent males' model indicated that effects were transmitted somewhat differently than in the model for females. Although all of the effects of parental problem behaviors (alcohol/drug use and serious crime by biological parents) on boys' internalization symptoms were indirect through the intervening variables in the path model, the effects of family abuse were split between direct and indirect effects (see Table 12A.3 in the Appendix). Unlike the girls' model, where the effects of family abuse were mediated by the intervening variables in the model, for boys there were strong direct effects of family abuse on internalization symptoms even when the intervening street behavior variables were taken into account. The effects of family abuse on street victimization were almost evenly split between direct and indirect effects. Similar to the girls' model, however, all of the effects of deviant peer affiliation on boys' internalization symptoms were indirect. The effects of deviant peer affiliations on street victimization were almost equally divided between direct and indirect effects.

Unlike the girls' model, the effects of family abuse were not mediated in the boys' model. However, the indirect effects of the intervening variables of the model contributed significantly and almost equally to internalization symptoms, indicating a concurrent effect of street experiences on internalization symptoms along with the main effects of family abuse.

A comparison of the two models indicated that they were very similar. Only two paths differed statistically, those between parental problem behaviors and dangerous sexual encounters and between time on own and deviant subsistence strategies. There was a significant direct path for males and the path for females was nonsignificant. The path between family abuse and dangerous sexual behaviors approached statistical significance ($p = .07$), as did the path between deviant subsistence strategies and street victimization ($p = .08$). In both of these cases the effects were stronger for males than females.

## DEVELOPMENTAL TRAJECTORIES OF RUNAWAY ADOLESCENTS

Without longitudinal data it is impossible to trace the developmental trajectories of runaway and homeless adolescents. However, these cross-sectional analyses in combination with the other findings reported in the this volume provide some theoretically intriguing insights into the developmental consequences of running away. Beginning in Chapter 3 we see progressive movement away from adult influence. This theme is repeated in analyses regarding social networks in Chapter 6, survival strategies in Chapter 7, and again in the amplification models just examined. As adolescents move away from adult spheres a process is set in motion that is difficult to reverse. Adult influences are replaced by the influence of "adultlike" peers. These affiliations provide information and support for runaways and socialize street survival skills. The deviant social networks themselves and the high-risk behaviors of the runaways in consort with the deviant peers increase the risk of serious victimization. Young people are assaulted and exploited within their new social networks. At the same time they engage in high-risk survival behaviors that increase their risk of victimization and exploitation. Revictimization and aggressive/coercive social networks reinforce what they have already learned in dysfunctional families.

The learning process develops its own inertia. After becoming "adultlike," submitting again to adult influence may not be an option. Attempts to force submission simply reinforce the adolescents' coercive/aggressive worldview. Inevitable encounters with the legal system do the same. The power struggle between coercive adults and aggressive/coercive youth is now reenacted continually. "Interactional continuity" is fully in process (Caspi & Bem, 1990; Caspi et al., 1989). They live in a social world characterized by coercive/aggressive interactions in their relationships with peers and with any adult who attempts to challenge their "adult" status.

At a more sinister level, the process of "cumulative continuity" is beginning to play itself out in the early lives of runaways. The progressive accumulation of the consequences of their own behaviors (Caspi et el., 1989) is becoming harder and harder to overcome even at this early stage. Asserting adult status has cut them off in large degree from prosocial adult influences. Deviant peer relationships have taken their toll directly through exploitation and victimization and indirectly by enhancing participation in high-risk behaviors. Repeated victimization at home and when on their own provides convincing evidence regarding what others are like and how they will treat you. Chronic runaways and homeless youth lose important developmental ground educationally and socially. The consequences of early drug use, early sexuality, and criminal behaviors are already being manifested.

To complete the process of cumulative continuity, runaway youth become a criminal justice problem, thus institutionalizing the basic conflict between too-early independence and adult controls. The child, pushed into precocious independence by neglecting or victimizing adults and then revictimized on the streets, may then be punished by the criminal justice system for engaging in survival strategies. Recognizing the developmental trajectories of chronic runaways does not mean we must sentimentalize them. These may be difficult, sometimes even dangerous young people with whom to work. However, understanding their developmental trajectories may help us create interventions that do not become part of this cumulative process. Punitive interaction with law enforcement and punitive interventions by the courts simply reinforce what chronic runaways already believe about the world. Those with the greatest coercive power win.

As is suggested in the amplification model, the psychological toll is also cumulative. Already experiencing emotional distress, the experiences runaways encounter when on their own magnify that distress. Whatever sense of sadness or hopelessness they experienced in a disorganized or abusive family is amplified by the trauma of homelessness itself (Goodman et al., 1991) and through relationships and experiences when on their own. If homelessness may be expected to be traumatic for adults, it is more so for these "too-early adults" who have neither adult emotional resources nor adult support systems to buffer the experience. No one has good information about what the future holds for chronic runaway and homeless adolescents. Theoretically, the trajectory into adulthood appears bleak. In the final chapter we address the futures of the runways with whom we spoke.

# 13

## Growing up on Society's Margins

*People get tired of the system, you know? I've been in the system ever since I was 12 . . . and you just get tired of it, you know, you get tired of being treated like a child. . . . I'm an independent person. . . . They failed to realize I'd already been through a lot and I already did a lot, you know what I'm saying? And, I give in a lot, you know, to change my life.*

—Seventeen-year-old male

One of the most striking things about the runaways we interviewed is that most have no acceptable placement options. Shelters are temporary, many of the adolescents can't or won't go home, and they have "outgrown" traditional foster homes and group homes. They have quite literally grown up too soon. Because they no longer fit society's definition of children, they have outgrown the system's ability to respond to them. As we have noted in earlier chapters, historically we have had room on society's margins for precocious independence, allowing those who were able to function on their own the opportunity to learn some work skills, and grow into society on their own terms. There are fewer such options today.

The young lives we have chronicled are on a trajectory leading them further away from traditional social controls and influences with each run or self-initiated life transition. As parental and family influences decrease, institutional and self-initiated changes increase. As system responses fail, these young people drift out of view. As one street worker sadly told us, "No one knows what happens to these kids." Certainly their futures are uncertain. In this chapter we will look to the future. First we will attempt to identify the resilient youth, the runaways with the greatest chance of making successful transitions to adulthood. Then we will look at the future through the eyes of the runaway adolescents at intervals of 3 months, 1 year, and 5 years. We will conclude with the policy implications of our study.

## RESILIENT RUNAWAYS

We know almost nothing about chronic runaways and homeless adolescents as adults. Available retrospective reports from homeless adults are not encouraging. Our research indicates that homeless adults with histories of running away when they were adolescents are worse off than those without such histories. Those who had runaway when young had higher levels of substance abuse and more adjustment difficulties than those who became homeless at a later age (Simons & Whitbeck, 1991). Interviews with homeless men in New York City shelters showed similar results. The men reported a high frequency of institutional separations from family when they were young and a childhood history of delinquent behaviors and running away (Susser, Struening, & Conover, 1987). However, not all of the stories will end badly. Many of the runaways we interviewed will find housing, return to school, or find regular employment.

Identifying resilient runaways poses some distinct challenges. Risk tends to be cumulative and all of these young people demonstrate multiple risk factors. Fergusson and colleagues (Fergusson, Horwood, & Lynskey, 1994) found that the 5% of children experiencing the most cumulative risk were 100 times more likely to become multiple-problem adolescents than the most advantaged 50% of their cohort. Rutter (1985) has shown that although one risk factor may not impair development, the cumulative risk of two or more stressors results in negative developmental outcomes. Chronic runaways and homeless adolescents represent the most disadvantaged group of young people in our society. The odds of resilience among these adolescents are reduced by the number and severity of developmental hazards they have endured. Street workers often point to the innovative adaptations and survival mechanisms employed by street kids as resilience. They are, in large measure, correct in their observations. The problem is that what is adaptive for early independence on the streets is often maladaptive for later adult developmental expectations.

Resilience is usually defined as the ability of those exposed to serious risk factors to overcome these factors and avoid negative developmental outcomes such as delinquency, psychological maladjustment, and academic difficulties (Rak & Patterson, 1996). Most researchers who specialize in childhood and adolescent resilience concur regarding basic factors that protect against or mitigate risk. Protective factors that contribute to resilience occur in three basic domains: the child's personality, family characteristics including parenting, and the social and community environment (Garmezy, 1983; Hauser, Vieyra, Jacobson, & Wertlieb, 1985). Stress-buffering personality characteristics include (1) being a good-natured, easily managed child from infancy onward (Werner, 1986), (2) having confidence and a sense of efficacy (Werner & Smith, 1982), (3) competence, intelligence (Garmezy, Masten, & Tellegen, 1984), and academic achievement (Rutter, 1980), (4) the ability from infancy onward to evoke positive attention from others (Garmezy, 1981), (5) adaptability and impulse control (Garmezy, 1981).

Protective factors that relate to the family involve both family structure and interaction. Being from a small family (less than four children), having an array of alternative caretakers who shared values and beliefs, and experiencing no prolonged separation from the primary caretaker during early years of life are important family structural buffers. Warm and supportive parenting and bonding with primary caretakers during the first years of life were important parenting characteristics, along with structure and rules within the household regardless of family stress level. Being an older child who cared for others also was a buffering factor. Required helpfulness such as supervising younger siblings or having the responsibility for others' well-being teaches the child coping skills and gave confidence (Werner, 1984).

In the social environment, the most important buffering factor is the presence of at least one caring adult who provides the child with support and with whom the child may identify (Beardslee & Podorefsky, 1988; Garmezy et al., 1984). When nuclear families are experiencing stress and disorganization, having caring adults to provide support that is absent in the home is extremely important. Finally, having a place or activity that is a refuge from the stress and a source of self-efficacy buffers stress. An activity or hobby contributes to self-confidence whether or not the child is particularly talented (Kauffman, Grunebaum, Cohler, & Garnett, 1979). Also, a place of refuge in the home, in a club, or at school where the child can escape the chaos in his or her life for periods of time can buffer stress (Anthony, 1974).

After reviewing factors that mitigate the negative effects of multiple stressors on children, it is evident that many of these factors are unavailable to chronic runaway and homeless youth. Family resources have been ineffective and largely left behind, contacts with academic resources have been interrupted, and there are few supportive adults available when adolescents are on their own. Resilient personality attributes may be diminished through family backgrounds of physical and sexual abuse and early substance abuse. To assess resilient adolescents in our sample, we used four indicators based on the research literature. First, based on evidence that a sense of confidence or self-efficacy was an important characteristic of resilient children (Brooks, 1994; Rutter, 1985) we took two items from the Rosenberg (1965) Self-Esteem Scale that clearly reflected a sense of efficacy: All in all I am inclined to feel that I am a failure (reverse coded); I am able to do things as well as most other people. The scores were cut at the median with 1 = at or above the median and 0 = below the median on self-efficacy. Second, based on research indicating that intelligence, problem-solving skills, and academic competency are factors in adolescent resilience (Fergusson & Lynskey, 1996; Herronkohl, Herronkohl, & Egolf, 1994; Kandel et al., 1988) we assessed academic resilience by the adolescents' ability to maintain school attendance (regular attendance or attendance most of the time). Response categories were recoded so that 1 = regular attendance or attendance most of the time and 2 = irregular or nonattendance. The third indicator of resilience was whether the adolescent had been able to maintain conventional means of self-support. Although there are no precedents in the literature for this indicator, it was selected to represent prosocial coping behaviors during early independence (see Chapter 7). This was measured by whether the adolescent reported regular employment or support via doing chores or odd jobs. Response categories were coded 1 = employment or odd jobs, 2 = no employment or odd jobs. Finally, to be considered resilient the adolescents had to score below the clinical cutoffs for externalization. Adolescent externalizing behavior is associated with less successful adult outcomes such as diminished educational attainment, employment troubles, and occupational success (Caspi, Elder, & Bem, 1987).

Cluster analyses were then performed to empirically group the adolescents (see Table 13.1). Six clusters emerged. Cluster 3 ($N = 103$) consisted of all of those adolescents who met the criteria for resilience: high self-efficacy, school attendance, employment as a means of self-support, and low externalization. A variable "resilience" was then constructed where cluster 3 was coded 1 for resilience and all other clusters were coded 0. A series of logistic regression models was then run to determine the effects of various background characteristics and street experiences on resilience. The panels were those investigated in the internalization and externalization chapters. Statis-

Table 13.1.   Cluster Analysis of Resiliency Factors

|  |  | Exceeds YSR |  |  |  |
| --- | --- | --- | --- | --- | --- |
| Cluster | Sample Size | Self-Efficacy | Employed | School Attendance | Externalization Cutoffs |
| 1 | 44 | 100.0 | 0 | 100.0 | 100.0 |
| 2 | 104 | 100.0 | 68.3 | 0 | 67.3 |
| 3 | 103 | 100.0 | 100.0 | 100.0 | 0 |
| 4 | 59 | 100.0 | 100.0 | 100.0 | 100.0 |
| 5 | 60 | 100.0 | 0 | 100.0 | 0 |
| 6 | 203 | 5.4 | 56.2 | 62.1 | 55.7 |
| All | 602 | 66.5 | 61.3 | 68.1 | 50.3 |

tically significant variables and significant interactions with gender were then run in a full model to determine the relative strengths of indicators of resilience when controlling for all others. Because there were so few significant indicators, only the full model will be discussed.


## FACTORS AFFECTING RESILIENCE

Adolescent males were three times more likely to meet the criteria we established for resilience ($b = 1.07$; (exp $b = 2.92$) than were adolescent females (Table 13.2). Having a parent who had been involved in serious criminal activity was negatively associated with resilience ($b = -.26$; exp $b = .49$) and decreased the likelihood of inclusion in the resilience cluster by 50%. Gender interacted with serious parent criminal activities so that the effect for adolescent males was negligible and the effect for adolescent females was very great ($b = .98$; exp $b = 2.67$). Parental monitoring had weak positive effects on resilience in the panel model but lost significance in the full model. Similarly, physical abuse by a caretaker was weakly negatively associated with resilience in the panel model, but did not remain significant when controlling for other influential factors. The interaction of gender and affiliation with deviant peers was negatively associated with resilience such that the effects of deviant peers were much stronger for adolescent males than females. Participating in victimizing subsistence strategies (e.g., taking money by force, burglarizing) decreased the likelihood of inclusion in the

Table 13.2.   Logistic Regression Model for Factors Influencing Inclusion in the Resiliency Cluster of Adolescent Runaways

| Variable | Unstandardized Coefficient | Standardized Coefficient | exp B |
|---|---|---|---|
| Intercept | −1.47 | — | — |
| Gender | 1.07 | .29* | 2.92 |
| Parent crime | −.72 | −.26* | .49 |
| Gender * parent crime | .98 | .25* | 2.67 |
| Monitor | .04 | .08 | 1.04 |
| Physical abuse | −.03 | −.06 | .98 |
| Deviant peers | −.03 | .00 | .97 |
| Gender * deviant peers | −2.27 | −.35* | .10 |
| Victimizing | −.57 | −.39** | .56 |
| Physical victimization | .02 | .03 | 1.02 |

$^*p < .05$.      $^{**}p < .01$.

resilience group by almost 50% ($b = -.57$; exp $b = .56$). Physical victimization although significantly negatively related to resilience in the panel model did not retain significance in the full model.

These findings indicate that the primary factors associated with our indicator of resilience were gender, parental criminal activity, deviant peer affiliation, and victimizing behaviors. Adolescent males were more likely to meet the criteria than were adolescent females. A history of serious parental crime reduced resilience for adolescent females but had little effect on adolescent males. Deviant peer affiliations reduced resilience more dramatically for adolescent males than for females. Victimizing behaviors reduced inclusion in the resilience cluster by almost 50% regardless of gender of adolescent.

## ASSESSING RESILIENCE AMONG RUNAWAY AND HOMELESS ADOLESCENTS

Defining resilience in a youthful population of runaways is especially problematic. Successful adaptation to a street environment such as developing "street wisdom" and survival skills certainly indicates one type of resilience. The fundamental adaptive tasks facing homeless adolescents are survival and avoiding harm. The problem is that such knowledge and skills typically are incongruent with successful adult adaptation. They run counter to the interpersonal and instrumental skills necessary to establishing conventional employment, conventional peer associations, and permanent housing. Skills necessary for conventional adaptation tend to be those that enhance education, employment, and the development of prosocial behaviors. It is difficult, if not impossible to develop these conventional skills in so unconventional an environment. The adaptive demands of early independence contradict those for prosocial development.

A second means of evaluating resilience would be the avoidance of internalizing symptoms. However, some research suggests that psychologically healthier young people are more likely to experience internalizing symptoms when faced with the stress of homelessness than are those who are less psychologically healthy. Stefanidis and colleagues found that homeless adolescents who manifested symptoms of depression were more responsive to treatment and more successful in transitional living programs than those who did not (Stefanidis et al., 1992). The more psychologically resilient young people, therefore, may be those who respond most dramatically to the trauma of homelessness (Goodman et al., 1991).

In our opinion, the only satisfactory assessment of resilience among runaway and homeless adolescents is their successful transition into adulthood. To fully understand the developmental effects of running away and periods of homelessness among adolescents, we need longitudinal data collected over a substantial period of time that includes a careful baseline assessment and follow-up assessments in early adulthood. Currently our knowledge of the developmental effects of running away is based solely on extrapolations from cross-sectional data. There is simply no systematic information about what happens to these youth when they become adults. In the absence of longitudinal data, we turned to the runaways themselves for their assessments of their futures.

## RUNAWAYS TALK ABOUT THEIR FUTURES

We asked the adolescents about their futures in a series of six open-ended questions. They were asked where they would like to be and what they would like to be doing in 3 months, 1 year, and 5 years from the date of interview. In response to where they would like to be in 3 months, most (59%) said they would like to be housed in some form or other. With the assumption that this goal would be accomplished in the near future, it became less important at 1 year (46%) and 5 years (29%). In terms of what they would like to be doing, most said that they would like to be employed: 44% at 3 months, 49% at 1 year, and 46% at 5 years. One-half wanted to be back in high school in 3 months, 39% in 1 year. Twenty-four percent said they would like to be in college in 5 years, although only 2% planned to be graduated by then. Only 6% wanted to be married in 5 years.

It was difficult to code the responses in terms of their chances of fulfillment. It was apparent, however, that the further into the future the young people projected themselves, the greater the element of fantasy. Some had very concrete plans. For example, a 17-year-old male told us:

I'd like to get stabilized for one. I don't see any immediate college plans. I want to, like I said, get stable and get back on my feet, a job, a permanent place to stay of my own. Then back to college. I want to get it done as soon as possible, but I don't want to rush into it before I'm financially and emotionally ready.

For some the future is uncertain and there are no specific plans:

Get a job, get somewhere to stay, be able to stay with Teresa and my little girl. Or if her don't work out, Alexis and my baby. Or if that don't work out then just by myself, have a job, save enough money for a car, and save enough money for a studio and then start making tapes . . . yeah . . . a rap studio because I like rap. (17-year-old male)

A number of the young people have never learned how to set goals and plan for them. Their responses about the future, therefore, seem incongruous with their developmental stage. For example, a 15-year-old girl told us that she wanted to be "a dentist, or an artist, but I really want to be an actress or a singer, because I'm really good at singing." A 16- year-old male told us, "My main goal, the main thing I want to do is play professional football, but I don't really see that in my near future." Like much younger children, there is a fantasy of the future, but no clear sense of how to achieve their goals.

To better distinguish the characteristics of youth who had concrete, achievable plans from those who did not, we coded their responses in terms of how realistic and how achievable they were. We then correlated characteristics of the young people against the quality of their future plans. It was noteworthy that the longer the adolescents had spent on their own, the less realistic their plans for the future at 3 months ($r = -.14$; $p < .01$) or 1 year ($r = -.16$; $p < .01$). Similarly, the more the adolescents had engaged in non-victimizing survival strategies (e.g., panhandling, begging, dumpster diving ) ($r = -.14$; $p < .01$), survival sex ($r = -.13$; $p < .01$), victimizing subsistence strategies ($r = -.13$; $p < .01$), the less realistic their future plans at 3 months. Having experienced physical victimization when on their own was also negatively associated with realistic future plans at 3 months ($r = -.18$; $p < .01$) and 1 year ($r = -.13$; $p < .01$). Sexual victimization when on their own had similar effects at 3 months ($r = -.09$; $p < .05$) and 1 year ($r = -.09$; $p < .05$). Affiliation with deviant peers also reduced realistic planning at 3 months ($r = -.14$; $p < .01$) and 1 year ($r = -.17$; $p < .01$). In general the longer on the streets, the more deviant behaviors engaged in while on their own, and the greater the victimization when on their own, the less evidence there was of realistic future plans.

In the life course literature, planned competency is a major contributor to young people's successful coping with hard times (Clauson, 1991). Among young people growing up during the economic hardships of the depression, the greater their ability to set plan their future, to set realistic and achievable goals, and to follow their plan, the more likely they successfully emerged from the depression. Among the runaways we interviewed, those most engaged in deviant behaviors and the culture of the street were less likely to have reasonable plans for a way out.

## POLICY SUGGESTIONS FROM THE RUNAWAYS

To get the runaways' impressions about the sorts of interventions that would work, we asked those who participated in the intensive qualitative interview to design a program for adolescents in situations such as theirs. As one would expect, their answers varied greatly in degree of thoughtfulness. However, some interesting points were raised. The most important was easy availability of shelter:

> [S]omeplace like this, you know, because if they don't want to live at home, or they need some time out, or some rest away from the house, then they can come and stay at some place like this to, you know, get a breather instead of going out there and risking their lives. (16-year-old male)

Several pointed out the need for easily accessible, safe places to go. The adolescents appeared very aware of the risks they were taking when they opted for the streets. One adolescent talked about the need for "safe places" such as businesses that are open late and to which street kids generally gravitate, for example, convenience stores. One 15-year-old female who had had trouble locating shelters in two separate cities told us:

> I think like Quik Trip, you know, how they put a safe place in there . . . do something like that, put more safe places around, like everywhere because that way a child knows that they have somebody to turn to.

They were also aware of one of the most important predictors of resilience, someone who cares. This would be someone, "just like a friend, usually kids don't like counselors or anything like that. They like to talk to friends and it gets them like a load off their chest" (15-year-old female). Knowing that the trajectory of influence has been from that of adult to that of peers, providing workers close to the runaways' own ages and perhaps peer counselors may speed attachments to shelters and outreach programs.

One young man, aged 16 years, had several negative experiences with shelters before ending up in the program where he was interviewed. He eloquently summed up the need for accepting, supportive outreach staff:

> I've been to three shelters, stayed at two but been to three where people were so cold-hearted that, I mean, I would rather be alone on the streets and cold. . . . We need really open-minded people, because close-minded people are just hurting the people even more. . . . The one that I went to and didn't stay . . . they had me sign a paper, they told me I would not be able to leave the shelter. They said that since they were government funded they had the right to sign me up for government aid organizations and accept the money for me. . . . We would be sleeping on the floor on a mat. . . . I figured I would be better off finding a place, a park bench.

There was also a concern among the older youth that they had somehow "fallen through the cracks" in the system. In one of the states, services were denied to youth aged 17 years, but they were still legally unable to sign a lease or exercise other rights of adulthood. The older youth felt many of the shelter services were designed for younger adolescents and children. As one 17-year-old male put it:

> We need more places for people who are like 16 to 19 years old because
> there's ages out there, those are the age that I see more girls turning to prosti-
> tution and dudes turning to gangs and so forth. . . . When you just put them on
> the streets, people lose their life.

The older adolescents knew that they were viewed as "more difficult" than
their younger counterparts. Some view all of the options as temporary
respites and hence not genuine options at all:

> It's very hard, like for me, my home isn't the best place to go home to and my
> sister's house isn't the perfect place for me, but because there ain't no other
> places, those are the only two options I have besides being homeless. (17-year-
> old male)

In some cases, no matter how hard the workers push the current policy of family reunification, the family resources are simply not strong enough to accom-
modate the adolescent. Too often, such policies result in sending children
back to difficult situations from which they run again. Current social policies
that build solely on family reunification are based on false assumptions: first,
that an organized family exists with whom the young person can be reunited;
second, that families so dysfunctional that a child opts for the known risks of
street life can be successfully rehabilitated through casework practices.

## THE NEED FOR A NATIONAL PLAN FOR HOMELESS YOUTH

In the past 25 years we have become a society that tolerates adult homeless people. Once considered a national social problem, they have blended
into the urban landscape to become part of certain downtown areas, another
nuisance like the traffic noise or littered streets. City governments pass laws
to restrain their behaviors, discourage their presence in certain areas, or push
them out of the community altogether. Even while living in the strongest economic times in recent history, our society has given little thought to providing basic living standards to the homeless.

If we tolerate our homeless adults, we ignore runaway and homeless
youth. They are less visible. For the most part, they look like the other kids
hanging out on the street. Because they can be so easily ignored, the societal response has been surprisingly passive. The first line of adult response typically has been law enforcement. As we have seen, police officers are viewed
primarily as adversaries by runaway youth. On the officers' part, the youth
are viewed at best as nuisances, at worst as potential criminals who should
be treated as adults.

There are no easy answers to the problem of homeless and runaway
youth. Our findings tell us that chronic runaways typically leave very disor-

ganized, dysfunctional families. They may drift out, be kicked out, or leave during a family crisis. They may be involved in "revolving door" placements from home to foster care to street to home to group home to street. The process is one of early and continuing disengagement from adult influences. All of this tells us what we have known for years: to prevent repeated runaways we need early and effective intervention in our most disturbed families. As a society, we are nowhere close to meeting these needs, nor is this a national priority.

However, our data also indicate possible interventions later in the developmental process. The goal at this point is to prevent further developmental harm. Runaways, particularly young women, are in immediate danger once they are on their own. The more time young people spend on the street the greater is the developmental risk. Aggressive outreach programs need to be established even in small and medium-sized cities to identify runaways and provide immediate and secure shelter the first time they run away. These programs need to be extended to include older adolescents, who are often viewed as more difficult and more dangerous. This is feasible and it is being done by effective street agencies such as the ones we worked with. Youth workers get to know local street cultures. They can identify new kids on the streets and intervene early. However, there are simply not enough outreach resources to meet the need. The work is difficult and can be dangerous. Often only entry-level salaries are offered. Shelters are too small, often shabby, and seriously underfunded.

Many shelters and transitional living programs already exist, particularly in larger cities. Because of underfunding, very few have sophisticated tracking and program evaluation components that would systematically guide their work and program development. Although many agencies that work with street youth have management information systems, the information collected too often is of little use, and even if it has scientific merit, it is seldom used, due to time and resource constraints. There is a need for partnerships with well-trained researchers to focus agency data collection and to evaluate it. We know that traditional services have failed these adolescents, but we are still uncertain about alternative approaches that will work.

Innovative programs require venture capital for systematic trials. Too often, agency-based demonstration programs, though well meaning, have lacked strong research components for guidance and evaluation. The urgency of the needs of runaways takes precedence, resulting in research components that are poorly formulated or simply inadequately carried out. Funding agencies need to aggressively encourage partnerships between established developmental scientists and practitioners who work with street youth to improve the quality of research on street youth. These partnerships are genuine. It is impossible for social scientists to access these youth without such cooperative agreements. In turn, the agencies need the systematic information to develop more effective programs and to demonstrate their need for continued community support.

Our data clearly indicate that the first program priority is safety. The developmental costs of victimization are too great to ignore. This may mean not waiting until runaway adolescents are "ready to commit to a program" but developing attractive safe havens for the young people to move in and out of during periods of independence. This approach may be controversial because it means changing the philosophy of intervention from "family reunification" to successful independent life skills. However, it may be simply too late for families, foster families, or the substitute families of group homes to guide many of these young people. Our findings suggest that these adolescents have turned away from adult influence to that of similarly aged peers. They have achieved a "too-early" adultlike status and they do not want to turn back. Peer or near-age mentors may be necessary to engage and guide them.

With our acceptance of adult homelessness, there appears to have developed a national willingness to write off chronic runaway children. The current policy emphasis is on deviance rather than development. Runaways are in danger of becoming a criminal justice problem. By criminalizing the behaviors, the system revictimizes young people who are likely to have already been physically and/or sexually abused at home and seriously harmed when on the streets. Criminalization would arrest them for getting away and trying to get by.

We need a national policy for runaway youth that focuses on the developmental consequences of "too-early" adult transitions. This policy should recognize the need to begin where the runaways currently are in their developmental trajectories and to build from there. It should recognize that no amount of wishful thinking will replace many of these young people in families, nor can we return them to childhood. "Too-early" adulthood represents an irreversible developmental transition. Essential parts of childhood socialization have been lost and the skills necessary to successfully cope may need to be taught in alternative ways, taking into account the adultlike status of these young people.

## WILL SOCIETY'S MARGINAL CHILDREN BECOME ITS MARGINAL ADULTS?

It is difficult to be optimistic about the futures of these young people. Theoretically, their developmental trajectories are very bleak. For many, life experiences thus far fit Moffitt's (1997) conceptualization of life course–persistent antisocial developmental trajectories. Early developmental disadvantages beginning in disorganized and often abusive families are perpetuated by chains of negative interactions and behaviors. The consequences of these negative interactions and behaviors begin to accumulate and prosocial options diminish. The process gains momentum as ties to the conventional world are broken. This momentum builds more rapidly for runaways than for any other high-risk adolescent populations. The assertion of adult status is more dramatic, conventional ties are more completely severed, and there are few if any prosocial options available on the streets.

For runaways and homeless adolescents, even "resilience" takes on a different meaning. Successful adaptation on the streets requires skills that often run counter to successful adult development. Acquiring these survival skills increases the momentum toward persistent antisocial outcomes. Conventionally "resilient" runaways are those who do not adapt well to street life. However, even among these adolescents, their experiences take an enormous psychological toll. Conventionally "resilient" runaways stay connected to prosocial options despite their "too-early" adult status. They maintain ties to family or to a significant adult, stay connected with school, are able to be employed, and perhaps most importantly, have realistic and achievable plans for their futures. The problem is that most of the factors typically associated with resilience among high-risk youth are less available to runaways and homeless youth than their continually housed counterparts.

Chronic runaways and homeless adolescents are literally learning to become marginal adults. For many runaway and homeless adolescents, early adult status has come at the cost of essential developmental experiences. These developmental losses are difficult to remedy under the best of circumstances and currently the resources available to intervene are woefully inadequate. Writing off these difficult children or a social policy based on a criminal justice response will undoubtedly continue or even expedite the process of marginalization. By not responding to the needs of runaway and homeless adolescents we are choosing to train them to become marginal adults, part of the criminal justice system, perhaps even part of the adult culture of homelessness.

# Appendix

**Table 2A.1:**  Provides frequencies of the adults who were designated as primary caretakers by the adolescents. The adult is the person named in response to the following question: "Now I would like you to think about all of the adults who helped raise you. Of all of these people, which one did you live with the longest and spend the most time with?"

**Table 2A.2:**  Presents the caretakers' reports regarding their marital situation and marital history.

**Table 2A.3:**  Reflects the interviewers' assessment of the degree to which the adolescents were over- or underreporting problem behaviors and traumatic experiences. The interviewers were told to base this assessment on their interviewing impressions of body language, voice inflection, consistency in reporting, previous knowledge of the respondent through their street or shelter work, and general comments made by the adolescents in response to various questions.

**Table 4A.1:**  Provides bivariate correlation coefficients, means, and standard deviations for the variables of the intergenerational path models presented in Table 4.4.

**Table 4A.2:**  Provides bivariate correlation coefficients, means, and standard deviations for the variables used in regression models presented in Figures 4.1 and 4.2.

**Table 5A.1:**  Provides bivariate correlation coefficients, means, and standard deviations for the variables used in regression models presented in Tables 5.4, 5.5, and 5.6.

**Table 6A.1:**  Provides bivariate correlation coefficients, means, and standard deviations for the structural equation model presented in Figure 6.1.

**Table 6A.2:**   Gives a complete list of adolescents' responses regarding reasons for being in the hospital during the past year.

**Table 7A.1:**   Provides bivariate correlation coefficients, means, and standard deviations for the path models presented in Figures 7.1, 7.2, 7.3, and 7.4.

**Table 8A.1:**   Provides bivariate correlation coefficients, means, and standard deviations for the logistic regression models in Tables 8.1, 8.3, and 8.4.

**Table 9A.1:**   Presents bivariate correlation coefficients, means, and standard deviations for the logistic regression model in Table 9.2.

**Table 10A.1:**   Provides bivariate correlation coefficients, means, and standard deviations for the regression models in Tables 10.1 and 10.2.

**Table 10A.2:**   Provides a complete listing of adolescents' responses to the PTSD screener that asked about "the most terrible or traumatic thing that has happened to you since being on your own."

**Table 11A.1:**   Provides bivariate correlation coefficients, means, and standard deviations for the regression models in Tables 11.2 and 11.3.

**Table 12A.1:**   Provides bivariate correlation coefficients, means, and standard deviations for the structural equation models presented in Figures 12.2 and 12.3.

**Table 12A.2:**   Provides a breakdown of the direct and indirect effects of the structural equation model for adolescent females in Chapter 12.

**Table 12A.3:**   Provides a breakdown of the direct and indirect effects of the structural equation model for adolescent males in Chapter 12.

**Table 13A.1:**   Provides bivariate correlation coefficients, means, and standard deviations for the regression model in Table 13.2.

*Table 2A.1.* Adolescent Report of His/Her Primary Caretaker

| | Percentage of Group | | |
|---|---|---|---|
| Caretaker | All (N = 602) | Male (N = 241) | Female (N = 361) |
| Biological relatives | | | |
| Mother | 64.0 | 59.3 | 67.0 |
| Father | 11.6 | 13.7 | 10.2 |
| Grandmother | 7.5 | 8.3 | 6.9 |
| Grandfather | 0.8 | 1.2 | 0.6 |
| Sister | 0.7 | 1.2 | 0.3 |
| Aunt | 2.3 | 2.1 | 2.5 |
| Uncle | 0.7 | 0.8 | 0.6 |
| Steprelatives | | | |
| Mother | 0.7 | 0.0 | 1.1 |
| Father | 1.2 | 0.8 | 1.4 |
| Adoptive relatives | | | |
| Mother | 3.3 | 3.3 | 3.3 |
| Father | 1.2 | 1.7 | 0.8 |
| Other (including biological) | 0.7 | 0.8 | 0.6 |
| Other caretakers | | | |
| Foster parents | 1.7 | 2.9 | 0.8 |
| Friend | 0.3 | 0.4 | 0.3 |
| Friend's parents | 0.2 | 0.4 | 0.0 |
| Professional person | 0.8 | 0.0 | 1.4 |
| Other | 1.8 | 1.2 | 2.3 |
| Refused | 0.7 | 1.7 | 0.0 |

*Table 2A.2.* Caretaker Report of His/Her Current Marital Status

| | Percentage of Group | | |
|---|---|---|---|
| Marital Status | All Adolescents (N = 201) | Male Adolescents (N = 71) | Female Adolescents (N = 130) |
| Married | 57.7 | 36.3 | 58.5 |
| Living with someone | 3.0 | 4.2 | 2.3 |
| Separated | 4.5 | 4.2 | 4.6 |
| Divorced | 25.4 | 25.4 | 25.4 |
| Widowed | 5.0 | 5.6 | 4.6 |
| Never married | 4.3 | 4.2 | 4.6 |

*Table 2A.3.* Interviewer Impression of Quality of Adolescent Responses

| Variable | Underreported 1 | 2 | Accurate 3 | 4 | Overreported 5 | Refused/missing |
|---|---|---|---|---|---|---|
| Physical abuse | | | | | | |
| All | 5.1 | 23.1 | 69.1 | 1.0 | 0.0 | 1.7 |
| Male | 3.3 | 22.8 | 70.1 | 1.7 | 0.0 | 2.1 |
| Female | 6.4 | 23.3 | 68.4 | 0.6 | 0.0 | 1.4 |
| Sexual abuse | | | | | | |
| All | 7.3 | 16.9 | 73.4 | 0.5 | 0.0 | 1.8 |
| Male | 4.6 | 12.9 | 79.7 | 0.4 | 0.0 | 2.5 |
| Female | 9.1 | 19.7 | 69.3 | 0.6 | 0.0 | 1.4 |
| Criminal activities | | | | | | |
| All | 5.6 | 22.6 | 68.3 | 1.2 | 0.5 | 1.8 |
| Male | 7.1 | 24.1 | 64.7 | 1.7 | 0.4 | 2.1 |
| Female | 4.7 | 21.6 | 70.6 | 0.8 | 0.6 | 1.7 |
| Drug/alcohol use | | | | | | |
| All | 5.6 | 26.7 | 62.3 | 2.8 | 0.7 | 1.8 |
| Male | 7.5 | 28.6 | 57.7 | 3.7 | 0.4 | 2.1 |
| Female | 4.4 | 25.5 | 65.4 | 2.2 | 0.8 | 1.7 |
| Other | | | | | | |
| All | 4.5 | 11.8 | 58.3 | 2.0 | 0.0 | 23.4 |
| Male | 5.0 | 10.4 | 58.9 | 2.1 | 0.0 | 23.7 |
| Female | 4.2 | 12.7 | 57.9 | 1.9 | 0.0 | 23.3 |

*Note:* $N = 241$ males and $N = 361$ females.

*Table 4A.1.* Bivariate Correlation Matrix for the Parenting Regression Models

|  | 1 | 2 | 3 | 4 | 5 | 6 | 7 | 8 | 9 |
|---|---|---|---|---|---|---|---|---|---|
| 1. Adolescent's substance use | — | | | | | | | | |
| 2. Parents' substance use | .20** | — | | | | | | | |
| 3. Grandparents' substance use | .07 | .16* | — | | | | | | |
| 4. Adolescent's crime | .31** | .14* | .08 | — | | | | | |
| 5. Parents' serious crime | .13 | .31** | .15* | .17* | — | | | | |
| 6. Grandparents' serious crime | .10 | .09 | .13 | .24** | −.01 | — | | | |
| 7. Family abuse | .21** | .39** | .04 | .13 | .13 | .06 | — | | |
| 8. Adolescent gender | −.15* | .07 | .06 | −.36** | −.13 | −.03 | .21** | — | |
| 9. Adolescent age | .06 | −.02 | .07 | .05 | −.08 | .05 | .15* | −.12 | — |
| Mean | 3.50 | 1.47 | .17 | .55 | .47 | .04 | .46 | .64 | 16.09 |
| SD | 2.91 | 1.43 | .38 | .94 | .64 | .19 | .31 | .48 | 1.80 |

*$p < .05$.   **$p < .01$.

*Table 4A.2.* Bivariate Correlation Matrix for the Intergenerational Path Models

|  | 1 | 2 | 3 | 4 | 5 | 6 | 7 | 8 | 9 |
|---|---|---|---|---|---|---|---|---|---|
| 1. Father's substance use | — | | | | | | | | |
| 2. Mother's substance use | .21** | — | | | | | | | |
| 3. Warmth | −.09* | −.13** | — | | | | | | |
| 4. Rejection | .08* | .10* | −.78** | — | | | | | |
| 5. Monitoring | −.01 | −.08 | .44** | −.36** | — | | | | |
| 6. Physical abuse | .17** | .22** | −.37** | .41** | −.18** | — | | | |
| 7. Sexual abuse | .11** | .15** | −.07 | .06 | −.00 | .27** | — | | |
| 8. Adolescent gender | .03 | .08 | −.11** | .13** | .09* | .13** | .19** | — | |
| 9. Adolescent age | .01 | −.01 | −.06 | .06 | −.05 | .14** | .06 | −.14** | — |
| Mean | .51 | .43 | 29.93 | 14.02 | 14.70 | 12.28 | .82 | .60 | 16.23 |
| SD | .50 | .50 | 9.82 | 4.44 | 4.01 | 4.69 | 1.72 | .49 | 1.90 |

*$p < .05$.   **$p < .01$.

Table 5A.1. Bivariate Correlation Matrix for Chapter 5 Regression Models

| | 1 | 2 | 3 | 4 | 5 | 6 | 7 | 8 | 9 | 10 | 11 | 12 |
|---|---|---|---|---|---|---|---|---|---|---|---|---|
| 1. Gender | — | | | | | | | | | | | |
| 2. Family structure | -.15** | — | | | | | | | | | | |
| 3. Geographic transitions | -.05 | .18** | — | | | | | | | | | |
| 4. Monitor | -.08 | -.06 | -.05 | — | | | | | | | | |
| 5. Warmth/support | .11** | -.10* | -.09* | .44** | — | | | | | | | |
| 6. Rejection | -.13** | .12** | .05 | -.36** | -.78** | — | | | | | | |
| 7. Neglect | -.02 | .07 | .07 | -.18** | -.18** | .19** | — | | | | | |
| 8. Physical abuse | -.09* | .14** | .06 | -.19** | -.32** | .32** | .53** | — | | | | |
| 9. Sex abuse | -.19** | .12** | .09* | .03 | -.04 | .04 | .33** | .30** | — | | | |
| 10. Age first time on own | -.02 | -.21** | -.10* | .12** | .05 | -.02 | -.31** | -.22** | -.26** | — | | |
| 11. Adolescent transitions after first run | -.03 | .06 | .07 | -.16** | -.21** | .22** | .15** | .18** | .18** | -.27** | — | |
| 12. First time ever on street | .13** | -.05 | -.03 | -.09* | -.05 | .05 | .07 | .05 | .06 | -.12** | .27** | — |
| Mean | 0.40 | 0.12 | 0.09 | 14.72 | 29.93 | 14.01 | 0.03 | 0.24 | 0.03 | 13.53 | 3.32 | 0.34 |
| SD | 0.49 | 0.14 | 0.14 | 4.02 | 9.87 | 4.45 | 0.06 | 0.18 | 0.07 | 2.51 | 3.52 | 0.47 |

* $p < .05$.  ** $p < .01$.

Table 6A.1.  Bivariate Correlation Matrix for the Chapter 6 Structural Equation Model

| | 1 | 2 | 3 | 4 | 5 | 6 | 7 | Mean | SD |
|---|---|---|---|---|---|---|---|---|---|
| 1. Parental warmth | — | -.06 | -.30** | -.10 | -.12* | .24** | -.20** | 28.98 | 10.16 |
| 2. Number of family transitions | -.16* | — | .12* | .06 | -.02 | -.09 | .14* | 2.03 | 2.05 |
| 3. Family abuse | -.35** | .21** | — | .29** | .19** | -.17** | .34** | 18.38 | 5.94 |
| 4. Number of child-initiated transitions | -.30** | .05 | .34** | — | .47** | -.15** | .26** | 5.49 | 4.68 |
| 5. Total time on own | -.24** | -.02 | .14* | .39** | — | -.15** | .23** | .48 | 1.81 |
| 6. Continued family support | .38** | -.05 | -.18** | -.20** | -.26** | — | -.14** | 2.08 | 2.11 |
| 7. Affiliation with deviant peers | -.13 | .05 | .29** | .28** | .23** | -.11 | — | .45 | .28 |
| Mean | 31.08 | 1.59 | 16.47 | 5.56 | .84 | 2.11 | .46 | | |
| SD | 9.29 | 1.78 | 5.71 | 4.38 | 1.80 | 2.18 | .27 | | |

* $p < .05$.    ** $p < .01$.

Note:  Coefficients above the diagonal are for females; coefficients below the diagonal are for males.

*Table 6A.2.*   Reasons for Hospitalization

| Hospitalization for Mental Conditions | |
| --- | --- |
| Suicidal ideation/Tried to hurt self | Mental health problems/Psychological treatment |
| Suicide attempt/Suicide | Psychological testing |
| Homicidal ideation | Defiance disorder |
| Depression | Behavior disorder |
| Bipolar | Anger problem |
| Overdose/Drug use | ADHD |
| Drug rehab/Intoxication | Counseling/Family problems |
| Runaway | Grief problem |

| Hospitalization for Physical Condition | |
| --- | --- |
| Stillbirth | Herpes |
| Miscarriage | Broken neck/Fracture in neck/Neck problems |
| Tumor | Ingrown toenail |
| Stomach Cancer | Bronchitis |
| Stomach pain/Stomach pumped | Tonsillitis |
| Rape | High blood pressure |
| Pneumonia | Heart problems |
| Flu | Infection/Abscess |
| HIV | Asthma |
| Ear Surgery/Ear infection | Burn |
| Strep throat/Throat problems | Diabetes |
| Laryngitis | Blood alcohol poisoning |
| Kidney infection/problem | Headaches/Head injury |
| Foot surgery/Knee surgery | Childbirth |
| STD/Trichomoniasis | Chicken pox |
| Yeast infection | Bladder problem/Urinary tract infection/Irritable bowel |
| Ovaries/Ovarian cyst | Blood problems/Low blood count |
| Parasite in blood | Seizures |
| Severe dehydration/Sun stroke | Spinal tap |
| Hypothermia | Someone slipped drugs in R's drink |
| Auto injury/Hit by car | Allergies |
| Wounds/Gunshot wound/Head wounds due to attack | Stitches |
| Broken bones/X-ray | Lupus |
| Injury: Ankle/Knee/Finger | Hernia |
| Beaten up/Assaulted | Pink eye |
| Stabbed | TB |
| Chemical balance testing | STD testing |
| Hyperventilated | Biopsy |
| Wisdom teeth removed/Infected teeth | Pregnancy testing |
| Appendectomy/Appendix surgery/Appendix problem | Thyroid problems |
| Bad cut | Bee sting |
| Uterine infection | Injury to testicles |
| Cyst removed | Blackout |

Table 7A.1. Bivariate Correlation Matrix of Variables for Chapter 7 Path Models.

| | 1 | 2 | 3 | 4 | 5 | 6 | 7 | 8 | 9 | 10 |
|---|---|---|---|---|---|---|---|---|---|---|
| 1. Change in family structure | — | -.06 | .08 | .12 | .09 | .11 | .07 | .01 | -.10 | -.09 |
| 2. Warmth/support | -.18* | — | -.10 | .03 | -.29** | -.03 | -.08 | -.06 | .05 | .24** |
| 3. Parental alcohol/drug use | .10 | -.09 | — | .27** | .25** | .24** | .03 | .04 | -.10 | -.04 |
| 4. Parental serious crime | .13 | -.14 | .41** | — | .19** | .16** | .13* | .02 | -.11 | .00 |
| 5. Family abuse | .22** | -.32** | .26** | .27** | — | .57** | .27** | .19** | -.22** | -.17** |
| 6. Sexual abuse | .04 | -.21** | .12 | .11 | .45** | — | .28** | .12 | -.20** | -.09 |
| 7. Number of child-initiated transitions | .05 | -.27** | .14 | .15* | .32** | .24** | — | .45** | -.32** | -.17** |
| 8. Total time on own | -.01 | -.21** | -.01 | .04 | .13 | .16* | .33** | — | -.20** | -.15* |
| 9. Age at first run | -.15* | .11 | -.23** | -.19* | -.28** | -.14 | -.25** | -.06 | — | .09 |
| 10. Continued family support | -.13 | .39** | .00 | .03 | -.17* | -.08 | -.16* | -.24** | .11 | — |
| 11. Affiliation with deviant peers | .05 | -.06 | .07 | .13 | .26** | .14 | .22** | .11 | -.15* | -.08 |
| 12. Alcohol/drug use | .10 | -.03 | .09 | .01 | .15* | .00 | .22** | .04 | -.09 | -.13 |
| 13. Number of different sexual partners | .01 | -.16* | .07 | .07 | .10 | .19** | .03 | .03 | .01 | -.07 |
| 14. Family subsistence | -.08 | .14 | -.06 | .03 | -.22** | -.08 | -.21** | -.11 | .00 | .22** |
| 15. Employment subsistence | .00 | -.07 | .06 | .02 | .14 | .18* | -.01 | .17* | .03 | -.15* |
| 16. Deviant subsistence | -.02 | -.10 | .04 | .03 | .15* | .06 | .10 | -.14 | -.11 | -.14 |
| 17. Drug dealing | .02 | .03 | .10 | .11 | .05 | .02 | .16* | -.01 | -.13 | -.03 |
| 18. Victimizing behavior | .00 | -.08 | .05 | .11 | .15* | .04 | .09 | -.19** | -.12 | -.07 |
| 19. Survival sex | -.06 | -.04 | .05 | .01 | .21** | .19* | .05 | .07 | .02 | -.09 |
| Mean | 1.61 | 30.64 | .93 | .47 | 16.78 | .12 | 6.00 | 1.09 | 13.56 | 2.07 |
| SD | 1.84 | 9.54 | .80 | .65 | 5.77 | .32 | 4.43 | 1.70 | 2.54 | 2.06 |

(Continued)

Table 7A.1 (cont.)

| | 11 | 12 | 13 | 14 | 15 | 16 | 17 | 18 | 19 | Mean | SD |
|---|---|---|---|---|---|---|---|---|---|---|---|
| 1. Change in family structure | .12 | .07 | -.01 | .02 | -.02 | .06 | .07 | .05 | .00 | 2.05 | 2.09 |
| 2. Warmth/support | -.13* | -.16** | -.03 | .09 | -.03 | -.07 | -.10 | -.10 | -.13* | 28.68 | 10.33 |
| 3. Parental alcohol/drug use | .15* | .13* | .11 | -.07 | .01 | .10 | .07 | .10 | .01 | 1.04 | .75 |
| 4. Parental serious crime | .19** | .10 | .12* | -.02 | .02 | .02 | .07 | .01 | -.06 | .48 | .65 |
| 5. Family abuse | .31** | .18** | .13* | -.16** | .13* | .17** | .23** | .18** | .24** | 18.77 | 5.92 |
| 6. Sexual abuse | .15* | .12 | .05 | -.09 | .12 | .11 | .09 | .11 | .08 | .31 | .46 |
| 7. Number of child-initiated transitions | .23** | .20** | .07 | -.11 | .10 | .22** | .20** | .15* | .11 | 6.02 | 4.89 |
| 8. Total time on own | .17** | .18** | .04 | -.15* | .13* | .09 | .21** | .05 | .12* | .71 | 1.72 |
| 9. Age at first run | -.15* | -.16** | -.08 | -.03 | -.06 | -.12* | -.08 | -.12* | -.16* | 13.61 | 2.48 |
| 10. Continued family support | -.11 | -.03 | .01 | .28** | -.03 | -.16** | -.09 | -.14* | -.18** | 1.97 | 2.12 |
| 11. Affiliation with deviant peers | — | .40** | .25** | -.04 | .05 | .38** | .31** | .33** | .30** | .48 | .27 |
| 12. Alcohol/drug use | .43** | — | .30** | .01 | .10 | .35** | .32** | .30** | .34** | 8.92 | 8.37 |
| 13. Number of different sexual partners | .13 | .01 | — | .01 | .09 | .20** | .21** | .14* | .37 | 3.00 | 4.95 |
| 14. Family subsistence | -.10 | -.06 | .11 | — | .06 | -.05 | -.02 | -.03 | -.08 | .99 | .84 |
| 15. Employment subsistence | .00 | .03 | .07 | .12 | — | -.04 | .07 | -.11 | .06 | .71 | .70 |
| 16. Deviant subsistence | .45** | .39** | .06 | -.01 | -.10 | — | .54** | .85** | .34** | .86 | 1.36 |
| 17. Drug dealing | .27** | .41** | .10 | -.16* | -.02 | .47** | — | .42** | .33** | .12 | .33 |
| 18. Victimizing behavior | .39** | .36** | .07 | .05 | -.17* | .87** | .37** | — | .26** | .39 | .79 |
| 19. Survival sex | .39** | .23** | .13 | -.11 | .05 | .30** | .14 | .19** | — | .07 | .26 |
| Mean | .49 | 12.56 | 3.00 | 1.04 | .88 | 1.99 | .40 | .98 | .09 | | |
| SD | .27 | 10.23 | 4.44 | .85 | .72 | 1.84 | .49 | 1.14 | .29 | | |

* p < .05.    ** p < .01.
Note: Coefficients above the diagonal are for females; coefficients below the diagonal are for males.

Table 8A.1. Bivariate Correlation Matrix of Variables for Chapter 8 Regression Models

| | 1 | 2 | 3 | 4 | 5 | 6 | 7 | 8 | 9 | 10 | 11 | 12 | 13 | 14 | 15 | Mean | SD |
|---|---|---|---|---|---|---|---|---|---|---|---|---|---|---|---|---|---|
| 1. Alcohol/marijuana use | — | .62** | .25** | .09 | .28** | .03 | .27** | .19** | .29** | .18** | .04 | -.33** | .07 | .07 | -.16** | 5.69 | 4.52 |
| 2. Hard drug use | .53** | — | .22** | .15** | .23** | .03 | .20** | .16** | .36** | .10 | -.05 | -.21** | .03 | .10 | -.23** | .94 | 1.58 |
| 3. Close friends sold sex | .22** | .18* | — | .09 | .23** | .07 | .11 | .09 | .33** | .12* | .02 | -.10 | .11 | .04 | -.04 | .21 | .41 |
| 4. CT sexual victimization | -.11 | .06 | .29** | — | .07 | -.02 | .05 | .00 | .18** | .07 | .09 | -.13* | .09 | .09 | -.12* | 1.06 | 1.87 |
| 5. Different sex partners | .12 | .07 | .12 | .14 | — | .11 | .22** | .01 | .29** | .25** | .18** | -.23** | .04 | .01 | -.07 | 2.43 | 3.92 |
| 6. AIDS concern | .05 | .02 | -.02 | -.12 | -.03 | — | -.01 | .08 | .06 | .05 | -.01 | -.04 | .01 | .03 | -.02 | 2.36 | 1.13 |
| 7. Early coitus | .25** | .17* | -.01 | -.04 | .19** | .08 | — | -.11 | .26** | .15** | .09 | -.22** | -.23** | -.01 | -.04 | .42 | .49 |
| 8. Sexual orientation | .02 | .07 | .23** | .23** | .15* | -.06 | -.03 | — | .00 | .08 | -.05 | -.08 | .14* | .09 | -.06 | .04 | .20 |
| 9. HIV risk behaviors | .33** | .46** | .39** | .22** | .16* | -.05 | .15* | .25** | — | .24** | .09 | -.16** | .05 | .08 | -.08 | .04 | .26 |
| 10. STD | .24** | .23** | .33** | .08 | .18* | .07 | .06 | .02 | .31** | — | .24** | -.22** | .17** | .04 | -.05 | .07 | .38 |
| 11. Pregnant | .16* | .17* | .03 | .04 | .09 | .07 | .12 | .12 | .22** | .18* | — | -.28** | .34** | .04 | -.01 | .25 | .44 |
| 12. Condom use | -.38** | -.35** | -.20** | -.04 | -.25** | .04 | -.17* | -.20** | -.22** | -.21** | -.30** | — | -.29** | -.01 | .04 | .42 | .49 |
| 13. Age | .24** | .13 | .27** | .12 | .15* | .21** | -.08 | .11 | .17* | .26** | .25** | -.29** | — | -.02 | .05 | 15.96 | 1.76 |
| 14. European American | .12 | .34** | -.06 | -.02 | -.04 | -.05 | -.18* | -.02 | .07 | .09 | .13 | -.18** | .08 | — | -.67** | .65 | .48 |
| 15. African American | -.13 | -.34** | .05 | -.04 | .11 | -.02 | .07 | .10 | -.02 | -.05 | -.10 | .13 | -.09 | -.70** | — | .20 | .40 |
| Mean | 7.34 | 1.53 | .19 | .44 | 2.56 | 2.45 | .44 | .04 | .12 | .10 | .17 | .48 | 16.59 | .55 | .28 | | |
| SD | 5.08 | 2.10 | .39 | 1.38 | 4.30 | 1.14 | .50 | .20 | .32 | .29 | .37 | .50 | 1.96 | .50 | .45 | | |

*p < .05.   **p < .01.
Note: Coefficients above the diagonal are for females; coefficients below the diagonal are for males.

Table 9A.1.  Bivariate Correlation Matrix of Variables for Chapter 9 Regression Models

| | 1 | 2 | 3 | 4 | 5 | 6 | 7 | 8 | 9 | 10 | 11 | 12 | 13 | Mean | SD |
|---|---|---|---|---|---|---|---|---|---|---|---|---|---|---|---|
| 1. Physical victimization | — | .27** | -.10 | .29** | .14* | -.14* | .12* | .35** | .20** | .17** | .21** | .22** | .19** | .65 | .48 |
| 2. Sexual victimization | .18** | — | -.11 | .20** | .07 | -.21** | .10 | .36** | .20** | .22** | .20** | .14* | .30** | .20 | .40 |
| 3. Age on own | -.06 | — | — | -.18** | -.14* | .05 | -.08 | -.14* | -.02 | -.11* | -.03 | -.10 | -.12* | 13.53 | 2.51 |
| 4. Time on own | .15* | — | -.01 | — | .30** | -.13* | .06 | .26** | .20** | .09 | .14* | .11* | .15* | 3.89 | 1.84 |
| 5. Ever on the street | .08 | — | -.05 | .17* | — | -.11 | .17** | .11* | .20** | .08 | .16** | .13* | -.00 | .29 | .45 |
| 6. Family support | -.27** | — | .05 | -.24** | -.19** | — | -.40** | -.14** | -.07 | -.05 | -.12* | -.13* | -.18* | 2.08 | 2.11 |
| 7. Friend support | .09 | — | -.13* | .03 | -.10 | -.31** | — | .16** | .18** | .14* | .09 | .07 | .05 | 2.58 | 2.42 |
| 8. Deviant peers | .41** | — | -.10 | .20** | .07 | -.10 | -.03 | — | .38** | .33** | .30** | .32** | .29** | .45 | .28 |
| 9. Alcohol/marijuana | .26** | — | .07 | .18** | .00 | -.05 | .05 | .43** | — | .44** | .31** | .18** | .12* | 2.05 | 1.15 |
| 10. Hard drugs | .30** | — | -.00 | .13 | .08 | -.22** | .21** | .41** | .43** | — | .25** | .20** | .29** | 1.01 | 1.66 |
| 11. Nonvictimizing behaviors | .27** | — | -.02 | .08 | .12 | -.27** | .06 | .42** | .33** | .28** | — | .46** | .22** | .42 | .74 |
| 12. Victimizing behaviors | .32** | — | -.10 | -.09 | .09 | -.14* | .06 | .42** | .30** | .28** | .48** | — | .27** | .38 | .78 |
| 13. Selling sex | — | — | — | — | — | — | — | — | — | — | — | — | — | .06 | .25 |
| Mean | .77 | — | 13.44 | 4.26 | .41 | 2.06 | 2.12 | .45 | 2.23 | 1.61 | .95 | .96 | | | |
| SD | .42 | — | 2.53 | 1.75 | .49 | 2.16 | 2.47 | .26 | 1.09 | 2.15 | .99 | 1.13 | | | |

* p < .05.    ** p < .01.

Note:  Coefficients above the diagonal are for females; coefficients below the diagonal are for males.

*Table 10A.1.* Bivariate Correlation Matrix for Chapter 10 Regression Models

| | 1 | 2 | 3 | 4 | 5 | 6 | 7 | 8 | 9 | 10 |
|---|---|---|---|---|---|---|---|---|---|---|
| 1. Gender | — | | | | | | | | | |
| 2. Change in family structure | -.11* | — | | | | | | | | |
| 3. Change in family residence | -.09* | .23** | — | | | | | | | |
| 4. Parental alcohol/drug use | -.07 | .11* | .02 | — | | | | | | |
| 5. Parental serious crime | -.03 | .14** | .15** | .32** | — | | | | | |
| 6. Parental depression | -.10* | .08 | .08 | .17** | .06 | — | | | | |
| 7. Warmth/support | .11* | .08 | .08 | -.13** | -.07 | -.09* | — | | | |
| 8. Monitoring | -.10* | -.11* | -.11* | -.03 | -.03 | -.01 | .43** | — | | |
| 9. Rejection | -.14** | -.07 | -.09* | .11 | .02 | .14* | -.79** | -.35** | — | |
| 10. Neglect | -.06 | .12** | .07 | .16** | .14** | .10* | -.23** | -.19** | .24** | — |
| 11. Physical abuse | -.13** | .05 | .01 | .27** | .14* | .17** | -.38** | -.19** | .40** | .42** |
| 12. Sexual abuse | -.26** | .17** | .08 | .24** | .20** | .18** | -.11* | -.01 | .13* | .19** |
| 13. Age at first run | -.04 | .12** | .10* | -.15** | .16** | -.04 | .06 | .15* | -.03 | -.25** |
| 14. Total time on own | .08 | -.09 | -.09 | .05 | -.14** | .08 | -.13** | -.16** | .08 | .12** |
| 15. Ever on street | .11* | -.02 | -.01 | .09* | .01 | .03 | -.05 | -.11* | .03 | .07 |
| 16. Continued family support | .02 | -.03 | -.02 | -.04 | .09* | -.09* | .30** | .18** | -.26** | -.21** |
| 17. Friend support | -.08 | -.09 | -.01 | .07 | .01 | .03 | -.19** | -.03 | .16** | .01 |
| 18. Affiliation with deviant peers | -.02 | .07 | .11* | .18** | .09* | .16** | -.16** | -.23** | .18** | .27** |
| 19. Alcohol/marijuana use | .14** | .13** | .08 | .16** | .19** | .10* | -.14** | -.24** | .16** | .13** |
| 20. Hard drug use | .16** | .10* | .05 | .10* | .09 | .15** | -.08 | -.21** | .09* | .12** |
| 21. Number of different sexual partners | -.06 | .06 | .05 | .17** | .02 | .16** | -.17** | -.21** | .19** | .26** |
| 22. Nonvictimizing strategy | .26** | .04 | .11* | .05 | .08 | .08 | -.05 | -.20** | .07 | .08 |
| 23. Survival sex | -.01 | -.01 | -.02 | .07 | -.01 | .13** | -.17** | -.20** | .18** | .16** |
| 24. Victimizing strategy | .31** | .00 | .10* | .09* | -.03 | .06 | -.07 | -.24** | .08 | .13** |
| 25. Physical victimization | .18** | .01 | .04 | .16** | .07 | .19** | -.10* | -.19** | .12* | .27** |
| 26. Sexual victimization | -.15** | .05 | -.01 | .16** | .17** | .14** | -.07 | -.06 | .16** | .18** |
| 27. Depressive symptoms | -.15** | .09* | -.05 | .12** | .10* | .17** | -.11* | -.06 | .13** | .12** |
| 28. Depression | -.14** | .11* | .03 | .09 | .11* | .13* | -.09 | -.07 | .07 | .07 |
| 29. PTSD | -.14** | .07 | .04 | .04 | .09* | .10* | -.06 | -.11* | | .15** |
| Mean | .39 | 1.89 | 1.38 | .97 | .47 | .25 | 29.83 | 14.75 | 14.07 | .32 |
| SD | .49 | 1.99 | 2.04 | .76 | .65 | .43 | 9.88 | 4.00 | 4.50 | .47 |

(cont.)

Table 10A.1 (cont.)

| | 11 | 12 | 13 | 14 | 15 | 16 | 17 | 18 | 19 | 20 |
|---|---|---|---|---|---|---|---|---|---|---|
| 1. Gender | | | | | | | | | | |
| 2. Change in family structure | | | | | | | | | | |
| 3. Change in family residence | | | | | | | | | | |
| 4. Parental alcohol/drug use | | | | | | | | | | |
| 5. Parental serious crime | | | | | | | | | | |
| 6. Parental depression | | | | | | | | | | |
| 7. Warmth/support | | | | | | | | | | |
| 8. Monitoring | | | | | | | | | | |
| 9. Rejection | | | | | | | | | | |
| 10. Neglect | | | | | | | | | | |
| 11. Physical abuse | — | | | | | | | | | |
| 12. Sexual abuse | .31** | — | | | | | | | | |
| 13. Age at first run | -.20** | -.18** | — | | | | | | | |
| 14. Total time on own | .15** | .09* | -.14** | — | | | | | | |
| 15. Ever on street | .08 | .05 | -.15** | .25** | — | | | | | |
| 16. Continued family support | -.18** | -.09* | .06 | -.17** | -.14** | — | | | | |
| 17. Friend support | .10* | .08 | -.07 | .07 | .05 | -.39** | — | | | |
| 18. Affiliation with deviant peers | .29** | .15** | -.14** | .21** | .09* | -.12** | .10* | — | | |
| 19. Alcohol/marijuana use | .16** | -.02 | -.09* | .22** | .12** | -.06 | .13** | .47** | — | |
| 20. Hard drug use | .16** | .08 | -.08 | .11* | .11* | -.12** | .15** | .37** | .60** | — |
| 21. Number of different sexual partners | .27** | .20** | -.09* | .14** | .02 | -.16** | .07 | .71** | .33** | .33** |
| 22. Nonvictimizing strategy | .05 | .01 | -.10* | .13** | .15** | -.16** | .09 | .34** | .39** | .34** |
| 23. Survival sex | .20** | .12** | -.06 | .07 | .01 | -.16** | .04 | .38** | .24** | .30** |
| 24. Victimizing strategy | .13** | .00 | -.15** | .09* | .13** | -.10* | .07 | .39** | .44** | .37** |
| 25. Physical victimization | .26** | .17** | -.16** | .27** | .21** | -.22** | .10* | .47** | .38** | .36** |
| 26. Sexual victimization | .19** | .27** | -.09* | .16** | .06 | -.19** | .05 | .33** | .14** | .17** |
| 27. Depressive symptoms | .23** | .16** | .02 | .00 | .08 | -.20** | .00 | .20** | .08 | .13** |
| 28. Depression | .16** | .15** | .03 | -.02 | .08 | -.17** | .01 | .13** | .07 | .10* |
| 29. PTSD | .09* | .08 | -.04 | .14** | .07 | -.16** | -.04 | .23** | .07 | .05 |
| Mean | 12.50 | .24 | 13.49 | .63 | .34 | 2.13 | 2.47 | .45 | 6.36 | 1.27 |
| SD | 4.72 | .43 | 2.49 | 1.77 | .47 | 2.16 | 2.44 | .27 | 4.81 | 1.92 |

Table 10A.1 (cont.)

| | 21 | 22 | 23 | 24 | 25 | 26 | 27 | 28 | 29 |
|---|---|---|---|---|---|---|---|---|---|
| 1. Gender | | | | | | | | | |
| 2. Change in family structure | | | | | | | | | |
| 3. Change in family residence | | | | | | | | | |
| 4. Parental alcohol/drug use | | | | | | | | | |
| 5. Parental serious crime | | | | | | | | | |
| 6. Parental depression | | | | | | | | | |
| 7. Warmth/support | | | | | | | | | |
| 8. Monitoring | | | | | | | | | |
| 9. Rejection | | | | | | | | | |
| 10. Neglect | | | | | | | | | |
| 11. Physical abuse | | | | | | | | | |
| 12. Sexual abuse | | | | | | | | | |
| 13. Age at first run | | | | | | | | | |
| 14. Time on own | | | | | | | | | |
| 15. Ever on street | | | | | | | | | |
| 16. Family support | | | | | | | | | |
| 17. Friend support | | | | | | | | | |
| 18. Deviant peers | | | | | | | | | |
| 19. Alcohol/marijuana use | | | | | | | | | |
| 20. Hard drug use | | | | | | | | | |
| 21. Different sexual partners | — | | | | | | | | |
| 22. Nonvictimizing strategy | .32** | — | | | | | | | |
| 23. Trade sex | .83** | .32** | — | | | | | | |
| 24. Victimizing strategy | .33** | .56** | .33** | — | | | | | |
| 25. Physical victimization | .46** | .45** | .37** | .48** | — | | | | |
| 26. Sexual victimization | .40** | .17** | .31** | .12** | .41** | — | | | |
| 27. Depressive symptoms | .22** | .09 | .20** | .10* | .28** | .30** | — | | |
| 28. Depression | .19** | .07 | .18** | .09* | .24** | .29** | .82** | — | |
| 29. PTSD | .26** | .15** | .21** | .07 | .26** | .29** | .34** | .24** | — |
| Mean | 1.09 | .60 | .45 | .77 | 2.84 | .16 | 22.05 | .33 | .39 |
| SD | 1.51 | .86 | 1.16 | 1.20 | 2.99 | .37 | 12.20 | .47 | .49 |

* $p < .05$.    ** $p < .01$.

*Table 10A.2.*   List of Traumatic Events from the PTSD Screener

Assaulted with a weapon/Beaten or hit with an item/Cut with a knife/Shot at/Being shot
Assaulted/Beaten up
Raped by acquaintance/friend/someone R knows
Gang raped/Raped by several people
Raped by stranger/Raped
Sexual assault/Sexual abuse
Unwanted sexual advances or requests
Victim of robbery/Armed robbery
Threatened with weapon/gun/knife/Had gun held to head/throat
Threatened with fists/People following R/Fear of trespassers/Threatened with bodily harm/
    Threatened by former abuser/Threatened with death
Parent threatened to take her to shelter/lock-up
Interrogated by police/Arrested by police/Police raid/Hiding from police/Fighting with police/
    Going to youth detention
Fight with friend/relative/Argument with parent/Yelled at
Physical fight with parent/boyfriend/friend
Kicked out of school/Suspended
Death of relative (not parent/caretaker)/Death of friend
Witnessed friend shot and killed/Friend/relative killed dealing drugs/Witnessed friends/
    significant other get shot
Cops forced R to return home/Forced to go back home/Being sent home/Not wanting to
    go home
Becoming homeless/Surviving on own/Being on streets/Sleeping in park/car/dumpster/vacant
    building/Cold and without shelter/Alone in the city/Worrying about where to stay/
    No money
Looking for place to stay/Almost evicted for trailer/Left family in different city
Unable to pay rent/Evicted from home with parent
Kicked out of foster home/relative's home/parent's home
Was in car wreck/Hit by car/Involved in car accident
Involved with people with bad criminal record
Jumping off train
Gang initiation
Getting pregnant and adopting child to others/R's child taken away/Becoming pregnant
Whole day without food/Going without food/Worried about starving/Had to steal food
Being on street during the holidays/Depressed not having normal life/Difficult to be on run
    on birthday
Injury to friend/relative/child
Not knowing what or who will be in your life/Feeling alone and abandoned/Feeling alone
    and humiliated/No one to give comfort and understanding/Having to be bad to get attention
Learned parent did not care about her/Parent did not want to see R/Caretaker no longer
    wanted R/Parent changed phone number
Living with father was a nightmare from hell, never knew what to expect or where to go
Dislikes shelter staff/Shelter staff always against you/Getting sent to shelter/Being in shelter so
long/Having to live in shelter
Friend's parents no longer respect R/R flipped out in front of friend's parents/significant other's
    parents mad at R
Went to a 24-hour study area and had to stay all night/No sleep
Nothing/No answer/None

*(cont.)*

*Table 10A.2.* *(Cont.)*

Friend died of AIDS
Dependency on friends
Breakup with boyfriend/girlfriend/Potential breakup
Finding out mother and stepfather might divorce/Parents divorce
Eating disorders
House burned down
Caught shoplifting
Victim of carjacking/Attempted carjacking
Physical abuse by boyfriend
Being stranded
Sent to hospital by parents & police for drug, alcohol, & suicide evaluation/Sent to detox/
    Stay in mental hospital
Perpetrator of an armed robbery
Shooting a friend while under the influence of drugs
Watching friend/someone die of overdose
R attempted/threatened suicide
Not being able to console mom because of fear of sexually abusive brother-in-law
Being taken away from boyfriend/Caseworker allowed no contact with boyfriend
Death of R's pet
R sustained injury/Had to go to hospital/R was sick
Sleeping on couch with another person
Being forced to do drugs and have sex with someone
Being depressed because unable to take part in social activities/Cannot use phone
Separated from siblings/Not able to have contact with sibling
Trying to stay away from parent
Friend tried to kill R and instead killed self
Witness someone getting beaten up and robbed/Witness sexual assault of friends/Witness fight
Physical abuse by caretaker and kicked out of house/Physical abuse by caretaker
Gang fight involved shooting/Witness to a shooting/Witness to death (not friends)
Concerns and worries about friend/girlfriend/parents/home/child
Becoming skinny and sickly because of drug use/Upset about drug use/Bad drug experience
Childcare worker losing job at placement
No clean clothing/Had to steal clothes/No clothing
Constantly reliving the abuse and walking scared/Abused (not specific)
Wanting to be with relative/parent/Wanting to go home
Victim of drive by shooting
Death of parent
Parent was worried/disappointed with R/R afraid parent would be upset with R because of run
Parent did not want R to attend school
Almost got caught with drugs
Involved in gang rape (perpetrator)
Relative turned R in
Parent's alcohol problem
Parent caught R on the run
Parent disappeared
Parent attempted suicide
Perpetrator of a drive by shooting
Kicked out of Job Corps
R developed drinking problem

*(cont.)*

*Table 10A.2.    (Cont.)*

Falsely accused of stealing
Parent physically abused by partner/other parent
Kidnapped by stranger
Drug deal went bad
Friend was arrested
Became a ward of state
Parent yelling and throwing things
Can't take care of child
Separated from parent because no room at adult shelter
People in house arguing/fighting
Parent/caretaker has medical condition
Friend threatened suicide
"Lost" friend
R has anger problems
Caseworker allowed police on R
State will not allow visits with parent
Prostitution

Table 11A.1.  Bivariate Correlation Matrix for Chapter 11 Regression Models

| | 1 | 2 | 3 | 4 | 5 | 6 | 7 | 8 | 9 | 10 |
|---|---|---|---|---|---|---|---|---|---|---|
| 1. Gender | — | | | | | | | | | |
| 2. Change in family structure | -.11* | — | | | | | | | | |
| 3. Change in family residence | -.10* | .21** | — | | | | | | | |
| 4. Parental alcohol/drug use | -.08 | .12** | .01 | — | | | | | | |
| 5. Parental serious crime | -.02 | .13** | .15** | .31** | — | | | | | |
| 6. Parental depression | -.11* | .08 | .08 | .17** | .06 | — | | | | |
| 7. Warmth/support | .10* | -.12** | -.12** | -.14** | -.08 | -.08 | — | | | |
| 8. Monitoring | -.11** | -.07 | -.10* | -.04 | -.03 | -.01 | .44** | — | | |
| 9. Rejection | -.13** | .13** | .07 | .12** | .02 | .13** | -.79** | -.35** | — | |
| 10. Neglect | -.06 | .06 | .02 | .16** | .14** | .09* | -.22** | -.19** | .24** | — |
| 11. Physical abuse | -.12** | .18** | .07 | .26** | .19** | .16** | -.36** | -.17** | .40** | .41** |
| 12. Sexual abuse | -.25** | .12** | .09* | .24** | .15** | .17** | -.11** | -.02 | .14** | .19** |
| 13. Age at first run | -.03 | -.10* | -.09 | -.15** | -.14** | -.04 | .06 | .14** | -.03 | -.24** |
| 14. Time on own | .09* | -.01 | -.02 | .06 | .01 | .07 | -.15** | -.18** | .10* | .13** |
| 15. Ever on street | .12** | -.04 | -.03 | .07 | .09 | .02 | -.05 | -.12** | .04 | .08 |
| 16. Family support | .02 | -.09* | -.01 | -.04 | .01 | -.09* | .29** | .19** | -.26** | -.21** |
| 17. Friend support | -.08 | .06 | .10* | .07 | .10* | .03 | -.19** | -.02 | .15** | .01 |
| 18. Deviant peers | .00 | .12** | .07 | .17** | .18** | .16** | -.17** | -.24** | .20** | .27** |
| 19. Alcohol/marijuana use | .15** | .08 | .05 | .15** | .09* | .10* | -.15** | -.24** | .16** | .13** |
| 20. Hard drug use | .15** | .06 | .06 | .11* | .03 | .15** | -.09* | -.22** | .10* | .12** |
| 21. Different sexual partners | -.06 | .05 | .10* | .16** | .08 | .15** | -.18** | -.22** | .20** | .26** |
| 22. Nonvictimizing strategy | .27** | -.02 | -.03 | .02 | -.03 | .07 | -.05 | -.21** | .07 | .07 |
| 23. Trade sex | .00 | .00 | .10* | .07 | -.03 | .13** | -.18** | -.21** | .18** | .15** |
| 24. Victimizing strategy | .32** | .00 | .04 | .06 | .06 | .05 | -.07 | -.25** | .08 | .12** |
| 25. Physical victimization | .20** | .04 | -.01 | .15** | .18** | .18** | -.11** | -.20** | .12** | .26** |
| 26. Sexual victimization | -.15** | .09* | -.06 | .16** | .11* | .14** | -.07 | -.06 | .09* | .19** |
| 27. Substance use | .14** | .05 | .01 | .13** | .04 | .10* | -.13** | -.19** | .12** | .09* |
| 28. Externalization problems | -.10* | .06 | .05 | .05 | .19** | .08 | -.09* | -.10* | .14** | .08 |
| Mean | .40 | 1.89 | 1.41 | .96 | .47 | .25 | 29.83 | 14.75 | 14.05 | .32 |
| SD | .49 | 1.97 | 2.06 | .77 | .65 | .43 | 9.91 | 4.01 | 4.49 | .47 |

(cont.)

*Table 11A.1 (cont.)*

| | 11 | 12 | 13 | 14 | 15 | 16 | 17 | 18 | 19 | 20 |
|---|---|---|---|---|---|---|---|---|---|---|
| 1. Gender | | | | | | | | | | |
| 2. Change in family structure | | | | | | | | | | |
| 3. Change in family residence | | | | | | | | | | |
| 4. Parental alcohol/drug use | | | | | | | | | | |
| 5. Parental serious crime | | | | | | | | | | |
| 6. Parental depression | | | | | | | | | | |
| 7. Warmth/support | | | | | | | | | | |
| 8. Monitoring | | | | | | | | | | |
| 9. Rejection | | | | | | | | | | |
| 10. Neglect | | | | | | | | | | |
| 11. Physical abuse | — | | | | | | | | | |
| 12. Sexual abuse | .31** | — | | | | | | | | |
| 13. Age at first run | -.20** | -.17** | — | | | | | | | |
| 14. Total time on own | .15** | .10* | -.14** | — | | | | | | |
| 15. Ever on street | .07 | .05 | -.13** | .25** | — | | | | | |
| 16. Continued family support | -.18** | -.09* | .06 | -.17** | -.14** | — | | | | |
| 17. Friend support | .11* | .09* | -.09 | .06 | .05 | -.38** | — | | | |
| 18. Affiliation with deviant peers | .29** | .16** | -.14** | .22** | .10* | -.12** | .09* | — | | |
| 19. Alcohol/marijuana use | .15** | -.02 | -.08 | .21** | .12** | -.06 | .12** | .47** | — | |
| 20. Hard drug use | .15** | .08 | -.08 | .12** | .10* | -.11* | .15—** | .36** | .59** | — |
| 21. Number of different sexual partners | .27** | .21** | -.09* | .15** | .03 | -.16** | .07 | .71** | .31** | .32** |
| 22. Nonvictimizing strategy | .04 | .01 | -.06 | .12** | .17** | -.17** | .07 | .34** | .39** | .31** |
| 23. Survival sex | .19** | .12** | -.05 | .07 | .01 | -.16** | .04 | .38** | .23** | .30** |
| 24. Victimizing strategy | .12** | .00 | -.13** | .08 | .14** | -.11* | .06 | .39** | .44** | .35** |
| 25. Physical victimization | .25** | .17** | -.15** | .27** | .21** | -.21** | .10* | .47** | .37** | .35** |
| 26. Sexual victimization | .21** | .28** | -.10* | .18** | .06 | -.18** | .06 | .34** | .14** | .17** |
| 27. Substance use | .10* | .01 | -.05 | .17** | .08 | -.04 | .07 | .40** | .82** | .53** |
| 28. Externalization problems | .17** | .14** | -.09 | .02 | .04 | .00 | .08 | .32** | .29** | .23** |
| Mean | 12.46 | .23 | 13.50 | .61 | .34 | 2.12 | 2.44 | .45 | 6.37 | 1.26 |
| SD | 4.74 | .42 | 2.50 | 1.78 | .47 | 2.15 | 2.43 | .27 | 4.79 | 1.91 |

Table 11A.1 (cont.)

| | 21 | 22 | 23 | 24 | 25 | 26 | 27 | 28 | 29 |
|---|---|---|---|---|---|---|---|---|---|
| 1. Gender | | | | | | | | | |
| 2. Change in family structure | | | | | | | | | |
| 3. Change in family residence | | | | | | | | | |
| 4. Parental alcohol/drug use | | | | | | | | | |
| 5. Parental serious crime | | | | | | | | | |
| 6. Parental depression | | | | | | | | | |
| 7. Warmth/support | | | | | | | | | |
| 8. Monitoring | | | | | | | | | |
| 9. Rejection | | | | | | | | | |
| 10. Neglect | | | | | | | | | |
| 11. Physical abuse | | | | | | | | | |
| 12. Sexual abuse | | | | | | | | | |
| 13. Age at first run | | | | | | | | | |
| 14. Total time on own | | | | | | | | | |
| 15. Ever on street | | | | | | | | | |
| 16. Continued family support | | | | | | | | | |
| 17. Friend support | | | | | | | | | |
| 18. Deviant peers | | | | | | | | | |
| 19. Alcohol/marijuana use | | | | | | | | | |
| 20. Hard drug use | | | | | | | | | |
| 21. Different sexual partners | — | | | | | | | | |
| 22. Nonvictimizing strategy | .32** | — | | | | | | | |
| 23. Trade sex | .82** | .32** | — | | | | | | |
| 24. Victimizing strategy | .32** | .57** | .33** | — | | | | | |
| 25. Physical victimization | .45** | .43** | .37** | .48** | — | | | | |
| 26. Sexual victimization | .41** | .15** | .32** | .10* | .40** | — | | | |
| 27. Substance use | .24** | .33** | .17** | .38** | .33** | .09* | — | | |
| 28. Externalization problems | .16** | .12** | .14** | .29** | .22** | .13** | .30** | — | |
| | | | | | | | | | |
| Mean | 1.09 | .62 | .45 | .80 | 2.84 | .15 | .43 | .50 | |
| SD | 1.50 | .88 | 1.15 | 1.21 | 3.01 | .36 | .50 | .50 | |

$p < .05.$    $p < .01.$

Table 12A.1. Bivariate Correlation Matrix for Chapter 12 Structural Equation Models

| | 1 | 2 | 3 | 4 | 5 | 6 | 7 | 8 | 9 | 10 | Mean | SD |
|---|---|---|---|---|---|---|---|---|---|---|---|---|
| 1. Parents behavioral problems | — | .26** | .12* | .18** | .12* | .10 | .09 | .16** | .09 | .02 | 0.77 | 0.42 |
| 2. Abuse | .24** | — | .20** | .31** | .14* | .21** | .18** | .39** | .20** | .05 | 0.52 | 0.34 |
| 3. Time on own | -.09 | .18** | — | .25** | .17* | .20** | .09 | .32** | .03 | .24** | 3.94 | 1.77 |
| 4. Deviant peers | .11 | .28** | .17* | — | .43** | .42** | .33** | .50** | .16** | .24** | 0.46 | 0.29 |
| 5. Drug use | .03 | .21** | .16* | .49** | — | .33** | .26** | .40** | .17** | .12* | 3.03 | 2.39 |
| 6. Deviant subsistent strategies | .13 | .18** | -.01 | .51** | .50** | — | .37** | .41** | .10 | .12* | 0.67 | 1.21 |
| 7. Survival sex | -.04 | .26** | .09 | .49** | .35** | .35** | — | .41** | .22** | .20** | 0.47 | 1.20 |
| 8. Victimization | .05 | .33** | .21** | .52** | .41** | .49** | .45** | — | .33** | .33** | 0.27 | 0.29 |
| 9. Depressive symptoms | .14* | .27** | .02 | .26** | .18** | .24** | .16* | .41** | — | .26** | 23.59 | 12.59 |
| 10. PTSD | .02 | .22** | .02 | .19** | .05 | .15* | .24** | .36** | .42** | — | 0.46 | 0.50 |
| Mean | 0.71 | 0.37 | 4.24 | 0.46 | 3.89 | 1.79 | 0.46 | 0.29 | 19.88 | 0.31 | | |
| SD | 0.45 | 0.29 | 1.71 | 0.26 | 2.84 | 1.74 | 1.15 | 0.25 | 11.56 | 0.46 | | |

* $p < .05$.　** $p < .01$.
Note: Females above diagonal and males below diagonal.

Table 12A.2.  Decomposition of Effects for Adolescent Females' Structural Equation Model

| Predictor Variable | Family Abuse | Time on Own | Deviant Peers | Drug Use | Outcome Variable — Deviant Subsistence | Risky Sex | Street Victimization | Internal Problems |
|---|---|---|---|---|---|---|---|---|
| **Parent Problems** | | | | | | | | |
| Direct | 0.46 *** | −0.15 * | 0.01 | 0.17 ** | 0.03 | 0.08 | — | — |
| Indirect | — | 0.13 *** | 0.15 *** | 0.02 | 0.09 * | 0.06 | 0.20 *** | 0.17 ** |
| Total | 0.46 *** | −0.03 | 0.16 ** | 0.20 *** | 0.12 * | 0.14 * | 0.20 *** | 0.17 ** |
| **Family Abuse** | | | | | | | | |
| Direct | | 0.28 *** | 0.32 *** | −0.08 | 0.07 | 0.02 | 0.21 *** | 0.08 |
| Indirect | | — | — | 0.16 *** | 0.15 *** | 0.11 *** | 0.18 *** | 0.22 *** |
| Total | | 028 *** | 0.32 *** | 0.08 | 0.22 *** | 0.13 * | 0.39 *** | 0.30 *** |
| **Time on Own** | | | | | | | | |
| Direct | | | — | 0.09 * | 0.07 | 0.00 | 0.17 *** | 0.00 |
| Indirect | | | — | — | — | — | 0.02 | 0.10 ** |
| Total | | | — | 0.09 * | 0.07 | 0.00 | 0.19 *** | 0.10 |
| **Deviant Peers** | | | | | | | | |
| Direct | | | | 0.42 *** | 0.40 *** | 0.34 *** | 0.22 *** | 0.04 |
| Indirect | | | | — | — | — | 0.18 *** | 0.25 *** |
| Total | | | | 0.42 *** | 0.40 *** | 0.34 *** | 0.40 *** | 029 *** |
| **Drug Use** | | | | | | | | |
| Direct | | | | | — | — | 0.14 ** | 0.06 |
| Indirect | | | | | — | — | — | 0.08 ** |
| Total | | | | | — | — | 0.14 ** | 0.14 |
| **Deviant Subsistence** | | | | | | | | |
| Direct | | | | | | — | 0.12 * | −0.16 |
| Indirect | | | | | | — | — | 0.06 * |
| Total | | | | | | — | 0.12 * | −0.09 |
| **Risky Sex** | | | | | | | | |
| Direct | | | | | | — | 0.22 *** | 0.21 ** |
| Indirect | | | | | | | — | 0.12 ** |
| Total | | | | | | — | 0.22 *** | 0.33 *** |
| **Street Victimization** | | | | | | | | |
| Direct | | | | | | — | — | 0.55 *** |
| Indirect | | | | | | | — | — |
| Total | | | | | | — | — | 0.55 *** |

Table 12A.3. Decomposition of Effects for Adolescent Males' Structural Equation Model

| Predictor Variable | Outcome | | | | | | | |
|---|---|---|---|---|---|---|---|---|
| | Family Abuse | Time on Own | Deviant Peers | Drug Use | Deviant Subsistence | Risky Sex | Street Victimization | Internal Problems |
| Parent Problems | | | | | | | | |
| Direct | 0.33 *** | -.20 ** | 0.11 | 0.04 | 0.12 | -0.27 *** | — | — |
| Indirect | — | 0.08 ** | 0.08 ** | 0.09 * | 0.11 ** | 0.17 ** | 0.12 * | 0.17 ** |
| Total | 0.33 ** | -0.11 | 0.19 *** | 0.13 | 0.22 *** | -0.10 | 0.12 * | 0.17 ** |
| Family Abuse | | | | | | | | |
| Direct | | 0.25 *** | 0.24 *** | 0.07 | 0.03 | 0.23 ** | 0.14 ** | 0.24 *** |
| Indirect | — | — | — | 0.12 *** | 0.09 ** | 0.10 ** | 0.18 *** | 0.15 ** |
| Total | | 0.25 *** | 0.24 *** | 0.19 ** | 0.12 | 0.33 *** | 0.32 *** | 0.39 *** |
| Time on Own | | | | | | | | |
| Direct | | | — | 0.07 | -0.09 * | -0.07 | 0.13 ** | -0.13 |
| Indirect | | | — | — | — | — | -0.03 | 0.05 |
| Total | | | — | 0.07 | -0.09 | -0.07 | 0.10 | -0.08 |
| Deviant Peers | | | | | | | | |
| Direct | | | | 0.43 *** | 0.48 *** | 0.48 *** | 0.19 ** | 0.08 |
| Indirect | | | | — | — | — | 0.24 *** | 0.21 *** |
| Total | | | | 0.43 *** | 0.48 *** | 0.48 *** | 0.43 *** | 0.29 *** |
| Drug Use | | | | | | | | |
| Direct | | | | | — | — | 0.05 | -0.12 |
| Indirect | | | | | — | — | — | 0.03 |
| Total | | | | | — | — | 0.05 | -0.09 |
| Deviant Subsistence | | | | | | | | |
| Direct | | | | | | — | 0.28 *** | 0.03 |
| Indirect | | | | | | — | — | 0.16 *** |
| Total | | | | | | — | 0.28 *** | 0.19 |
| Risky Sex | | | | | | | | |
| Direct | | | | | | | 0.18 ** | -0.01 |
| Indirect | | | | | | | — | 0.10 ** |
| Total | | | | | | | 0.18 ** | 0.09 |
| Street Victimization | | | | | | | | |
| Direct | | | | | | | | 0.59 *** |
| Indirect | | | | | | | | — |
| Total | | | | | | | | 0.59 *** |

Table 13A.1. Bivariate Correlation Matrix for Chapter 13 Regression Model

| | 1 | 2 | 3 | 4 | 5 | 6 | 7 | 8 | 9 | 10 |
|---|---|---|---|---|---|---|---|---|---|---|
| 1. Resiliency | — | | | | | | | | | |
| 2. Gender | -.04 | — | | | | | | | | |
| 3. Family transition | .05 | -.09 | — | | | | | | | |
| 4. Geographic transitions | .00 | -.11* | .23** | — | | | | | | |
| 5. Parent drug | .00 | -.05 | .10* | .04 | — | | | | | |
| 6. Parent's serious crimes | .10* | -.01 | .11* | .12* | .33** | — | | | | |
| 7. Parent's depression | .05 | -.11* | .05 | .09 | .16** | .09 | — | | | |
| 8. Warmth | -.08 | .09 | -.12* | -.13** | -.11* | -.03 | -.12* | — | | |
| 9. Monitor | -.10* | -.13** | -.06 | -.09 | -.03 | -.02 | -.03 | .45** | — | |
| 10. Rejection | .10* | -.11* | .13** | .09 | .09* | -.04 | .18** | -.78** | -.36** | — |
| 11. Neglect | -.05 | -.08 | .06 | .05 | .17** | .17** | .10* | -.19** | -.17* | .22** |
| 12. Physical abuse | .08 | -.12* | .17** | .09 | .25** | .20** | .20** | -.35** | -.17** | .38** |
| 13. Sexual abuse | .06 | -.22** | .10* | .11* | .23** | .17** | .18** | -.10* | -.03 | .15** |
| 14. Age at first run | -.06 | -.01 | -.15** | -.07 | -.15** | -.15** | -.08 | .05 | .14** | -.05 |
| 15. Time on own | .04 | .10* | .01 | -.05 | .03 | .00 | .09 | -.11* | -.16** | .06 |
| 16. Ever on the streets | .09 | .12* | -.02 | -.05 | .06 | .11 | .02 | -.03 | -.08 | .01 |
| 17. Family support | -.05 | .03 | -.11** | -.03 | -.04 | -.00 | -.11* | .31** | .17** | -.26** |
| 18. Friend support | .02 | -.11* | .07 | .08 | .11* | .10 | .06 | -.20** | .01 | .15** |
| 19. Deviant peers | .17** | .01 | .08 | .08 | .12* | .16** | .17** | -.12* | -.20** | .14** |
| 20. Alcohol/marijuana use | .13** | .19** | .07 | .03 | .11* | .08 | .08 | -.09 | -.18** | .11* |
| 21. Hard drugs | .13** | .17** | .04 | .06 | .08 | .01 | .15** | -.04 | -.19** | .06 |
| 22. Number of different sexual partners | .09 | -.00 | .02 | .11* | .07 | .07 | .05 | -.14** | -.11* | .16** |
| 23. Nonvictimizing strategy | .09 | .30** | .01 | -.02 | .01 | -.01 | .09 | -.03 | -.17** | .06 |
| 24. Survival sex | .03 | .01 | -.02 | .03 | .03 | -.06 | .10* | -.09 | -.17** | .10* |
| 25. Victimizing strategy | .19** | .35** | .00 | .02 | .06 | .06 | .07 | -.06 | -.23** | .07 |
| 26. Physical victimization | .13** | .22** | .03 | .00 | .13** | .19** | .21** | -.08 | -.17** | .09 |
| 27. Sexual victimization | .04 | -.13** | .07 | -.04 | .14** | .10* | .13** | -.06 | -.06 | .08 |
| Mean | .84 | .39 | 1.87 | 1.36 | 1.00 | .48 | .25 | 29.36 | 14.49 | 14.35 |
| SD | .37 | .49 | 1.96 | 1.99 | .76 | .65 | .43 | 10.05 | 4.08 | 4.52 |

(cont.)

Table 13A.1 (cont.)

| | 11 | 12 | 13 | 14 | 15 | 16 | 17 | 18 | 19 | 20 |
|---|---|---|---|---|---|---|---|---|---|---|
| 1. Resiliency | | | | | | | | | | |
| 2. Gender | | | | | | | | | | |
| 3. Transition family | | | | | | | | | | |
| 4. Tran Geo | | | | | | | | | | |
| 5. Parent drug | | | | | | | | | | |
| 6. Parent's serious crimes | | | | | | | | | | |
| 7. Parent's depression | | | | | | | | | | |
| 8. Warmth | | | | | | | | | | |
| 9. Monitor | | | | | | | | | | |
| 10. Rejection | | | | | | | | | | |
| 11. Neglect | — | | | | | | | | | |
| 12. Physical abuse | .41** | — | | | | | | | | |
| 13. Sexual abuse | .23** | .33** | — | | | | | | | |
| 14. Age at first run | -.26** | -.25** | -.20** | — | | | | | | |
| 15. Time on own | .10* | .15** | .11* | -.17** | — | | | | | |
| 16. Ever on the streets | .08 | .08 | .07 | -.15** | .23** | — | | | | |
| 17. Family support | -.23** | -.20** | -.10* | .11* | -.18** | -.14** | — | | | |
| 18. Friend support | .02 | .09 | .11* | -.14** | .04 | .08 | -.36** | — | | |
| 19. Deviant peers | .29** | .25** | .14** | -.18** | .15** | .07 | -.10* | .07 | — | |
| 20. Alcohol/marijuana use | .11* | .13** | -.04 | -.10* | .11* | .09 | -.03 | .11* | .41** | — |
| 21. Hard drugs | .09 | .13** | .08 | -.10* | .07 | .10* | -.10* | .14** | .34** | .57** |
| 22. Number of different sexual partners | .05 | .16** | .05 | -.04 | -.00 | -.00 | -.03 | .12* | .32** | .33** |
| 23. Nonvictimizing strategy | .08 | .04 | .01 | -.08 | .07 | .10* | -.15** | .09 | .32** | .36** |
| 24. Survival sex | .17** | .18** | .11* | -.07 | .08 | -.01 | -.13** | .02 | .34** | .22** |
| 25. Victimizing strategy | .13** | .13** | .01 | -.12* | .02 | .06 | -.10* | .06 | .37** | .42** |
| 26. Physical victimization | .27** | .23** | .17** | -.17** | .21** | .17** | -.21** | .08 | .43** | .33** |
| 27. Sexual victimization | .21** | .22** | .26** | -.14** | .19** | .05 | -.18** | .07 | .33** | .10* |
| Mean | 0.33 | 12.77 | 0.24 | 13.58 | 0.82 | 0.36 | 2.06 | 2.51 | 0.48 | 6.96 |
| SD | 0.47 | 4.68 | 0.43 | 2.51 | 1.70 | 0.48 | 2.13 | 2.44 | 0.27 | 4.64 |

Table 13A.1 (cont.)

| | 21 | 22 | 23 | 24 | 25 | 26 | 27 |
|---|---|---|---|---|---|---|---|
| 1. Resiliency | | | | | | | |
| 2. Gender | | | | | | | |
| 3. Transition family | | | | | | | |
| 4. Tran Geo | | | | | | | |
| 5. Parent drug | | | | | | | |
| 6. Parent's serious crimes | | | | | | | |
| 7. Parent's depression | | | | | | | |
| 8. Warmth | | | | | | | |
| 9. Monitor | | | | | | | |
| 10. Rejection | | | | | | | |
| 11. Neglect | | | | | | | |
| 12. Physical abuse | | | | | | | |
| 13. Sexual abuse | | | | | | | |
| 14. Age at first run | | | | | | | |
| 15. Time on own | | | | | | | |
| 16. Ever on the streets | | | | | | | |
| 17. Family support | | | | | | | |
| 18. Friend support | | | | | | | |
| 19. Deviant peers | | | | | | | |
| 20. Alcohol/marijuana use | | | | | | | |
| 21. Hard drugs | — | | | | | | |
| 22. Number of different sexual partners | .28** | — | | | | | |
| 23. Nonvictimizing strategy | .32** | .16** | — | | | | |
| 24. Survival sex | .26** | .27** | .23** | — | | | |
| 25. Victimizing strategy | .35** | .24** | .56** | .25** | — | | |
| 26. Physical victimization | .34** | .19** | .42** | .29** | .47** | — | |
| 27. Sexual victimization | .16** | .13** | .15** | .29** | .11* | .41** | — |
| Mean | 1.39 | 2.34 | 0.66 | 0.07 | 0.86 | 3.17 | 0.17 |
| SD | 1.99 | 1.76 | 0.89 | 0.26 | 1.25 | 3.12 | 0.38 |

$^*p < .05.$    $^{**}p < .01.$

# References

Achenbach, T. (1991). *Manual for the Youth Self-Report and 1991 Profile.* Burlington: University of Vermont.

American Psychiatric Association (1994). *Diagnostic and Statistical Manual of Mental Disorders,* 4th edition. Washington: DC: Author.

Anthony, E. (1974). The syndrome of the psychologically invulnerable child. Pp. 529–44 in *The Child and His Family: Vol 3, Children at Psychiatric Risk,* edited by E. Anthony & C. Koupernik. New York: Wiley.

Armsden, G., McCauley, E., Greenburg, M., Burke, P., & Mitchell, J. (1990). Parent and peer attachment in early adolescent depression. *Journal of Abnormal Child Psychology* 18:683–97.

Athey, J. (1991). HIV infection and homeless adolescents. *Child Welfare* 70:515–28.

Beardslee, M., & Podorefsky, M. (1988). Resilient adolescents whose parents have serious affective and other psychiatric disorders: Importance of self-understanding and relationships. *American Journal of Psychiatry* 145:63–69.

Belle, D., ed. (1989). *Children's Social Networks and Social Supports.* NY: Wiley.

Berger, I., & Schmidt, M. (1958). Results of child psychiatric and psychological investigations of spontaneous and reactive runaways. *Praxis Kinderpsychologie und Kinderpsychiatrie* 7:206–10.

Boney-McCoy, S. & Finkelhor, D. (1996). Is youth victimization related to trauma symptoms and depression after controlling for prior symptoms and family relationships? A longitudinal prospective study. *Journal of Counseling and Clinical Psychology* 64:1406–16.

Brennan, T. (1974). *Evaluation and Validation Regarding the National Strategy for Youth Development.* Boulder, CO: Behavioral Research Evaluation Program.

Brennan, T. (1980). Mapping the diversity among runaways: A descriptive multivariate analysis of selected social psychological background conditions. *Journal of Family Issues* 1:189–209.

Brennan, T., Huizinga, D., & Elliott, D. (1978). *The Social Psychology of Runaways.* Lexington, MA: D. C. Heath.

Brooks, R. (1994). Children at risk; Fostering resilience and hope. *American Journal of Orthopsychiatry* 64:545–53.

Bucy, J., & Obolensky, N. (1990). Runaway and homeless youths. Pp. 333–53 in *Planning to Live: Evaluating and Treating Suicidal Teens in Community Settings,* edited by M. Rotheram-Borus, J. Bradley, & N. Obolensky. Tulsa: University of Oklahoma Press.

Burbach, D., & Borduin, C. (1986). Parent-child relations and the etiology of depression: A review of methods and findings. *Clinical Psychology Review* 6:133–53.

Burge, D., & Hammen, C. (1991). Maternal communication: Predictors of outcome at follow-up in a sample of children at high and low risk for depression. *Journal of Abnormal Psychology* 100:174–80.

Carelton-Ford, S., Paikoff, R., & Brooks-Gunn, J. (1991). Methodological issues in the study of divergent views of the family. Pp. 87–102 in *New Directions for Child Development: Shared Views in the Family during Adolescence,* edited by R. Paikoff. San Francisco: Jossey-Bass.

Caspi, A., & Bem, D. (1990). Personality continuity and change across the life course. Pp. 549–75 in *Handbook of Personality Theory and Research,* edited by L. Pervin. New York: Guilford.

Caspi, A., Bem, D., & Elder, G. (1989). Continuities and consequences of interactional styles across the life course. *Journal of Personality* 57:375–406.

Caspi, A., & Elder, G. (1988). Emergent family patterns: The intergenerational construction of problem behavior and relations. Pp. 218–40 in *Relationships within Families,* edited by R. Hinde & J. Stevenson. Oxford England: Clarendon.

Caspi, A., Elder, G., & Bem, D. (1987). Moving against the world: Life-course patterns of explosive children. *Developmental Psychology* 23:308–13.

Cauce, A. M., Felner, R., & Primavera, J. (1982). Social support in high-risk adolescents: Structural components and adaptive impact. *American Journal of Community Psychology* 10:417–28.

Cauce, A. M., Paradise, M., Embry, L., Lohr, Y., & Wagner, V. (1997). Homeless youth in Seattle: Youth characteristics, mental health needs, and intensive case management. Pp. 257–67 in *Outcomes for Children and Youth with Emotional and Behavioral Disorders and Their Families: Programs and Evaluation Best Practices,* edited by M. Epstein, K. Kutash, & A. Duchnowski. Austin, TX: Pro-Ed.

Cauce, A. M., & Srebnik, D. (1989). Peer social networks and social support: A focus for preventive efforts with youth. Pp. 235–54 in *Primary Prevention in the Schools,* edited by L. Bond & B. Compas. Newbury Park, CA: Sage.

Center for Disease Control (1996). Youth Risk Behavior Surveillance—United States, 1995, MMWR:45 (No. ss-4), 1–86.

Claes, M. (1992). Friendship and personal adjustment during adolescence. *Journal of Adolescence* 15:39–55.

Clauson, J. (1991). Adolescent competence and the shaping of the life course. *American Journal of Sociology* 96:805–42.

Coie, J., & Dodge, K. (1983). Continuities and changes in children's social status: A 5-year longitudinal study. *Merrill-Palmer Quarterly* 29:262–82.

Committee on Health Care for Homeless People (1988). *Homelessness, Health, and Human Needs.* Washington, DC: National Academy Press.

Compas, B., Howell, D., Phares, V., Williams, R., & Ledoux, N. (1989). Parent and child stress and symptoms: An integrative analysis. *Developmental Psychology* 25:550–59.

Conger, R. & Elder, G. (1994). *Families in a Changing Society: Hard Times in Rural America*. Hawthorne, NY: Aldine de Gruyter.

Cotteral, J. (1994). Analyzing the strength of supportive ties in adolescent social supports. Pp. 196–270 in *Social Networks and Social Supports in Childhood and Adolescence*, edited by F. Nestman & K. Hurrelmann. Hawthorne, NY: Aldine de Gruyter.

Crystal, S. (1986). Psychosocial rehabilitation and homeless youth. *Psychosocial Rehabilitation Journal* 10:15–21.

Daddis, M., Braddock, D., Cuers, S., Elliott, A., & Kelly, A. (1993). Personal and family distress in homeless adolescents. *Community Mental Health Journal* 29: 413–22.

Daniels, D., & Moos, R. (1990). Assessing life stressors and social resources among adolescents: Applications to depressed youth. *Journal of Adolescent Research* 5:268–89.

Deblinger, E., McLeer, S., Atkins, M., Ralphe, D., & Foa, E. (1989). Post-traumatic stress in sexually abused, physically abused, and nonabused children. *Child Abuse & Neglect* 13:403–8.

Dodge, K. (1983). Behavioral antecedents of peer social status. *Child Development* 54:1396–99.

Donovan, J. & Jessor, R. (1985). Structure of problem behavior in adolescence and young adulthood. *Journal of Counseling and Consulting Psychology* 53:890–904.

Downey, G., & Walker, E. (1992). Distinguishing family-level and child-level influences on the development of depression and aggression in children at risk. *Development and Psychopathology* 4, 81–95.

East, P., Hess, L., & Lerner, R. (1987). Peer social support and adjustment of early adolescent peer group. *Journal of Early Adolescence* 7:153–63.

Feital, B., Margetson, N., Chamas, J., & Lipman, C. (1992). Psychosocial background and behavioral and emotional disorders of homeless and runaway youth. *Hospital and Community Psychiatry* 43:155–59.

Fergusson, D., Horwood, L. & Lynskey, M. (1994). The childhoods of multiple problem adolescents: A 15 year longitudinal study. *Journal of Child Psychology and Psychiatry* 32:1123–40.

Fergusson, D., & Lynskey, M. (1996). Adolescent resiliency to family adversity. *Journal of Child Psychology and Psychiatry* 37:281–92.

Ferran, E. & Sabatini, A. (1985). Homeless youth: The New York experience. *International Journal of Family Psychiatry* 6:117–28.

Finkelhor, D. (1984). *Child Sexual Abuse: New Theory and Research*. New York: Free Press.

Finkelhor, D., Hotaling, G., & Sedlak, A. (1990). Missing, abducted, runaway, and thrownaway children in America. Washington, DC: Office of Juvenile Justice and Delinquency Prevention.

Forehand, R., Brody, G., Slotkin, J., Fauber, R., McCombs, A., & Long, N. (1988). Young adolescents and maternal depression: Assessment, interrelations, and family predictors. *Journal of Consulting and Clinical Psychology* 56:422–26.

Furman, W., & Buhrmester, D. (1992). Age and sex differences in perceptions of networks of personal relationships. *Child Development* 63:103–15.

GAO (1989). Homeless and runaway youth receiving services at federally funded shelters. Report HRD-90-45. Washington DC: Author.

Garmezy, N. (1981). Children under stress: Perspectives on antecedents and correlates of vulnerability and resistance to psychopathology. Pp. 196–270 in *Further Explanations in Personality,* edited by A. Rubin, A. Aronoff, J. Barclay, & R. Zucker. New York: Wiley.

Garmezy, N. (1983). Stressors of childhood. Pp. 43–84 in *Stress, Coping, and Development in Children,* edited by edited by N. Garmezy & M. Rutter. New York: McGraw-Hill.

Garmezy, N., Masten, A., & Tellegen, A., (1984). The study of stress and competence in children: A building block for developmental psychopathology. *Child Development* 55:97–111.

Ge, Xiaojia, Lorenz, F., Conger, R., Elder, G., & Simons, R. (1994). Trajectories of stressful life events and depressive symptoms during adolescence. *Developmental Psychology* 30:467–83.

Godwin, J. (1985). Post-traumatic symptoms in incest victims. Pp. 157–68 in *Post-Traumatic Stress Disorder in Children,* edited by S. Eth & R. Pynoos. Los Angeles: American Psychiatric Association.

Goodman, L., Saxe, L., & Harvey, M. (1991). Homelessness as psychological trauma. *American Psychologist* 46:1219–25.

Hagen, J., & McCarthy, B. (1997). *Mean Streets: Youth Crime and Homelessness.* New York: Cambridge University Press.

Hauser, S., Vieyra, M., Jacobson, A., & Wertlieb, D. (1985). Vulnerability and resilience in adolescence: Views from the family. *Journal of Early Adolescence* 5:81–100.

Herronkohl, E., Herronkohl, R., & Egolf, B. (1994). Resilient early school age children from maltreating homes: Outcomes in late adolescence. *American Journal of Orthopsychiatry* 64:301–9.

Hersch, P. (1988). Coming of age on city streets. *Psychology Today,* January, pp. 28–37.

Homer, L. (1973). Community-based resources for runaway girls. *Social Casework* 54:473–79.

House Committee on Education and Labor, Subcommittee on Human Resources (1984). *Juvenile Justice, Runaway Youth, and Missing Children's Act,* amendments 98th Congress, 2nd session, 7 March, Y4, E8, 1:J98/15.

Hoyt, D., Whitbeck, L., & Cauce, A. (1999). Street Victimization and psychological distress among homeless adolescents: A longitudinal investigation of the risk amplification model. *American Journal of Community Psychology* (under review).

Haupt, D., & Offord, D. (1972). Runaways from a residential treatment center: A preliminary report. *Corrective Psychiatry and Journal of Social Therapy* 18:14–21.

Huesmann, L., Eron, L., Lefkowitz, M., & Walder, L. (1984). Stability of aggression over time and generation. *Developmental Psychology* 20:1120–34.

Jacobsen, R., Lahey, B., & Strauss, C. (1983). Correlates of depressed mood in normal children. *Journal of Abnormal Child Psychology* 11:29–39.

Janoff-Bulman, R. (1992). *Shattered Assumptions: Towards a New Psychology of Trauma.* New York: Free Press.

Janus, M., Burgess, A., & McCormack, A. (1987). Histories of sexual abuse in adolescent male runaways. *Adolescence* 22:405–17.

Janus, M., McCormack, A. Burgess, A., & Hartman, C. (1987). *Adolescent Runaways: Causes and Consequences.* Lexington, MA: Lexington.

Jessor, R., & Jessor, S. (1977). *Problem Behavior and Psychological Development: A Longitudinal Study of Youth.* New York: Academic Press.

Joreskog, K., & Sorbom, D. (1993). *PRELIS 2: A Program for Multivariate Data Screening and Data Summarization.* Chicago, IL: Scientific Software International.

Kandel, E., Mednick, S., Kirkegaard-Sorenson, L., Hutchings, B., Knop, J., Rosenberg, R., & Schulsinger, F. (1988). IQ as a protective factor for subjects a high risk for antisocial behavior. *Journal of Consulting and Clinical Psychology* 56:224–26.

Kauffman, C., Grunebaum, H. Cohler, B., & Garnett, E. (1979). Superkids: Competent children of psychotic mothers. *American Journal of Psychiatry* 36:1398–1402.

Kennedy, M. (1991). Homeless and runaway youth mental health issues: No access to the system. *Journal of Adolescent Health* 12:576–79.

Kipke, M., Montgomery, S., & MacKenzie, R. (1997). Substance abuse among youth seen at a community based clinic. *Journal of Adolescent Health* 14:289–94.

Kipke, M., Montgomery, S., Simon, T., & Unger, J. (1997). Homeless youth: Drug use patterns and HIV risk profiles according to peer group affiliation. *AIDS and Behavior* 1:247–59.

Kipke, M., Simon, T., Montgomery, S., Unger, J., & Iverson, E. (1997). Homeless youth and their exposure to violence while living on the streets. *Journal of Adolescent Health* 20:360–67.

Kipke, M., Simon, T., Montgomery, S., Unger, J., & Johnson, L. (1997). Homeless youth: drug use patterns and HIV risk profiles according to peer group affiliation. *AIDS and Behavior* 1:247–59.

Kiser, L., Ackerman, B., Brown, E., Edwards, N., McColgan, E., Pugh, R., & Pruitt, D. (1988). Post-traumatic stress disorder in younger children: A reaction to purported sexual abuse. *Journal of the American Academy of Child and Adolescent Psychiatry* 25:645–49.

Koopman, C., Rosario, M., & Rotheram-Borus, M. (1994). Alcohol and drug use and sexual behaviors placing runaways at risk for HIV infection. *Addictive Behaviors* 19:95–103.

Kufeldt, K., & Nimmo, M. (1987). Youth on the Street: Abuse and neglect in the eighties. *Child Abuse and Neglect* 11:531–43.

Kurtz, P., Kurtz, G., & Jarvis, S. (1991). Problems of maltreated runaway youth. *Adolescence* 26:544–55.

Larsen, R., & Prescott, S. (1977). The ecology of adolescent activity and experience. *Journal of Youth & Adolescence* 6:281–94.

Libertoff, K. (1980). The runaway child in America: A social history. *Journal of Family Issues* 1:151–64.

March, J. (1990). The nosology of posttraumatic stress disorder. *Journal of Anxiety Disorders* 4:61–82.

McCleer, S., Callagnan, M., Henry, D., & Wallen, J. (1994). Psychiatric disorders in sexually abused children. *Journal of the American Academy of Child and Adolescent Psychiatry* 33:313–19.

McLanahan, S., & Sandefur, G. (1994). *Growing Up with a Single Parent.* Cambridge, MA: Harvard University Press.

McNally, R. (1996). Assessment of posttraumatic stress disorder in children and adolescents. *Journal of School Psychology* 34:147–61.

Moffitt, T. (1997). Adolescent-limited and life-course-persistent offending: A complementary pair of theories. Pp. 11–54 in *Developmental Theories of Crime and Delinquency,* edited by T. Thornberry. New Brunswick, NJ: Transaction.

Moos, R., & Moos, B. (1981). *Family Environment Scale Manual.* Palo Alto, CA: Consulting Psychology Press.

Mundy, P., Robertson, J., Greenblatt, M., & Robertson, M. (1989). Residential instability in adolescent outpatients. *Journal of American Academy of Child and Adolescent Psychiatry* 28:176–81.

Mundy, P., Robertson, M., Robertson, J., & Greenblatt, M. (1990). The prevalence of psychotic symptoms in homeless adolescents. *Journal of the American Academy of Child/Adolescent Psychiatry* 29:724–31.

National Network of Runaway and Youth Services (1991). *To Whom Do They Belong? Runaway, Homeless, and Other Youth In High-Risk Situations in the 1990s.* Washington, DC: Author.

North, C., Smith, E., & Spitznagel, E. (1993). Is antisocial personality a valid diagnosis among the homeless? *American Journal of Psychiatry* 150:578–83.

Nye, I. (1980). Some social characteristics of runaways. *Journal of Family Issues* 1:147–50.

Parker, J., & Asher, S. (1988). Peer relations and later personal adjustment: Are low accepted children at risk? *Psychological Bulletin* 102:358–89.

Parker, G., Tupling, H., & Brown, L. (1979). A parental bonding instrument. *British Journal of Medical Psychology* 53:1–10.

Patterson, G. (1982). *Coercive Family Processes.* Eugene, OR: Castilia.

Patterson, G., Dishion, T., & Bank. L. (1984). Family interaction: A process model of deviancy training. *Aggressive Behavior* 10, 253–67.

Pelcovitz, D., Kaplan, S., Goldenberg, B., Mandel, F., Lehane, J., & Guarrera, J. (1994). Post-traumatic stress disorder in physically abused adolescents. *Journal of the American Academy of Child and Adolescent Psychiatry* 33:305–12.

Pennbridge, J., Freese, T., & Mackenzie, R. (1992). High risk behaviors among male street youth in Hollywood, California. *AIDS Education and Prevention* (Supplement):24–33.

Pennbridge, J., Yates, G., David, T., & Mackenzie, R. (1990). Runaway and homeless youth in Los Angeles Country, California. *Journal of Adolescent Health Care* 11:159–65.

Radloff, L. (1977). The CES-D scale: A self-report depression scale for research in the general population. *AppliedPsychological Measurement* 1:385–401.

Radloff, L. (1991). The use of the center for epidemiologic studies depression scale in adolescents and young adults. *Journal of Youth and Adolescence* 20:1991.

Rak, C., & Patterson, L. (1996). *Journal of Counseling and Development* 74:368–73.

Robertson, J. (1992). Homeless youths: An overview of the recent literature. Pp. 33–68 in *Homeless Children and Youth,* edited by J. Kryder-Coe, L. Salamon, & J. Monar. New Brunswick: Transaction.

Rosenberg, M. (1965). *Society and Adolescent Self-Image.* Princeton, NJ: Princeton University Press

Rotherum-Borus, M., Koopman, C., & Ehrhardt, A. (1991). Homeless youths and HIV infection. *American Psychologist* 46:1188–97.

Rotheram-Borus, M., Luna, G., Marotta, T., & Kelly, H. (1994). Going nowhere fast: Methamphetamine use and HIV infection. Pp. 155–83 in *The Context of HIV Risk among Drug Users and Their Sexual Partners* (National Institute on Drug Abuse Monograph No. 143), edited by R. Battjes, Z. Sloboda, & W. Grace. Roackeville, MD: U.S. Department of Health and Human Services.

Rotherum-Borus, M., Meyer-Bahlburg, H., Koopman, C., Rosario, M., Exner, T., Henerson, R., Matthieu, M., & Gruen, R. (1992). Lifetime sexual behaviors among runaway males and females. *Journal of Sex Research* 14:229–44.

Rotherum-Borus, M., Parra, M., Cantwell, C., Gwadz, M., & Murphey, D. (1996). Runaway and homeless youths. Pp. 369–91 in *Handbook of Adolescent Health Risk Behavior,* edited by R. DiClemente, W. Hansen, & L. Ponton. New York: Plenum.

Rotherum-Borus, M., Rosario, M., & Koopman, C. (1991). Minority youth at high risk: Gay males and runaways. Pp. 181–200 in *Adolescent Stress: Courses and Consequences,* edited by S. Gore & M. Colton. Hawthorne, NY: Aldine de Gruyter.

Rowe, D., Rodgers, J., Meseck-Bushey, S., & St. John, C. (1989). Sexual behavior and deviance: A sibling study of their relationship. *Developmental Psychology* 25:61–69.

Ruble, D., & Martin, C. (1998). Gender development. Pp. 933–1016 in *Handbook of Child Psychology,* vol. 3, edited by W. Damon & N. Eisenberg. New York: John Wiley.

Rutter, M. (1980). School influences on children's behavior and development. *Pediatrics* 65:598–611.

Rutter, M. (1985). Resilience in the face of adversity: Protective factors and resistance to psychiatric disorders. *British Journal of Psychiatry* 147:598–611.

Scientific Analysis Corporation (1974). The sick, the bad, and the free: A review of the runaway literature. San Francisco: Unpublished.

Saltonstall, M. (1984). *Street Youth and Runaways on the Streets of Boston: One Agency's Response.* Boston: The Bridge.

Schaffer, D., & Caton, C. (1984). *Runaway and Homeless Youth in New York City: A Report to the Ittleson Foundation.* New York: Division of Child Psychiatry, New York State Psychiatric Institute and Columbia University College of Physicians and Surgeons.

Schweitzer, R., & Hier, S. (1993). Psychological maladjustment among homeless adolescents. *Australian and New Zealand Journal of Psychiatry* 27:275–80.

Schweitzer, R., Hier, T., & Terry, D. (1994). Parental bonding, family systems, and environmental predictors of adolescent homelessness. *Journal of Emotional and Behavioral Disorders* 2:39–45.

Shalwitz, J., Goulart, M., Dunnigan, K., & Flannery, D. (1990). Prevalence of sexually transmitted diseases (STD) and HIV in a homeless youth medical clinic in San Francisco. Presentation at the Sixth Annual International Conference on AIDS, San Francisco.

Shane, P. (1996). *What About America's Homeless Children?* Thousand Oaks, CA: Sage.

Shellow, R., Schamp, J., Liebow, E., & Unger, E. (1967). Suburban runaways of the 1960s. *Monographs of the Society for Research in Child Development* (Serial Number 111, 32, 3). Chicago: University of Chicago Press.

Silbert M., & Pines, A. (1981). Sexual child abuse as an antecedent to prostitution. *Child Abuse and Neglect* 5:407–11.

Simons, R. (1996). *Understanding Differences between Divorced and Intact Families: Stress, Interaction, and Child Outcome.* Thousand Oaks, CA: Sage.

Simons, R., & Whitbeck, L. (1991). Running away as a precursor to adult homelessness: An investigation of the consequences of leaving home during adolescence. *Social Service Review* 65:224–47.

Sirles, E., Smilth, J., & Kusama, H. (1989). Psychiatric status of intrafamilial child sexual abuse victims. *Journal of the American Academy of Child and Adolescent Psychiatry* 28:225–29.

Smart, R., & Walsh, G. (1993). Predictors of depression in street youth. *Adolescence* 28:41–53.

Stefanidis, N., Pennbridge, J., MacKenzie, R., & Pottharst, K. (1992). Runaway and homeless youth: The effects of attachment history on stabilization. *American Journal of Orthopsychiatry* 62:442–46.

Straus, M., & Gelles, R. (1990). *Physical Violence in American Families.* Brunswick, NJ: Transaction.

Stricof, R., Novick, L., & Kennedy, J. (1990). HIV-1 seroprevalence in facilities for runaways and homeless adolescents in four states. Presentation at the Sixth Annual International Conference on AIDS, San Francisco.

Susser, E., Struening, E., & Conover, S. (1987). Childhood experiences of homeless men. *American Journal of Psychiatry* 144:1599–1601.

U.S. Employment Service (1991). *Dictionary of Occupational Titles.* Washington, DC: Author.

Wells, M., & Sandhu, H. (1986). The juvenile runaway: A historical perspective. *Free Inquiry in Creative Sociology* 14:143–47.

Werner, E. (1984). Resilient children. *Young Children* 40:68–72.

Werner, E. (1986). The concept of risk from a developmental perspective. *Advances in Special Education* 5:1–23.

Werner, E., & Smith, R. (1982). *Vulnerable but Invincible: A Longitudinal Study of Resilient Children and Youth.* New York: McGraw-Hill.

Whitbeck, L. B., Conger, R., Simons, R., & Kao, M. (1993). Minor deviant behaviors and adolescent sexual activity. *Youth & Society* 25:24–37.

Whitbeck, L. B., Hoyt, D., & Ackley, K. (1997a). Abusive family backgrounds and later victimization among runaway and homeless adolescents. *Journal of Research on Adolescence* 7:375–92.

Whitbeck, L. B., Hoyt, D., & Ackley, K. (1997b). Families of homeless and runaway adolescents: A comparison of parent/caretaker and adolescent perspectives on parenting, family violence, and adolescent conduct. *Child Abuse & Neglect* 21:517–28.

Whitbeck, L. B., Hoyt, D., & Ackley, K. (1999). A risk-amplification model of victimization and depressive symptoms among runaway and homeless adolescents. *American Journal of Community Psychology* (April).

Whitbeck, L. B., & Simons, R. L. (1990). Life on the streets: The victimization of runaway and homeless adolescents. *Youth & Society* 22:108–25.

Whitbeck, L. B., & Simons, R. L. (1993). A comparison of adaptive strategies and patterns of victimization among homeless adolescents and adults. *Violence and Victims* 8:135–52.

Windle, M. (1989). Substance use and abuse among adolescent runaways: A four-year follow-up study. *Journal of Youth and Adolescence* 18:331–34.

Wright, J. (1991). Health and the homeless teenager: Evidence from the National Health Care for the Homeless program. *Journal of Health and Social Policy* 2:15–36.

Yates, G., Mackenzie, R., Pennbridge, J., & Cohen, E. (1988). A risk profile comparison of runaway and non-runaway youth. *American Journal of Public Health* 78: 820–21.

Zide, M., & Cherry, A. (1992). A typology of runaway youths: An empirically based definition. *Child and Adolescent Social Work Journal* 9:155–68.

# Index